INTEGRATED PROJECT MANAGEMENT

EARL HALL
University of St. Thomas, Retired

with

JULIANE JOHNSON
Project Management Consultant
Best Buy Corporation

Prentice Hall

Upper Saddle River, New Jersey
Columbus, Ohio

Libary of Congress Cataloging in Publication Data

Hall, Earl.
Integrated project management / by Earl Hall with Juliane Johnson.
p. cm.
Includes bibliographical references and index.
ISBN 0-13-067449-4
1. Project management. I. Johnson, Juliane. II. Title.
HD69.P75 H347 2003
658.4'04--dc21

2002014822

Editor in Chief: Stephen Helba
Assistant Vice President and Publisher: Debbie Yarnell
Editorial Assistant: Sam Goffinet
Production Editor: Alexandrina B. Wolf
Design Coordinator: Diane Ernsberger
Cover Designer: Thomas Borah
Production Manager: Brian Fox
Electronic Text Management: Karen L. Bretz
Product Manager: Jimmy Stephens

This book was set in Times by D&G Limited, LLC. It was printed and bound by Maple Press. The cover was printed by Phoenix Color Corp.

Pearson Education Ltd.
Pearson Education Australia Pty. Limited
Pearson Education Singapore Pte. Litd.
Pearson Education North Asia Ltd.
Pearson Education Canada Ltd.
Pearson Educación de Mexico, S.A. de C.V.
Pearson Education—Japan
Pearson Education Malaysia Pte. Ltd.
Pearson Education, Upper Saddle River, New Jersey

Prentice Hall

10 9 8 7 6 5 4 3 2 1
ISBN: 0-13-067449-4

PREFACE

Projects are facts of life. A project is an effort to create a unique product or service with a desired outcome that is precisely defined and a completion that can be demonstrated.

Project management does not work nearly as well as it should. Projects end up costing far more than expected, they finish late, and often the finished product is not precisely what it was originally intended to be. Some projects are abandoned altogether and left to die. The ideal project goal of finishing on time, within budget, and to specifications is seldom met.

Mistakes in project management affect projects large and small and are costly: overruns of time and money often reach, or exceed, 500 percent. According to survey data, around 30 percent of projects are never completed.[1]

A body of knowledge on project management exists that explains the various steps and procedures to accomplish a project. Software for planning, budgeting, resource leveling (not assigning more than 100 percent of a person's time), and monitoring a project is also readily available. Yet something is still missing; the

[1]*P. M. Network*, (Newton Square, PA: Project Management Institute, Publishing Division, September 1996): 24 (Selin Corp. Reports for 1995).

projects continue to get into trouble. Does this mean that the ideal project goal of finishing to specifications and on time is impossible? Should the goal be abandoned and project management be left in its current mess? Or, should the missing information be pursued and added to the existing body of knowledge? This book will offer the information and practices that are currently missing.

How is Integrated Project Management different from other project management methods? IPM follows the same steps and concepts found in *A Guide to the Project Management Body of Knowledge* (PMBOK®), however IPM adds new procedures for following these steps, and these procedures make a big difference. IPM also adds a special method of creating useful time buffers, or "risk factors." But most importantly, IPM employs step-by-step activities whereby the project manager involves everyone who is responsible for project tasks in planning the project.

THE ORGANIZATION OF THIS BOOK

Integrated Project Management is written for college juniors and seniors with projects in their future and for graduate students needing help with projects in technical fields.

The book follows a project, step by step, explaining the what, why, and how of executing project steps. These steps are tightly linked together, ending with a completed project. The style is informal, which makes it easier to read. This book is about our life work and is written to help you with your life work.

We present a basic approach to project management with leadership, teaming, tools, and methods all integrated into one seamless planning and execution process. Using this integrated project management method, projects will finish to their specifications, and will be both on time and within budget!

Chapter 1 discusses leadership and its importance in project management. In addition, collaborative leadership between a project manager and team is also discussed in this chapter.

Chapter 2 describes the many ways projects emerge and how an individual comes to be a project manager. It is important for a new project manager to realize that a lot of work is required even before project planning begins—such as helping the customer examine the circumstances that justify the project and also identify the project's outcome. A new project manager often is unprepared for these roles.

Chapter 3 deals with developing the work breakdown structure and recruiting the project team. The project manager should be prepared with a system for getting help from within the organization, and for facilitating drawing this information into a project plan. The skills in developing collaborative leadership that were first considered in Chapter 1 now become the project manager's working role. In addition, selecting and recruiting a project team, whose members will collaboratively help plan and execute the project, is also explained in this chapter.

Chapter 4 describes the kickoff meeting, which brings the entire team together for the first time. Some team members will be leading a workgroup to accomplish a project task; others will work alone on a particular task. The project manager will explain to them how they will work collaboratively to plan and execute the project. *This kind of collaboration is unique to Integrated Project Management.*

Chapter 5 describes the effort to create the project's task list, which involves one or two two-hour team meetings. The "affinity diagram exercise" is used to consolidate and organize the individual task lists, which each team member created following the kickoff meeting, into a composite task list. Each team member will work on the affinity diagram exercise and help to create the task list.

Chapter 6 deals with the Gantt chart development, or the process of determining task sequences, the duration of each task, and who will do each task. The work of defining and sequencing tasks, identifying task start dates, providing careful and unbuffered time estimates of each task, and identifying who will do the task will be the focus of one or several successive two-hour meetings. The project manager will facilitate the Gantt chart development by displaying the emerging project Gantt chart on a screen in the front of the meeting room, using a PC loaded with Microsoft Project 2002® software and a projector. Anyone not familiar with this equipment can rest easy because instructions for its use are covered. This chapter also describes the project planning effort that concludes with the completion of the basic project Gantt chart. A 120-day trial version of Microsoft Project 2002 is found on the CD-ROM packaged with this text.

Chapter 7 explains and demonstrates how the project manager can create a critical path chart. Several ways of displaying the critical path will be introduced. One method in particular, the arrow diagram, is a very useful tool for managing the execution of the project.

Chapters 8 and 9 explain time buffer-risk analysis. The task time estimates in the Gantt chart are just that—*estimates*—and are subject to uncertainty. Due to the nature of the processes used throughout project planning, the original working Gantt chart—the pre-risk analysis Gantt chart—defines a completion date that is unrealistic. Because the project will take longer, a time buffer must be added to define a realistic completion date. These chapters will explain how to get it right.

Chapter 10 explains how the project budget is created. Modern software makes this task easy, and its application is explained in this chapter.

Chapter 11 explains the steps to create a graphic display for the customer/manager. The means to effectively make this presentation and to bring the customer into a discussion are also described. Along the way, the customer may want some changes. Because shortening a project is the most requested change, this procedure is explained.

Chapter 12 follows the project from launch to completion—the point at which the project objectives have been fully met. **Chapter 13** deals with project change. Procedures for dealing with change will be discussed in this chapter.

Chapter 14 explains the steps to achieve project closure. **Chapter 15** describes the duties and responsibilities of a project team member. In this chapter, we also restate the process of planning and executing the project from the perspective of a project team member.

Chapter 16 defines basic, major, and macro projects and expands on the project management role required for each project type. The means by which someone with basic project management experience can grow into the role of a major, and later, macro project manager is also noted.

ACKNOWLEDGMENTS

Thousands of people have contributed directly and indirectly to this book. They include project colleagues, customers, and project management practitioners who have discussed project management with us in the intense project management workshops that we lead. Thank you all very much. In a sense, this is your book. We have simply compiled it.

Some of you have been particularly important.

In 1982, Len Gross, who had a long and strong IBM project background, invited Earl to help with a corporate project management workshop that he was teaching. It was Len who made the importance of integration in project management explicit.

Professor Dan McNamara joined with Earl to develop the first project management course for the MBA program at the University of St. Thomas in St. Paul, Minnesota. Dan helped to develop the curriculum in many ways, but it was his knowledge and skill at using one of the early project management software packages, Timeline, that particularly enriched the course and has continued to influence the development of this book.

About seven years ago, Earl Hall was happily teaching and consulting when a very bright, insightful, and experienced project manager named Juliane Johnson appeared in his workshop. Once Juliane came aboard, this book became a "we" effort.

John Ely, Surface Conditioning Division president for FSI International, of Chanhassen, Minnesota, challenged Earl to make project management principles clear for project managers and the managers of project managers during the years that Earl taught and consulted for FSI. John also read an early draft of *Integrated Project Management* and made useful suggestions.

Everton King, Rochester Institute of Technology; Rick Wilson, Oklahoma State University; Ralph Rogers, Old Dominion University; Anthony A. Olinzock, Mississippi State University; and Ajay K. Mishra, SUNY Binghamton, all reviewed the manuscript for Prentice Hall and provided helpful feedback.

Among these reviewers, Anthony Olinzock provided particularly insightful and valuable suggestions. Thanks, Andy. It is a better book because of your feedback.

Joyce Vogt, assisted by her engineer husband, Guy Vogt, did a great job of prodding us and pulling together the first draft for the publisher. Thank you, Joyce and Guy, for typing, formatting, and creating diagrams and for your editorial advice.

Sue More, who is responsible for graphics, design, and prepress at the University of St. Thomas, prepared the final draft for the publisher. Thanks, Sue!

I have a spunky little Norwegian wife with a big, fat university degree in journalism and experience in community news and magazine writing, who believes her background qualifies her to force an engineer-economist and an information specialist to write readable and understandable prose for college and graduate school students. After my many long, loud protests of "but Carol, you are changing the meaning," I have come to believe her corrections work! Carol Hall has been the prepublish manuscript editor. If you can read this book easily and understand it, it is because of Carol. For that, Juliane and I are most grateful.

There is a lovely young woman I know only through the telephone and e-mail. She laughs at my attempts at email humor, even though everyone else says I have no sense of humor. She has guided the book along and is constantly cheerful and understanding. Debbie Yarnell is our editor at Prentice Hall, and we love her. Project editor Julie Frigo has also been very good to work with and copyeditor Jan Lynn did a great job of making this difficult subject more readable.

Earl Hall

ABOUT THE AUTHORS

This book is based on almost 60 years of project management experience on the part of the senior author, Earl Hall, and more than 15 years experience for the junior author, Juliane Johnson. Both Earl and Juliane have worked on a wide range of projects of all types and sizes.

Dr. Earl Hall has graduate training as an engineer and as a sociologist and economist. Although his engineering career focused mainly on projects—particularly jet engine projects—he also found time to design and develop servomechanism control systems that produced patents in his name, which are assigned to General Electric.

Juliane Johnson is an information systems specialist who has applied her project management skills in a variety of settings where information systems were needed to implement new concepts, including Internet technologies.

In the early 1980s, Earl, with Professor Dan McNamara, developed the first graduate course in project management for the MBA program at the University of St. Thomas, in St. Paul, Minnesota.

Earl and Juliane have taught more than 2,500 senior managers and project managers in intensive seven-week project management workshops hosted by the University of St. Thomas Management Center.

Dedicated to
Carol Hanson Hall

CONTENTS

2 THE PROJECT, THE STATEMENT OF WORK, AND THE SPECIFICATION 15

3 PROJECT WORK BREAKDOWN STRUCTURE AND TEAM RECRUITMENT 41

4 THE KICKOFF MEETING 47

11 PROJECT PLAN REVIEW 167

12 PROJECT EXECUTION 185

13 PROJECT CHANGE 205

14 ACHIEVING CLOSURE 215

1 THE IPM PROJECT MANAGER

INTRODUCTION

To manage a project well is demanding and challenging, yet a widespread belief exists that just about anyone can do it. This belief alone accounts for many project failures. The skills needed to manage a project and lead a team are described in this chapter. These skills are not very different from those of any other managerial role, however, they are significant in that the objective is to win the support of project team members who often must be treated as if they were volunteers. Armed with these particular leadership skills and an understanding of the Integrated Project Management (IPM) step-by-step method, a project manager will be able to consistently complete projects to specifications and finish on time and within budget.

LEADERSHIP OF A PROJECT TEAM

A project manager with limited technical skills who is somewhat awkward in interpersonal relationships can still successfully lead a project. A project manager who possesses outstanding technical skills and plans and organizes well, can blow a project.

The success of a project depends not on the project manager's technical expertise or know-how, but on the project manager instilling in the team the fact that they are the lifeblood of the project: That their input, expertise, and collaborative efforts are critical in every phase of the project from planning through execution. This is the job the IPM project manager is charged with doing!

As noted earlier, the authors have managed many projects. We have received praise, promotions, and rewards for what fellow workers and managers have described as good leadership abilities. Although not experts on the subject, we do know something about leadership as it applies to projects. In this chapter, we emphasize the points we believe are important and invite you, the reader, to think about them, fit them to your personality, and tuck them away for future reference.

THE DEFINITION OF IPM LEADERSHIP

When a project manager strives to help members of a project team share objectives and participate cooperatively and creatively in achieving these objectives, he or she is practicing IPM leadership.

To put this principle into practice, the project manager first must consider the situation of the people on the project team: They are typically workers who have special skills and expertise needed for the project, and *have been assigned temporarily or part-time to the project.* Each team member reports to a supervisor or resource manager and also has work assigned by that boss. In addition, some members may be working on other projects. Consequently, it is not surprising that many of these individuals feel they are already overscheduled—yet, they are essential to the project team. They must attend several team meetings, arriving prepared to share and consolidate information about the durations, resources, and risks of the project task! Most of these workers are competent and intrinsically motivated to do a good job, but they can easily achieve job satisfaction by working at their other jobs and giving only scant attention to the project. Therefore, to ensure their full participation, the project manager is forced to treat them as volunteers! What this means is unlike regular employees who can be expected to do to do their job, volunteers must be "persuaded" to do their job. This "persuasion" requires the use of several motivation techniques that are explained in the next section of this chapter. These techniques can be implemented only in an atmosphere of mutual trust and respect between the project manager and team.

Because trust is based largely on credibility, a project manager must strive to be truthful in all communications with the team members. Thus, lies of any kind are out. Information concerning the organization associated with the project and the technology required for the project must be shared honestly. Under *no* circumstances should the project manager heap praise on a team member in order to manipulate that person, nor should the project manager take credit for the work of others.

The surest way to gain the respect of any employee is to demonstrate that the person is valued for the skills and dedication that they bring to the job. Listening to a team member's suggestions and offering feedback provides solid assurance of that person's value, as does showing sensitivity to their feelings. This is especially important if it becomes necessary for the project manager to offer criticism, which should be only constructive criticism and conducted in private on that person's turf. The best way for a project manager to implement this principle, however, is to admit that his or her understanding of the technical areas of the project is not expert—which is usually the case—and to defer to those workers who are the experts.

MOTIVATION

To ensure the team's full participation, every team member must trust and respect the project manager. However, this is not enough. They also must put forth their best work. For example, team member Tom may think project manager Sue is a nice person whom he trusts and respects. Yet the reality is nothing about Sue's project influences Tom to make a special effort to do the job well. Sue must use motivating practices to gain Tom's full task effort and cooperation.

Motivation through Individual Attention: About 70 years ago, a major experiment was conducted at a large manufacturing facility to determine what motivates people in the workplace. The answer came back loud and clear: *If you pay attention to workers and they discover that they are respected for what they do, they will try to live up to those expectations.* In the previous example, Sue clearly must demonstrate to Tom that she respects his ability, which she can do best through individual attention.

The need for individual attention arises over and over. It can be accomplished in many different ways and requires just a little extra effort, such as a short note recognizing a special contribution left on a computer screen, for example, or an e-mail message or personal visit to the worker's workplace. Or, it can be in the form of a one-on-one conversation.

In recent years, "empowerment" has become a buzzword for motivation. Exactly what it means is not always clear. Self-managing work teams are empowered to manage themselves, which seems to have a motivating influence for many, but not all, people. Some people prefer a "just tell me what to do and let me do it" approach. This also occurs in a project team, and because IPM is built around full team participation, the project manager must go easy on those individuals who resist and draw their contributions in other ways. This can mean a dose of individual attention in the form of a one-on-one conversation with the "resister" between meetings.

Another instance where this approach works well is that of a team member needing help to solve a problem, such as how to prepare the all important task time and effort estimates. Here the project manager can step in and review similar past projects with the team member or identify knowledgeable people who can be queried to obtain a good estimate.

If help is given by leading a team member through a series of questions, the questioning itself may bring forth the answer to the problem, or at the very least, open up a new train of thought. Giving individual attention is good; however, recognition with rewards is the strongest motivator.

Motivation through Recognition with Rewards: The project manager must recognize each significant contribution made by a team member and develop mechanisms to reward that person. The reward policy should be announced at the beginning of the project to create an added incentive toward good performance. The task-by-task nature of project work makes outstanding contributions easy to recognize; those contributions for planning and execution are always a matter of record, as they are noted in the project Gantt chart.

It is part of the project manager's job to record such contributions. Recognition and rewards, if possible, should follow soon afterward. Recognition can take many forms. At the very least, a memorandum of recognition, an "orchid letter," a special written pat on the back, should be sent to the team member's regular manager, human relations department, and to the team member. Regular postings of team member achievements are good—provided that no one is left out. If the project manager has an opportunity to give time off, free entertainment tickets, or other perks, they should be husbanded carefully, with criteria set up for their disposal, and used as much possible. However, sometimes the informal gesture of leaving an "attaboy" note on a computer monitor, or surprising the team member with a handful of balloons or a batch of cookies works even better! Regardless of form, the project manager must be sincere with recognition.

COMMUNICATION SKILLS

The project manager and the team must "speak the same language" in order to work together. If they are not absolutely clear on all the terminology used in the project, chaos will reign. For example, to an engineer the term "quality" means "all parts for the product fall within the plus or minus tolerance specifications on design drawings." To the person leading the quality movement, "equaling or exceeding the expectations of the customer," is generally the interpretation. (This last statement raises this question: What is meant by 'the expectations of the customer?') To others, quality simply means a pleasant appearance. A product manager, however, may think of quality in terms of "99.6 percent of the products falling within specified tolerance limits defined in a performance-sampling test."

A project manager must never assume that the term "quality," or for that matter anything else he or she says to the team, will mean the same to them as it does to him or her! What is required to ascertain agreement between them is *feedback*.

Feedback is the give and take of information between the project manager and team members to clarify the meaning of terms. Team members must provide feedback to the project manager: During team meetings, they can ask for clarification of a term or statement, or they can restate the project manager's words differently to be certain that both parties agree on the meaning. (Even if fairly sure of the meaning of a key statement, a team member may request that it be restated.) The project manager must encourage team members to use feedback at all meetings to ensure that everyone understands the intended meaning of the terms and key statements.

Good communication requires a collaborative effort between the project manager and the team. It facilitates good decision-making and encourages cooperation.

COLLABORATIVE LEADERSHIP

Collaborative leadership is critical to Integrated Project Management (IPM). It is at the heart of every accomplishment involved in planning and executing the project. Collaborative leadership can be defined as the team working together to reach a mutual agreement whenever a decision is required. A project manager, acting as a trainer, will explain collaboration leadership, as presented here, at the kickoff meeting (see Chapter 4 for more details).

Team Norms: A procedure that builds team awareness and a "we are a team" attitude is the creation of team norms, or rules of engagement. The process of creating norms takes place at the start of the kickoff meeting, with the project manager directing a 15-minute activity in which team members choose norms to guide them as they interact with each other. This activity helps build a sense of teamwork, and the norms themselves help keep meetings running smoothly.

The procedure is simple. The project manager asks the team to think of a set of rules that will be useful in making meetings more efficient. It is good to recruit a team member to lead this activity because it enables the project manager to join the others and act as a team member and to suggest a few norms as starters. One norm that is basic to IPM procedure is *team meetings will never exceed two hours.*

Limiting meetings to two hours helps gain meeting participation from the "volunteers," or team members with other pressing job responsibilities. Longer meetings could well discourage them from coming, but a two-hour meeting with a clear agenda will generally be doable for these busy people, particularly if they believe the project is important. The project manager is responsible for convincing them of the project's importance and for preparing the agenda, all of which is discussed later in Chapters 3 and 4.

Some other norm suggestions are:

- We will attend all meetings and arrive on time. (The project manager will explain the importance of all team members attending all planning meetings. [See Chapter 3.])
- We will stick closely to the agenda.
- We will come prepared to the meetings.
- We will not interrupt each other during the discussions.
- We will encourage participation by all team members.

Although the project manager may offer the first suggestions, norms must come primarily from the team. The team member leading the session will invite suggestions from the group. Each person who is suggesting a norm will explain its importance, and the leader will ask other team members for their comments. Acceptance of a norm can be done by general agreement. When each norm is agreed upon, it should be displayed on a blackboard, flip chart, overhead projector, or by other display means.

Note that the process of creating norms is as important to team building as it is to promoting meeting efficiency.

CONFLICT RESOLUTION AND CONSENSUS DECISIONS

One norm the project manager should suggest to the team is a norm to resolve team conflict. Because differences of opinion among team members concerning task execution, length, risk, and so forth could arise, a procedure is needed to resolve these differences. Conflicts during meetings must be dealt with because if allowed to develop and simmer, they can cause team members to lose their enthusiasm for the project. Conflict also can slow down a meeting. Although no magic solution exists, one procedure generally works if team members are familiar with it and are prepared to use it before conflict occurs.

The conflict resolution norm can be stated as follows: We agree that when two individuals or two groups of team members advance conflicting proposals, *each will explore the other's concept*, develop a clear statement of it, gather information and data to support it, and report their findings to the team.

Should this norm be invoked, the meeting may have to be interrupted and completion rescheduled, but it will be worth it. Afterward, the project manager usually can guide the team to a consensus. A consensus decision does not necessarily mean that every team member—or the project manager—fully supports it. It does mean that all recognize the position of the majority and are willing to accept it and move on. Consensus should be accomplished with a discussion, not a vote.

In IPM, much energy is invested in keeping team members connected as a team and in moving forward with planning as quickly as possible.

SHARED LEADERSHIP

At the heart of collaborative leadership is the concept that, when appropriate, any team member can spontaneously share the leadership role. This action becomes appropriate when a meeting, for some reason, is drifting away from its objective or when the expertise of a team member is not being drawn into the decision-making process. The team member who first notices either problem must speak up and get the attention of the project manager. Then, that team member can intervene by reminding the team that urgent business is at hand and time is limited, or that team members with important expertise are not speaking up or being heard.

Some questions to prompt intervention are

- Are we forgetting some team norms?
- Do we all agree on the meaning of the term we are using?
- Do we not generally agree that "this" task sequence belongs in our task list? Can we now accept that and move on?
- Are we letting our discussion focus on personalities rather than project outcomes?
- Are we giving everyone the opportunity to participate?
- Are we aware of our time limit and of what we have to accomplish?

Often those who want to ask such questions to better focus and expedite a meeting feel uncomfortable about actually doing so, but with IPM, these questions are encouraged. One aspect of the integrating principle is that all team members share in team leadership as previously described. The project manager must emphasize this point and issue the invitation, but should never completely surrender the responsibility to lead the meeting.

All team members are asked to take this shared leadership responsibility seriously, and at the same time, not abuse it with lengthy discussions. An opportunity to share leadership will motivate many workers to work diligently toward the team's goals.

ESTABLISHMENT OF THE INTERNAL CUSTOMER PHILOSOPHY

The internal customer philosophy has proven to be a powerful tool to improve quality and productivity in the modern quality movement. It has given great personal satisfaction to those individuals who have learned to use it. The principle is simple: We in the project are all, one way or another, each other's customer. This is best explained in the following project management setting:

An engineering group begins a project to build, for example, a control system, by creating a design. The manufacturing department reviews the design and makes suggestions about manufacturability; they then pass the design onto the shop floor where it is created. Manufacturing personnel then may suggest changes to the engineers. From there, it goes to testing and the testers determine whether the system actually works. So far, no one has simply passed or rejected the project, they have made evaluations and suggestions. The design then returns to engineering to be refined and finalized. The persons in each group do not just "do it and dump it" on the next group: They discuss each other's needs as they go along. By doing good work, each group helps the next group down the line, and together they proceed to produce an excellent control system.

When team members begin thinking in these terms, they will seek out the best way to help each other do a good job. If I, as a team member, explain my tasks to the "customers" who receive the outputs, I will discover how to time task processing to best serve them. However, I, too, am a "customer" to my "customers," and for me to better serve them, they must inform me of their needs. At this point, my "customer"—who has supplied me with information—becomes my "supplier," and this information enables me do a better job of performing my tasks.

This is a powerful concept. Convincing team members to adopt it will improve project quality and productivity, but it will not be easy. The project manager must explain, demonstrate, advise, and coach the team. It will take time to make their responses automatic. This concept will be revisited again at the project launch meeting where task execution begins.

PROJECT MANAGERS AS TRAINERS AND TEACHERS

Training the Team: IPM team members must be trained to do the many tasks expected of them, and they must have their questions about the project answered. Because several meetings are necessary, the question, "Why do I have to attend all these meetings?" is sure to be asked.

The project manager should explain that decisions concerning the project plan will be made at every meeting and that each team member must be there to contribute his or her unique body of knowledge and experience to such decisions. In addition, each team member's project role also will be clarified at the meetings.

Team meetings are limited to two hours so as not to overwhelm team members' other commitments, and they are scheduled collaboratively for the same reason.

This information, which was spelled out to each team member during recruitment, is repeated at the kickoff meeting in more detail. In addition, the project manager will explain action items and will offer assistance for getting outside help for them by identifying useful resource people to query.

Although usually not sufficiently skilled to mentor team members on technical matters involving tasks, the project manager must know who can help and must assist team members to gain access.

The project manager performs team training at the kickoff meeting. Consequently, a concise lesson plan and a clear objective for each teaching unit are absolutely essential. The object of the first teaching unit is to encourage team member attendance at every meeting. The lesson plan also must include the basics of what, why, and how, and also check on team-member understanding. (Skilled project managers will use brief examples, called memory markers, to emphasize such points.) A project manager cannot be expected to be a master trainer but must be conscious of the trainer/mentor role and plan to deliver whatever training is needed.

Training Resource Managers: It is rare that resource managers who control the people and resources needed for the project fully understand project planning and management. Explaining to resource managers the IPM planning process of plan first and then execute the plan, falls to the project manager when he or she recruits workers and resources for the team. Many resource managers benefit from this explanation, which is made by explaining the project planning Gantt chart to them. They discover how their people will be involved in the project and recognize the need for their time commitments.

NEGOTIATION SKILLS

The project manager will conduct two sets of negotiations, one with the project customer and another with the various function managers who control the workers needed for the project.

Negotiating with the Customer: Negotiations with a customer occur at a project's outset and are done to arrive at a project's specification. It would seem to be a straightforward task: Thc customer explains what is wanted, and the project manager captures it in the specification and goes ahead with the project. This is not always the case, however. Some customers may come up with only a fuzzy idea of their desired product and may need help from the project manager to discover what is possible to be produced for them. This is where negotiating enters in the process: The project manager identifies the various tradeoffs to the customer and negotiates decisions regarding these tradeoffs.

The customer may not understand project feasibility, or what can and cannot be produced—and also may have come up with time and cost expectations that are inconsistent with what experience dictates. Resolving these types of problems also requires negotiating.

Basically, the key to negotiating is to clearly identify the needs of the person with whom you are negotiating. Then, you must tell this person exactly how you propose to meet those needs, discover the constraints limiting their efforts to help you meet those needs, and discover what they would accept as an incentive for their help.

It is important never to negotiate with a chip on your shoulder. The person being negotiated with is a collaborator, not an adversary. The more a project manager can help this person, the more successful he or she will be in achieving desired goals.

Negotiating with Resource Managers: These negotiations center on borrowing the desired workers needed for the project from their respective resource managers. In so doing, it is desirable to involve the manager as much as possible in the project, for a manager who feels involved in the project will be more likely to encourage his or her staff to participate. If the desired employee is already overcommitted, the involved manager will likely cooperate in helping to find a second choice. Such negotiations will work if the project is of high priority to the organization. If not, the project may have to be delayed.

The critical thing to remember is that negotiations involve give as well as take. A project manager must be prepared to provide everything possible in return for the necessary help.

THE ABILITY TO MAINTAIN ORDER AND DISCIPLINE

From time to time, an individual assigned to a project will not cooperate. This person opposes the planning process and goofs off when doing the assigned planning work. The project manager must step in and correct this situation. Failure to do so will lose the support of the team, and worse, their respect; it may even lead to undermining the project.

It is very difficult to get a team member, who chooses not to do so to contribute to project planning. Often the person calls the planning process "Mickey Mouse," and cannot be talked out of it. The first step in dealing with this situation, if it is feasible, is to bring in a replacement with similar expertise. This step begins with a one-on-one discussion with the offender, with the project manager asking whether he or she would voluntarily leave the project. If this works, the project manager should go for it. The project is always better off with a lesser skilled individual who will try, than someone who will not. It is important to speak frankly in discussions with the problem individual without being aggressive. However, the project manager, by no means, should be wishy-washy.

If the project is stuck with an uncooperative team member, the project manager will have to enforce the member's participation. This process will be time consuming and will slow project planning but is necessary. Whenever necessary planning input must be gotten from others with appropriate experience and knowledge, this input should be referred to the troublemaker for comment. Through this process, the project manager will be able to identify the troublemaker's tasks and add them to the task list. At this point, the troublemaker may or may not choose to participate.

If the project manager must search for the necessary input, the troublemaker should be told, and the input should be passed on to the team, along with any comments the troublemaker may have made.

With risk analysis, the project manager will have to consider the validity of the troublemaker's time and overrun estimates. It is best not to expect a conscientious effort. Then again, the troublemaker may try; risk analysis will allow for a "not try."

An even bigger problem is that of a team member who ignores assigned tasks. While walking about and talking to people occupied with tasks, the project manager will note progress and compare it with the task performance projections in the project Gantt chart. If a task appears to be moving slowly, the key question is, "Are we slowed down because of factors deemed possible in risk analysis, or is this a case of a substandard performance on the worker's part?"

The project manager must talk to the worker in question, identify the problem, and ask, "What can we do about it?" If the problem is caused by a source discovered in risk analysis, some risk-reducing resources must be brought into play, and the delay absorbed by the risk factor. If the problem is the worker, the project manager is faced with a classic discipline problem that must be dealt with in a forthright manner, by holding a private discussion on the worker's turf, as soon as possible. If adjustments to bolster work performance are possible, the task then should proceed. These adjustments also must be put into writing, dated, and signed, and copies must be provided for both parties.

If the unsatisfactory performance continues, the project manager's options will depend on the organization's practices and must always be documented carefully and shared with the problem individual. If dealing with a programmer, for example, the project manager may determine that in similar situations programmers typically write 400 lines of code each day, while he or she writes only 100 lines, at best. Different situations call for different measures, but the uncooperative person's poor performance must be written up. This is very important in any disciplinary situation. If it could somehow get to the National Labor Relations Board, documentation is absolutely necessary. The problem individual must be given a written statement describing the perceived problem and have ample opportunity to respond in writing.

Depending on the organization's practice, the project manager may ask the problem individual to join in a discussion with their resource manager. This conversation may resolve things, or it could result in the manager taking formal disciplinary action. The project manager may, alternatively, seek to replace the problem individual. Another option is to have someone work with that person. In any case, the action should be taken with the problem individual's full knowledge.

If no resolution can be reached, the project manager should give the individual's manager a carefully documented description of the problem and the processes used to try to resolve it.

If another person is brought in to replace the problem individual, the project manager and the team should identify how to best bring the new person up to speed. This can be done through a formal plan or with someone acting as a mentor. The chosen method should be used whenever a new team member is added to the project.

Throughout this process, the rest of the team will realize that the project manager cares deeply about good performance and is willing to take uncomfortable steps to ensure it in addition to going to great lengths to be fair and just.

THE PROJECT DIARY

In 1995, Tetra Pak, a Swedish food packaging machine-manufacturing firm with facilities around the world, published an excellent handbook titled *Project Working Model.*[1] The Tetra Pak CEO described his firm as "the project oriented company." Many project management principles found in this unusual and excellent manual echo those we have developed during years of experimentation and experience. One principle most emphasized is that project management should be a continuous learning experience. To that end, both we and Tetra Pak insist that a project manager keep a project diary.

In the 1940s and 1950s, a project manager carried a 3 1/2 by 5 inch loose-leaf notebook in a hip pocket for project notes. There are obviously better ways to do this today, but no matter how it is done, *a project manager should keep a diary!*

This diary must cover the highlights of project planning. This includes the agenda for every planning process meeting, meeting notes, and activity notes, such as the effort to create a critical path chart. The key elements of these notes should be 1) what we did, 2) why we did it, 3) what problems came up, 4) how they were solved, and 5) what we learned.

When project execution is underway, the project manager should fill a page or section of the diary for every task that is performed. During the walkabout, the five key elements should be kept in mind while communicating with workers, and appropriate records should be kept. If e-mail is used to communicate, all e-mail including the replies should be added to the notes. These notes and the information accumumlated within the project planning software package will provide source material for the project report and for the discussion of "what we learned," which is held with the team at project's end.

By keeping a diary, the project manager will be able to provide the customer with a valuable project report. A diary also will help both the project manager and the team grow in their project management skills.

[1]Leif Ögárd, *Project Working Model, a guide for project managers*, Effect, Effectusgruppen Malmö, Illustrations, layout, and original: TPM Information: Váxjö AB, Sweden, 1995, Tetra Pak, Lund Sweden.

The best way to keep a project diary today is to set up a file and format in a computer word processing package, and, on a daily or at least a weekly basis, bring it up to date. If using Microsoft Word® and Microsoft Project Management® software, the project manager can "paste" in project information and e-mail material to create a useful record.

SUMMARY

A project manager should have good technical knowledge in the field of the project being undertaken, but he or she need not be an expert. Because team members are on temporary assignment, the project manager must treat them like volunteers. Because they have other responsibilities outside the project, the project manager must have exceptional leadership skills to keep these "volunteers" on track with project work. Facilitator and leadership skills are particularly important for IPM projects because success depends heavily upon each team member's input in both planning and execution.

DISCUSSION QUESTIONS

1. Is there such a person as a natural born project manager?
2. Why are leadership skills particularly important for project managers?
3. How does the role of "facilitator" differ from the traditional manager's role?
4. When is it appropriate to take a vote to resolve conflicting positions?
5. If a project manager is not the technical expert in one area, when and how might he or she play the role of mentor to someone who is?
6. Is maintaining discipline and order in a project different from what a good line operations supervisor does?
7. What is the difference in management roles for a project manager working with team members who are unfamiliar with IPM and team members who are used to the IPM approach to projects?

EXERCISES

1. Find a condensed version of "Undaunted Courage."[2] Were Lewis and Clark leaders as this chapter describes leadership?

[2]Ambrose, Stephen E. *Undaunted Courage*, the Simon & Schuster, Rochefeller Carter, NY, NY, 10020, 1996.

2. Find someone who has worked on two or more projects at once. (Someone in a school's maintenance department probably has.) Ask how they decide which project to work on first.
3. If you were taking two courses pass or fail and had a term paper to write for each, what would influence the amount of time you spent on each paper?
4. Pick three people you know something about who have been characterized as leaders. Explain why or why not they would have been good IPM project managers.
5. Interview someone who has or had management responsibilities. Ask this person to define leadership. How does their definition compare with the IPM description of leadership?

2 THE PROJECT, THE STATEMENT OF WORK, AND THE SPECIFICATION

INTRODUCTION

A project begins taking shape long before it reaches the project manager. The first step occurs when a need or opportunity for a project comes to the attention of someone who has the authority to initiate a project. This person examines the feasibility, cost/benefit considerations, resource availability, and external problems associated with initiating the project, and in so doing, becomes the project's sponsor.

At this point, the sponsor chooses someone to act as the project manager. Working together, the sponsor and the project manager draw up a statement of work, or outline, which explains how the project manager will migrate the project from a general idea to a precise, measurable outcome statement. The outcome statement is called the project specification. The project manager may develop several revisions of the specification and discuss them with the sponsor before they are both entirely satisfied. After they reach an agreement, the project manager sets forth to recruit a team and to develop the project plan.

THE DEFINITION OF A PROJECT

The world is full of projects. Planning a holiday party or publishing an in-house newsletter to inform employees of "what is going on" are examples of projects. Reconfiguring an office layout for a new facility also is a project. Building an atomic power plant is a project—a very big project. Because holiday party and newsletter projects have loosely defined outcomes and the characteristics of collaborative happenings, they do not necessarily require managing. However, more complicated projects that have precisely defined outcomes, such as reconfiguring an office layout or building atomic power plant, must be managed.

A Guide to the Project Management Body of Knowledge (PMBOK®), the guide created by the Project Management Institute, defines a project as "A temporary endeavor undertaken to create a unique product or service. 'Temporary' means that every project has a definite beginning and end. 'Unique' means that the product or service is different in some distinguishing way from all similar products or services. The project ceases when its declared objectives have been obtained."[1]

This is a good definition, but it is incomplete.

The publication, *Project Working Model*, is a guide for project managers that was produced for Tetra Pak, of Lund, Sweden, a world leader in the manufacture of packaging machines. It states: "The project objective must be clear and measurable."[2] We share this need for measurement precision, as do many other practitioners and authors of project management literature.

IPM defines a project as any unique activity sequence having a beginning and a precisely and measurably defined outcome that requires the cooperative efforts of a number of people over time, and that is managed by one person.

The term "unique" in the IPM definition means that a project is a one-time activity and not something done the same way again and again—that type of effort is called a process. "A precisely and measurably defined outcome" defines exactly where the project is going. "Managed by one person" means that one person is responsible for ensuring the achievement of the project outcome and will remain with the project from beginning to end.

"Measurable" as used in the IPM definition does not mean measurable by numbers only, as is depicted in the following project specification example:

> Deliver 20 gallons of Brand X house paint to the building at 100 First Street by 11:00 A.M. on November 3, 2002. Color must match the attached sample.

[1]A Guide to the Project Management Body of Knowledge (PMBOK®), Sylva, NC: Project Management Institute, Publishing Division, 1996 edition.P. 4 (A CD-ROM or Hard Copy of the more recent update of PMBOK are available upon request.)

[2]"Op Sit"

'Twenty gallons' *is numerical.* However, 'Brand X house paint' and 'the building at 100 First Street' are *identifiably measurable*; '11 A.M.' is *measurable with a clock* and 'November 3, 2001,' *a calendar.*

'Matching the color sample' is not precisely measurable until a color chart with a graduation of colors is referenced, and an expert at matching samples to colors on the chart is designated. In short, precise measurements can be designated in terms other than numbers, and the writer must be careful not to let a fuzzy criterion slip in.

Projects rarely fall into a project manager's lap with their precise measurable objectives all spelled out, however, there are exceptions. For example, a human resources department may be faced with a new government requirement to report monthly on the number of people who have filed claims for carpal tunnel syndrome disability. Here, the precise, measurable outcome is specified, and the human resources department can go ahead and design a system to gather this information and report it. Most projects, however, reach this go-ahead point only following a great deal of analyzing, and data gathering, and after considering alternatives.

PROJECT FEASIBILITY

Before embarking on a project, it must be determined that the project is feasible—that it actually can be done. Whether or not a project is feasible depends on whether enough information and data exist so that a project team can fully plan the project, and whether the people available to do the project have the knowledge and skills necessary to plan and execute it.

Designing and developing the first jet engine to perform at and above the speed of sound (MACH-1) raised feasibility questions. The characteristics of airflow change dramatically as the airflow speed reaches the speed of sound. However, in the early 1950s, jet engine design did not deal with this "shock-wave" phenomenon. This brought up the question of whether it was feasible to create a MACH-1 engine design. Significant wind tunnel testing had been done on critical engine elements. This testing led to the conclusion that the necessary information and data for the project existed. The contractor project team then was able to demonstrate that they had and could combine research information and create the engine. The project was deemed feasible, and the jet engine was produced.

Projects like this one which advance the state of the art, must be judged carefully as to their feasibility. Analysis may show that more research—more mucking around gathering data—is needed before it is possible to attempt a project's execution. (Research is not pursued with on-time objectives as is a project.)

THE BIRTH OF A PROJECT

Project possibilities emerge whenever problems or opportunities occur. Generally, events over time come together to bring project possibilities into focus. The following examples explain several different ways that a project can come into being. These examples also illustrate some of the types of projects that are commonly undertaken.

The Internal Process Improvement Project: The production cost of a product produced by a manufacturing firm is running high, which concerns the firm's top manager. The top manager instructs the manufacturing manager to reduce the production cost. To do so, the manufacturing manager will consider various process improvement projects.

The manufacturing manager begins by discussing options with the firm's director of quality and discovers several production lines that seem to be good candidates for process improvement. Some analysis of process details and improvement possibilities is needed, so the manufacturing manager undertakes a cost/benefit analysis to help identify the level of improvement to be sought. Questioning feasibility, he asks, "What cost reduction benefit can be achieved from a 1 percent improvement in the key process output measure?" "Is the benefit from a 1 percent improvement enough to justify the project, or do we need a 10 percent improvement?" "Have we reason to believe that a 10 percent or even a 1 percent improvement is feasible?" If this analysis suggests that the project is feasible and can offer a good cost reduction, it is necessary to compare the project to other potential projects, because resources for process improvement are always limited. If analysis suggests that improvement of this specific process is a good use of scarce resources, a project is "born."

Because the manufacturing manager has sponsored the project, or undertaken to get it done, he has become the *project sponsor*. His responsibilities include: issuing an order announcing the project and its purpose, assigning a project manager, authorizing resources, defining the relationships between the project team and the process operators, clearly defining reporting channels, and reporting to higher authorities the reason for the project. This project order is sometimes called a project contract or project charter. It precedes discussions to precisely define project outcomes.

The Product Improvement Project: This type of project often begins in a firm's marketing department, which is always a good source for project concepts. In this setting, a process improvement project takes shape when a marketing product line specialist, who keeps in touch with his customers, discovers certain improvements one customer would like to have. In a company like Lincoln Electric of Cleveland, Ohio, this product line specialist would be a welding engineer who would regularly visit the customer's shop floor to see firsthand how the product is being used.

Discovering the need for improvement, the product line specialist would inform the development and design engineers at the home office. Together they would discuss improvements and offer this information to the product line manager in the marketing department, who then develops some general estimates for project costs and the expected return on the investment.

In most cases, deciding on a project involves the allocation of scarce resources. Discussion with the leader of the engineering department and with manufacturing management also must occur to ensure technical feasibility and the availability of resources both for product development and new product production. If the proposed project is feasible and financially advantageous, the product line manager will take on the role of project sponsor. He may choose a product engineer to act as project manager, and ask him to work closely with the product specialist who first discovered the need for the product's improvement.

Every year, thousands of product improvement projects and new product development projects follow this general pattern.

The Information Systems Project: Information systems projects follow a similar pattern with a wide range of variations. An information systems department, like an engineering department, exists to do projects. In some organizations, it serves as a service department for the entire organization and develops software and hardware packages to meet the needs of all its operating units. An information systems department in a bank or other financial house faces a steady stream of demand for new or improved information processing services. Typically, others in the organization come up with the information on what needs to be accomplished. The information specialist tells them what can be developed and how to do it. The information package user typically sponsors the project and acts as the customer for the project. The appropriate person to act as the project manager for this type of project is a systems analyst/information specialist.

The Salesperson-Produced Project: In many organizations, salespersons are the contact people who identify potential customers. They send out a project manager who is a representative from the product development staff to negotiate unique product specification and delivery conditions with the customer. This makes for a good product, which is delivered when expected to a happy customer. The procedures that flow from specification to delivery are spelled out in a developed project plan. The customer is sometimes presented with a flow chart describing the plan. The project manager keeps the customer informed as to how the workflow is progressing, and a well-defined specification change procedure exists. Some companies that produce high-ticket custom products have developed a cadre of project managers—former engineers—to manage their projects.

The Marketing Project: Marketing organizations, which often sponsor product improvement and new product development projects, generate many internal projects. Part of their job is market research, and market research teams continually are involved in gathering market data that may be used for new product development or advertising and sales campaign decisions. A sponsor for such a project typically is a product line manager or the marketing general manager. As always, scarce resources are involved, and cost benefit and feasibility questions must be addressed.

The Small Basic Internal Project: A department manager often sponsors small basic internal projects. These projects emerge at a level where the manager has discretionary control over the resources and has the responsibility for unit performance that can be improved with projects. Two conditions must be met: 1) The manager must have authority to commit resources to a project, and 2) the manager must have the motivation to do so. There are always many project possibilities and never enough resources for most of them. Costs, and particularly benefits, are often hard to estimate. Yet, week after week, managers still initiate projects. It is a rare manager who understands the importance of a project manager using IPM procedures to lead a project. However, the assigned project manager often has the flexibility to pursue the IPM approach, win the manager's support for it, and proceed with a successful project.

THE PROJECT SPONSOR

Every project must have a sponsor. As mentioned in the preceding text, a sponsor is someone within an organization who first discovers the need for a project and proceeds to get the project off the ground. If the project serves an external customer, the sponsor acts as the official contact with that customer. For new products and product improvement projects, the marketing manager is often the sponsor and the customer. For process improvement projects and Information Technology projects for operating departments, *the sponsor is also the customer,* because he or she has discovered the need and ordered that the work be done. The sponsor must be a person who is an executive or manager who has discretionary control over committing people and other resources or has a direct channel for requesting such commitments. After the go ahead to begin is ensured, the sponsor chooses a project manager.

The sponsor directs the project manager to draft a statement of work. The statement of work can be defined as an outline of what will be done to migrate the project from a general concept to a precise specification.

The statement of work goes by different names in different organizations. It is sometimes only a verbal agreement, but it should be put in writing to prevent confusion later on. The adage, "If it isn't in writing, it hasn't been said," applies here.

PROJECT HAZARDS

Problems brought on by outside sources can negatively impact a project or even jeopardize its feasibility. Before deciding to undertake a project, the sponsor may assess these potential problems or require that the project manager do so as a part of the statement of work. Either way, a project should not get underway without some assessment of potential problems stemming from events in the external world, in either the environment of project development or the application of project outcome.

Another type of problem to be considered beforehand is that the project will not be well planned and executed. This, however, can be mitigated by IPM procedures, especially internal risk analysis.

THE DAILY LIFE OF A PROJECT MANAGER

Making decisions is part of daily life for any manager or executive. Some decisions may result in a change of strategy in personnel policy or employee training. Other decisions may result in undertaking a project to launch a new product line. A gamble often is associated with important decisions. Newspapers frequently report the names of executives who were rewarded for "making the right decision" and those who were fired for being wrong. More than likely, those who were rewarded had weighed the pros and cons of the situation and had become thoroughly informed before deciding on the venture.

Making informed decisions is the dilemma at the heart of assessing potential project hazards. It plagues the project manager whose sponsor requests that he or she prepare an assessment of potential project hazards for the statement of work.

How does a project manager go about making informed decisions concerning potential external project hazards? By going out and talking to as many people as possible who have knowledge of every conceivable aspect of the project—and by gathering as much input from them as possible.

Armed with this information, the project manager should be able to formulate key questions for the experts who have the answers. For example, if a project involves building a new atomic power plant, a critical question for a politician from the affected district would be, "Will the government become so environmentally concerned during the construction phase of the plant that they might close us down before we can complete it?" A seismologist could be asked, "What is the earthquake possibility on the land where we propose to build?"

The weather must be considered for some projects. For a pipeline project in Alaska, where it can get very cold and snowy, a situation called "whiteout" can occur, which severely limits the distance a person can see while outdoors. In fact, a whiteout can be so bad that with an arm fully extended, it is impossible to see one's own hand. Under these conditions, all outdoor work must stop, which would bring most pipeline work to a halt. Surely the project manager will query an Alaskan climate expert on the possibility of whiteout occurring during the pipeline's construction.

For any type of project, it is important to ask a crucial supplier, "What is the likelihood of your firm getting involved in a long labor dispute and cutting off our supplies?"

And *the* question for each and every project is "Assuming the project is feasible, do we have the right people to work on it?" Surprisingly, some organizations proceed with a project when the answer to this question is no.

ASSESSMENT OF THE PROBLEM

Although business, industry, government, nonprofit organizations, and project sponsors would pay handsomely for a sure technique to correctly assess potential project hazards, no such system exists and probably never will. There are, however, guidelines to follow. Raising the right questions and asking them of experts, as previously noted is crucial. There are, however, thousands of questions one might ask and no one has the time or resources to explore them all.

When significant possibilities of potential hazards have been identified, the next step requires developing strategies to mitigate them. There are no magic solutions here either. Again, guidance from others and good judgment can lead to plans to lessen the impact of a significant external risk.

Sometimes problem assessment warns, "Do not try this project."

EMERGENCY PROJECT SHUTDOWN

If worse actually came to worst and an external hazard did shut down a project, the team must proceed in a certain way. They should be prepared for this eventuality, because no project manager ever wants task workers to simply stop working and walk away. Proper procedure calls for an orderly and disciplined shutdown, wherein all activities are brought to a point where they can be easily and reasonably resumed in the future. Each task leader, therefore, should be instructed to write a description of the exact point that his or her task has reached at shutdown. Measurements may be needed in this description to create restart conditions. It may be desirable to back off on some processes to reach a good shutdown point. Material and equipment locations also must be planned and documented, and backup procedures must be used.

Different kinds of projects require different emergency shutdown procedures. A project manager must discuss the proper procedures with the project team. Although preparing for shutdown is not generally a long or costly process, it is well worth the effort if a shutdown is ever necessary.

When restarting a project, it is not possible to simply begin where the project left off. Changes will have taken place, requiring adjustments to the original project plan. This delay should not be merely inserted into the Gantt chart; rather, the project manager should reconvene the team and review the Gantt chart construction step and re-examine the task risks. The project plan then should be replanned before the team proceeds to finish it. Some situations may call for paying a second source supplier to stand by to help if something happens to a project's key supplier.

DOCUMENTATION OF PROJECT DECISIONS FOR PROJECT APPROVAL

A project must receive final approval before it can be actually undertaken. The competent, conscientious sponsor will document the cost and benefits analysis, the feasibility analysis, and the hazards involved in doing the project in a report to request final approval. Many organizations have established procedures to ensure this report is done. The report typically is a form with questions that are specific to the project decision-making process. The financials are always in it. A feasibility analysis also may be required. The current state of the operation, relative to problems and needs, also may be addressed. A gap analysis of the current situation of products or practices as related to a desired situation may be requested. The probability of losing the investment made in the project and mitigating strategies for dealing with such a hazard must be examined. This report basically says, "We have done our homework," to whomever has the power to grant approval for the project to continue.

Many companies have highly structured procedures to ensure that the investment in a project is well justified. The documents for justifying the project usually go one of two routes. They may go directly to the project file. Then the sponsor proceeds to initiate the project and commit resources to it as appropriate. More often, the documents go through a review procedure, where a project review board has the responsibility for coordinating and controlling project investments across the organization. This board may approve, delay, or reject the project, and they also may assign it a priority level. Once their approval is granted, the project manager can take over the project.

A CASE STUDY

A real example of a sponsor identifying an opportunity to initiate a project and recruiting a project manager follows. In this example, the project manager acts as the sponsor's agent in developing information to clarify an opportunity and focus on one particular way to take advantage of it. The project manager helps the sponsor to understand the benefits of taking advantage of the opportunity. He or she suggests a feasibility study to be the first project in a series of projects, and determines reasonable time and resource requirements for the feasibility study.

Details of the example follow: Executives from other insurance companies told the vice president for operations at Macro Insurance Company that better utilization of computers has improved their efficiency and reduced costs. Macro Insurance has a Management Information Systems (MIS) department and significant mainframe and PC capacity, used primarily by human resources, payroll in particular, and analysts. Vice President Bill wants to explore other possibilities, and he believes that purchasing manager Nancy is the right person to lead a project to reduce costs through more effective computer utilization.

Bill tells Nancy his thoughts. Nancy has heard about electronic forms and thinks that the company spends too much money on paper forms for printing and processing. She shares these thoughts with Bill.

Bill likes Nancy's ideas and asks her to "look into this." Nancy tells Bill she will call some people in other companies and talk to Macro's MIS manager and some of his staff. Bill and Nancy agree that Macro can save money and improve operations by making greater use of computers; however, Bill is conservative and wants to proceed in small steps. They agree that Nancy should prepare a definition of terms and descriptions of relevant processes and then report back.

Nancy asks Bill what size project he has in mind, and they agree that the first effort should be something doable in at least three to four months, using some of Nancy's staff and some people from MIS, working part-time.

Nancy then refines the project's scope in the following memo:

Memorandum

To: Senior Management Team

From: Purchasing Manager

Subject: Electronic Forms Systems: Definitions and Processes

Electronic Forms are computer-generated formats, usually incorporating a series of organizational graphic elements (for example, lines, boxes, captions—on computer screen they resemble the paper forms we use to collect data) used for recording, collecting, and transmitting variable data.

Electronic Forms Design is the use of computer software to create the static structure of a form that will organize and guide the entry of variable data. Forms creation is achieved by using forms design software. (One such package is WYSIWYG.)

Electronic Forms are passed electronically from the creation/integration workstation to the mainframe for storage. Output of the forms can be from a mainframe laser printer or a mainframe-controlled remote printer.

Electronic Forms Print on Demand refers to a current revision of a form that is electronically printed when needed, in the quantity needed for a short or reasonably short time.

Electronic Development Publishing is a mainframe process, outputting multi-page or multi-copy documents at a high-speed, large-volume mode.

Electronic Forms Print on Demand produces blank forms on demand from centralized or remote laser printers.

Advantages of print on demand:

- Eliminates printing by an outside source
- Eliminates storage charges
- Decreases turnaround time
- Avoids obsolescence and waste

As the next step, Electronic forms may be used:

- To replace preprinted paper forms
- As a template for entering the appropriate variable data on the computer screen by the information processing person (which may or may not ever be printed on paper)
- As a vehicle for transmitting partially completed documents to other computer network stations for data addition and/or approval
- As the static structure for organizing and displaying the collected variable data as a computer-printed form

As the next step, electronic forms can be used as a basis for business analysis.

Relational Database refers to a software system that will accept a number of different files for data in such a way that relationships of one category in one file can be compared to a different category in a different file in many ways.

Electronic File Data Entry enables an operator to pull up an electronic form on a PC, enter data in the fields of the form, and then cause the form's data to be stored in a relational database. This allows for both paperless filing of data and for many options of summarizing and analyzing different categories of form data.

Setting up a paperless form filing system and a relational database provides for a very fast retrieval of file information and processing of clients claims. It also provides for analyzing client data and claims data categories, which is almost impossible with only paper files. However, a relational database will be expensive to set up and requires the development of new complex systems, which will take time.

We recommend that we first explore and consider developing an Electronic Forms Print on Demand System before we proceed with more sophisticated elements of electronic data processing.

The executives, in discussion with the purchasing manager and the members of Nancy's staff who helped put together the memo, decide to pursue Nancy's recommendations. They direct her to prepare the following working paper to be used to help finalize project objectives.

Working Paper

To: Senior Management Team

From: Purchasing Manager

Subject: Key considerations for the implementation of an Electronic Forms Print on Demand System

We recommend starting the analysis in the Classic Care Underwriting and Customer Service area. We believe that each form should be examined to see whether it is a form candidate based on a cost/benefit analysis.

Goals:

- Reduce cost and time needed for designing forms
- Reduce time and cost needed to print forms
- Reduce cost and time needed to distribute forms
- Eliminate storage of forms and cost of storage
- Reduce waste due to forms revision

Guidelines and standards will need to be established to determine:

- When a form is printed by an outside vendor versus an internal print shop
- When a form is printed on the 9700 laser printer versus a 5090 copier
- When a form is to be printed by a local laser printer versus a 9700 laser printer

Resource Requirements:

1. The project staff will have to review current information flow via forms as well as other methods of information flow that could be handled by forms. Project staff members will need to be relieved on a part-time basis from other duties over a period of one to two months.
2. The forms design staff, who are members of the project team, will have to analyze forms to determine what can be converted.
3. The systems people, who are members of the project team, will have to examine the printing schedules for the feasibility of printing on demand with the present equipment.
4. A schedule will have to be determined with person power requirements for redesigning forms for the electronic form system.

Project Objective Statement:

Prepare a feasibility study based on the cost/benefit analysis for the development of an Electronics Forms Print on Demand System for forms used in the Classic Care Underwriting and Customer Service Area. Forms to be considered are those that are used at least 50 times a week. The system will be judged feasible if the cost of developing it can be recovered by benefits within one year.

THE SPECIFICATION AND THE STATEMENT OF WORK

The document that measures project objectives is called the project specification. In literature and practice, it goes by many names, but in every case it states exactly what the project is going to accomplish. The project manager has the lead role in drawing up the specification.

The statement of work is the document used to clarify the project manager's effort to create the specification. It must state that the specification is to be clear, that it identifies measurable outcomes, and how the achievement of these outcomes will be demonstrated.

DEVELOPMENT OF THE PROJECT SPECIFICATION

The following checklist is to be used when developing a project specification:

A. What are we concerned about?

- Improving a process
  - Reducing costs
  - Reducing time
  - Improving performance of the process deliverable
- Addressing an opportunity
  - Meeting an emerging demand
  - Creating a new product or service
  - Entering a new market
  - Adding value to a product or service
- Taking advantage of Information Systems Technology
  - Acquiring better information for decision making
  - Providing faster, more reliable customer service
  - Managing production and inventory operations
  - Providing faster, more reliable, more extensive employee services
  - Automating paper processes
  - Upgrading an information system
- Improving customer relations
  - Attracting new customers
  - Entering a new market
  - Servicing a particular customer

B. Why are we concerned?

- We have a policy of continuous improvement.

- Customers are asking for it.
- Employees are asking for it.
- Competitors are challenging us.
- We must reduce costs.

C. What alternative approaches have been considered?

- What are the assumptions?
  (If we can do "this," "that" result will follow. What evidence supports this?)
- What is the cost of not doing the project?
- Could we outsource this project?

D. What is achievable after the project is completed that is not achievable now?

E. Are we very sure that the terms we are using mean the same thing to everyone involved with this proposed project? (Are we giving and receiving feedback?)

F. What processes are known to be associated with the problem(s) to be overcome or with the achievement of the desired result? Can we chart these processes?

G. What sources of expertise can help us best understand the proposed project?

- Subject matter experts
- Reading material
- Histories and Gantt charts from similar projects
- Reports on new developments in this field

H. What are our mutual (sponsor and project manager) expectations regarding the time and resources to be used in the project?

THE PROJECT SPECIFICATION

After the foundation has been laid, the project manager, assisted by key task leaders, is ready to write a draft project specification. This specification defines the project outcomes. (It does not deal with how the team will achieve these outcomes.)

Note: The project outcomes must be measurable.

Developing a software package for materials and manufacturing management, for example, would involve a broad range of required outputs that must be clearly specified so that the performance of the completed package can be demonstrated. Such packages, however, can typically perform thousands of complex processes, with hundreds of particular outcomes, so testing all the processes cannot be done. Therefore, the specification must include the details of a Beta test.

A Beta test is a performance demonstration of the project's product at the customer's facility, using the customer's staff. The customer and the project manager collaborate to develop the test's details. They also agree that if the package passes the Beta test, it reasonably can be expected to perform all the functions set forth in the specification.

For example, a jet aircraft engine is expected to perform over a broad range of flight speed and altitude conditions. In the experimental development of military jet engines, several representative performance points were identified for demonstration in a test call. If the engine met these performance points, it could be expected to reach the full range required of it. The engine developer and the customer collaborated to determine these points and the measure of successful achievement.

Note that ambiguities or vague generalizations are forbidden in a project specification! When this is ignored, a product that is not what the customer wanted can result.

Obtaining a good specification is the project manager's responsibility. If the project's sponsor is unwilling to help with details, the project manager must go it alone, redoing the project specification until it meets the customer's approval. (The project change committee and the change procedures provide the mechanism for adjusting the specification later if the customer asks for this. The change process is discussed in Chapter 13.)

Producing a good project specification is the very first step in executing a project. The project manager and sponsor(s) begin by creating the draft specification, which is reviewed by all interested parties. Everyone must be comfortable with the specification, and consider it a document that could provide directions a team would readily understand for executing the project. The specification also must identify specific ways of measuring project deliverables so that a knowledgeable third party examining the deliverables could easily determine that the specification had been met. This requires holding a specification review meeting. The group of reviewers must include members of the customer's organization who will be primary users of project deliverables, representatives of the proposed project team who have key roles in producing the deliverables, third parties with similar project experience, writers who will produce user guides and service manuals, and key suppliers who need to understand the project goal(s).

The specification must be distributed to attendees beforehand. At the meeting, it may be displayed on flip charts or overhead slides, clearly written in large print. It also can be displayed as the product of computer word processing through a computer-driven projector. (Some specifications will require many pages.) A specification can be written on a software word processing package. As overhead projectors scroll page-by-page, the project manager should read the specification, pausing for discussion and/or questions. A team member must take notes; using a tape recorder also is reasonable. Modifications can be made on the computer keyboard during the presentation, if necessary.

After the meeting, the specification will have to be rewritten. Often this rewrite will involve minor adjustments. It can be distributed to meeting attendees for review and comments before it is finalized. If major revisions are necessary, a second meeting also is necessary.

Everyone must understand that this specification will guide the planning process without any adjustments, unless and until a project outcome change is processed (see Chapter 13). If changes are required, the specification will be rewritten and reviewed before adjustments are made.

This process must not be long and drawn out. However, some projects, like Information Systems projects, have much detail in the specification and require a series of meetings. Getting such a specification correct may take time.

EXAMPLES OF PROJECT SPECIFICATIONS

Specification: Develop a project marketing launch plan for the A to Z sheet metal washer that will cost effectively identify and gain the attention of all potential customers, produce sales of 100 units during the first six months of product availability, and ensure field support for every machine sold according to the corporate-defined commitment to product support.

Discussion: This specification is fairly clean, but "cost effective" is not an acceptable statement for a specification. The statement must either define how cost effectiveness is to be measured or provide a specific cost target for the project. In addition, the term "all potential customers" is not measurable. This might be marginally acceptable for an experienced marketing organization, but a clearer specification would call for a potential customer list of "10,000" customers who meet the stated characteristics. "Field support for every machine according to the corporate-defined commitment to product support" is only satisfactory for the specification if there is a document defining this commitment. Otherwise, the product support part of the specification needs to be extensively expanded. It is easy to refine this specification and well worth the time to do so.

Specification: Design a year-round vacation cottage that will conform to the standards of the Bloomington, MN, building code, with 900 square feet of living space in three rooms—a living/dining/kitchen room, a bedroom, and a bathroom. The bathroom shall have a shower, sink, and toilet. The bedroom shall accommodate a king-size bed, and the living/dining/kitchen room will be the largest room in the cottage. You must provide a concrete slab foundation, an R18 heat transmission value in the walls, and an R24 value in the ceiling. In addition, you must provide a fireplace sufficient to keep the cottage at 60 degrees inside with a −20 degree temperature and −40 degree windchill outside. Indoor plumbing, electricity for operating a cooking stove, a refrigerator, and a washer/dryer also must be provided. The cost is not to exceed $100,000.

Discussion: This specification is a good first try, but it still needs work. First, the architect must know what lot the cottage will be built on or at least the characteristics of the soil that will support it so that a foundation can be designed.

Knowing the location of the lot and its surroundings also will guide the architect in placing the entryway and windows.

The specification also references the Bloomington, MN, building code. This is important. Without such a reference, much of the content of the building code would have to appear in the specification.

Some reference to outside appearance also must be provided to guide the architect. Wood siding, logs, aluminum siding, brick, and so on, need to be considered and chosen. Some guidance regarding the interior trim, windows, and doors also is needed.

Nine hundred square feet of living space is not sufficiently precise. A very unusual architect might design a house 10 feet wide by 90 feet long. To avoid confusion some reference to the layout of the cottage is needed. In general, this is a situation often found where the initial specification calls for a design that must be developed collaboratively between the designer and the customer.

The specification may direct the architect to produce three cottage layouts and three exterior view sketches referencing the stated details. It can further state that the architect and the customer will review the sketches and agree on one or a composite taken from the three sketches. Then, the architect will finish the design. The architect's finished design and layouts will become the specification that the builder will use in constructing the cottage. The cost statement must be a target and must clearly refer to either the architect charges or the cost of the finished cottage.

The interaction between project manager and customer noted here as layouts are discussed, is frequently necessary in a project. It therefore, must be noted in the specification and built into the project plan.

Specification: Write a program for providing a firm with a computer-based accounting system containing up to 500 accounts. Note that the program will provide 1) the entry of sales information of accounts receivable for up to 200 customers, with entries accurate to the penny and up to $100,000; 2) an accounts payable entry system for 100 vendors with the same dollar constraints; 3) the ability to automatically bill customers monthly, specifying a finance charge option of 1 percent a month for accounts 30 days overdue; 4) the ability to automatically write checks for vendors when the accounts come due, with a manual override for those checks that are issued selectively; and 5) a monthly profit and loss statement and balance sheet. The program will be written in C++ language to run with a UNIX operating system on a machine with 9 GB of disk storage.

Discussion: The critical consideration regarding this specification is the clarity of the communication between the customer and the project software developer. To an accountant familiar with small business double-entry bookkeeping, this specification may be clear. However, it would still require the development of a Beta test. This Beta test would demonstrate the functions so that the customer and the software developer could agree that if the package passed the Beta test, it could be expected to perform all the functions the customer desires.

This assumes, however, that the software developer also is trained and somewhat experienced in double-entry bookkeeping. There are thousands of details buried in the statement of requirements that demand knowledge of accounting. The details of how a double-entry bookkeeping system works and what its inputs and outputs are must be understood by anyone who is going to develop a software package to perform bookkeeping functions. Thus, the customer or a third party must explain these and train the software developer. A course in accounting also is indicated. At the same time, the customer must be briefed in what a software package can be designed to do and must understand the advantages and disadvantages of the different design approaches. Sometimes software package customers do not feel that they can agree on a specification until the software developer explains to them what they can have.

In fact, many big problems have emerged in software development and in other areas when a customer and a provider have not communicated clearly. A specification that both parties can agree on that describes the project's objectives adequately and accurately in language that both understand is necessary for any project.

Specification: (An old one, but a good one!) This project has the following four planning objectives:

1. Upgrade the computer hardware used to support the existing shop floor document management and tool crib system in Macon, GA. The existing systems will be migrated from a UNIX platform to a 32-bit Windows®-based distributed processing client/server network. In addition, server software will utilize the existing NT 4.0 file server. All of the client's PCs are to be at least Compaq Pentium 650s with 128 MB of RAM, running Windows 98®. The software language used to support existing business applications will not change.
2. Integrate an enhanced Electronic Tool Design Requestor (ETDR) system with the existing Material Requirements Planning (MRP) system. Known integration requirements are

   - Avoid duplicate data entry
   - Provide existing on-line application client PC interfaces for
     – Machine tool operators
     – Tool crib personnel
     – Manufacturing engineers
     – System administrators
   - Receive tool requests from the shop floor to issue specialized tools for the fabrication of specific parts identified by the MRP system
   - Send and receive problem reports from the shop floor to the Manufacturing Engineer Production Control Center

3. Determine the feasibility of completing all computer hardware and software tasks by no later than January 15, 2003.
4. Develop a jointly agreed-upon systems requirements document and acceptance test (Beta test) for the final acceptance of all hardware and software capabilities before beginning migration and upgrade activity. Customer and contractor officers will sign off on the requirements document and acceptance test.

Discussion: The shop floor document management system upgrade and migration specification is as stated, "The project has four planning objectives," which is A project to plan for a project that subsequently will be executed.

Paragraph one identifies the specific site where the project will be executed. An existing system at this site has been defined and documented. The PC network hardware to be used also is precisely defined, as is the software file server.

The general statement specifies that the existing systems will be migrate from a UNIX platform to a 32-bit Windows®-based distributed processing client/server network.

Paragraph two sets forth in some detail what the project outcomes should be. The MRP system that is to be part of the total systems also exists. The enhanced ETDR system also exists, or it must be identified. If the ETDR system has been identified but not enhanced, it is necessary to spell out that a part of the project is to enhance this system, and it is critical that what is meant by "enhanced" be precisely stated in a system performance terms. Words like "enhance," "improve," "better," "best," and "highest quality," are not satisfactory for a project specification. Their meaning must always be spelled out in precise, measurable terms.

The statement "known integration requirements" is to be followed by the specifics as an effective way of identifying deliverables, but the word "known" suggests that this requirement is open-ended. This is not satisfactory as it stands. Either the systematic process of inquiry and discussion with a clear definition of closure must be specified, or the word "known" is dropped. It can be dropped with the understanding that if and when additional integration requirements are identified, the project change procedure can be followed to batch the new requirements and include them in a new, expanded project specification, which will then be followed by a replanning session. It is reasonable to expect that in this situation, while the replanning will extend the project, it also will follow the direction indicated by the initial project plan, which will have substantial value.

Paragraph three sets forth the primary project requirement. This project is a feasibility study. A complete project plan to provide the outcomes identified in paragraph two is necessary to determine whether it is feasible to meet the stated date requirements. Feasibility is measured by the fact that a complete project plan has been developed and that it either does or does not fall into the indicated time window.

Paragraph four adds the critical requirements that the customer and contract officers must mutually agree up on the details for a Beta test, which can satisfactorily demonstrate that the specification has been met. Note that paragraphs two and four are closely related.

It is clear that only people who are familiar with shop floor management and with the use of information systems tools to achieve shop floor management will fully understand this specification. If the customer and the project team all understand and clearly communicate about these processes and issues, it is not important that anyone else understand the specification.

What we end up with is not some poorly stated specification that needs to be rewritten, but a very good start on a specification that still needs some refinement.

Specification: (This example is a specification that is jointly produced by members of the quality department and the process plant managers at a Fortune 100 company.) Investigate the current finishing and polishing operation in the XYZ product plant and propose improvements that will enable scheduling cycles to be reduced from two weeks to one week in converting and from one month to one week in slitting. This also will include a proposal to implement kanban between slitting and converting. These proposals also will include estimated cost savings and are to be completed on September 1, 2003.

Discussion: The reduction of cycles to one week and implementing kanban also is measurable. An estimated cost saving is a clear deliverable.

The customer, plant manager, the process operators, and the quality improvement team know exactly what the specification refers to. They know exactly what kanban means in their organization (it refers to a tight, just-in-time type of processing). They also know how to measure costs. If they all know this information, it is not important who else does or does not understand the specification.

A review of the similar operations in the company and in the other organizations supports the feasibility of the project. The date of September 1, 2003 is a target date.

There is one serious flaw in this specification, however. It does not state that the resulting process improvement must produce products that meet the same quality standards required of the present process. The project leader, in this case, can argue that in the quality program this condition is assumed to be a given. You should note, however, specifications should never include assumptions. The process products' quality requirements should have been stated in the specification.

Many project specifications require much more than one paragraph or page. Often, the marketing department creates a specification, providing input regarding customer needs and feedback from the engineering department on how these needs may be met. Collaboratively, marketing and engineering will arrive at a detailed project specification. The following specification for repackaging the ABCD Shielded Electronics Console is such a specification.

Some specifications can require more details, such as with some information systems specifications that may go into detail in regard to what information will be input into each input screen and how each output item will be displayed.

It is not important that the general public understand the language of a specification. It is important, however, that the customer and project team be precisely clear and agree on the meaning of each term of the specification.

Specification:

1. The existing ABCD electronics console assembly must be repackaged into a stainless steel, EMI/RFI-shielded enclosure.

   This shielded enclosure will be contained within a flame retardant polypropylene (FRPP) skin; areas of the shielded enclosure that are not covered by the FRPP skin will be straight line, grit-finished stainless steel like that used on XYZ ISR.

   The components will be mounted in drawers that may be extended out of the enclosure, either to the front or the rear. The goal is to build it with a front/rear access.

   The same components as the existing design must be used, except as noted elsewhere.

   Space for future I/O expansion must be allowed.

2. The following remote control boxes must be incorporated into the new electronics console, and a single 208–240 volt single-phase power line must be brought in. The main GFI breaker will change, depending on which of the following options are present:

   HELIOS 52 (This control box is powered by the 480-volt supply to the HELIOS 52 heater column.)

   IR heater

   Nitrogen heater (This will not be powered by the UPS.)

   Thornton resistively/pH monitor

   Remote touch screen switch box

3. Each set of the previous control circuitry will have dedicated realestate in the cabinet. If the option is not present, the designated space will be empty.
4. The heated recirculation control box will remain in the existing console; EMI/RFI shielding will be added as necessary, based on test results.
5. The booster pump will be powered off the UPS. The cabinet design will be modified only as necessary to meet the EMC requirements. The electrical box will still be mounted in the pump console.

6. The UPS will still have a separate control box, but it will power the ZIP booster pump and IR heater. The separate control box is required because the UPS may be remotely located and must have an EPO on it. The UPS will be redesigned for 10 kVA capacity under Project 9605. Any EMI/RFI shielding modifications following testing will be done under the EMC Project 9611.
7. Primary user interface:

   Phase I: The existing touch screen interface will be centered 5 feet up from the floor, and it will be covered by a clear shielded panel that flips up during use. Allowance will be made in this area for the incorporation of the ZETA GUI at a later date. EPO buttons will be placed on the front and rear, and a single rotary main disconnect switch on the front will remove power from all options in the spray processor system. The touch screen, EPO/main disconnect, IR heater/Nitrogen heater/HELIOS 52 controllers, resistivity monitor, disk drive, and pressure gauges will be visible without removing any of the panels.

   Phase II: Incorporate The ZETA GUI, keyboard, and its associated CPU as a touch screen emulator. Use Factory Link and OS/2 software. Other primary interface aspects are the same as Phase I.
8. Remote user interface:

   Phase I: The remote touch screen will be contained in a shielded enclosure with an FRPP skin. This screen will still be an optional feature. The customer will no longer have the option to have a single touch screen remotely mounted.

   Phase II: To use the GUI from the rear of the electronics console, a rear pullout drawer will be provided that will contain either a fixed or remote laptop PC.
9. The electronics console will be field upgradeable to all installed ZIP MPs. If the customer purchases the upgrade, he or she must operate on the latest software version (that is 9.071).
10. The following are the facility power requirements at 208–240 volts single-phase 50/60 Hz; these requirements have not changed from the existing design. A fully loaded system will require a 10 kVA UPS. The Nitrogen heater will not be powered by the UPS because it is not necessary for personnel and product safety, and the Nitrogen heater chamber is not remotely located from the ZIP. Here are the facility power requirements:

    ZIP: 10 amps

    ZIP with IR heater: 40 amps

    Dual booster pump: 14 amps
11. The identical shielded electronics console also will be used for the ZIP OC Front/Rear Access.

12. All wiring diagrams and installation diagrams will be revised. The O&M manual must be revised for this new configuration.
13. Make the nitrogen inlet tube 3/4 of an inch instead of 3/8 of an inch for greater flow capacity.
14. Make the following modifications prior to the first pass EMC test:
    Add EMI/RFI filters to all I/O cables.
    Ensure all shields are properly grounded.

Discussion: This is a somewhat longer and more detailed specification that has survived review. It is specific for persons with special technical knowledge. Other specifications may follow this pattern and may require dozens of pages.

Project size does not determine the length of the specification. The specification is properly sized if it describes precisely and completely the project's deliverables.

CUSTOMER AND SPONSOR START-UP EXPECTATIONS

Customers often want a project to begin before they have decided on a precise outcome. However, IPM is based on the premise that a precise outcome statement, or specification, must come first: Experience and logic support this proposition. Nevertheless, when thinking is at the scope level—the level of general awareness of a problem or opportunity—it is often reasonable for the customer to be uncertain of such a precise outcome. Can an integrated project be started under these conditions? The answer is, necessarily, yes. The project manager can begin the project by leading the creation of the specification.

As the project manager helps migrate the project from scope to specification, he or she will aim for precision. This will capture the current best estimate of what the outcome should be. The specification will be used to plan and execute the project. At the same time, the project manager will put in place a project specification change procedure to efficiently deal with outcome changes that may come later.

Experience has proven that this approach is more efficient than starting in a general direction and then adjusting, redirecting, and reorganizing as a precise outcome concept emerges. It must be understood, however, that in IPM replanning will be a major event and will not be done piecemeal, nor will it occur often during the life of the project. Small and frequent modifications must be prevented. Such practices kill projects.

When replanning occurs, as it does in most projects, all the small, new modifications that have been considered can be batched and integrated into the specification and detailed project plan.

PROJECT MANAGEMENT ALTERNATIVES

Some efforts, called "projects," never arrive at a precise specification. In these situations, the project manager is directed by the sponsor or customer to begin an activity at a point that seems to be a promising place to deal with a general problem or opportunity. As initial tasks approach completion, the next step is decided upon. At this point, the sponsor may be making the decisions, or the project manager may be expected to make them. The project manager, backed by the sponsor, recruits and assigns people for the next step. This process continues, and desirable outcomes are identified. If and when useful outcomes are finally achieved, the project is declared a success and is stopped. If, after a while, no good outcome emerges, the project is stopped.

However, there is no "right" way to manage a project. There are many different management approaches to choose from.

- Some project managers believe in planning a project completely before starting work: "Plan the Work and Work the Plan." Others prefer "fast track:" Start by executing the obvious first step and then plan the steps as you go.
- Some project managers do the planning themselves. Others collaboratively plan with the project team. A variety of approaches are available for gaining collaboration of the project team members.
- Some project managers plan from the project completion date backward. For others, the only efficient way is to plan, step by step, from start to finish.
- Some project managers make their planning fit the project management software that they are using. The very sophisticated project managers make the software fit the needs of their planning approach and then add longhand tools where their software is inadequate.
- Some project managers do not do risk analysis nor plan for catastrophes. They are simply hoping to successfully ad lib when problems emerge. They do not believe that it is possible to plan and manage a project to finish on time, and they take pride in their expediting skills when deviating from the plan.

IPM is designed to complete a project to specifications, on time and within budget, using only the planned resources and without the occurance of serious injury or loss of time due to accidents. (The latter condition is particularly important for construction projects.)

IPM requires the following:

1. A technically knowledgeable project manager who is a skilled leader. He or she must be able to lead the team into collaboratively planning and cooperatively taking responsibility for the project.

2. A detailed and precise analysis of what is required to complete the project, prepared before the work begins.
3. A well-planned and structured change procedure to be in place at the beginning of the project. Then, when the inevitable requests for change in outcome occur, a smooth effort can be initiated to redefine and replan the project.
4. The project's feasibility to be addressed before project planning.

SUMMARY

In this chapter, we examine various circumstances and situations in business and industry in which project possibilities have emerged. We identify the role of the project sponsor and the considerations a sponsor must review before making a general project decision. In addition, we identify the point at which a project manager typically enters into the project identification and project-defining procedure. We also discuss the role of a statement of work and explain the way a project manager proceeds from a general project concept to a precise project specification.

DISCUSSION QUESTIONS

1. Why is it not reasonable for a project to be created in business and industry without a project sponsor?
2. Could the project manager also be the project sponsor?
3. Why would a manufacturing manager, a product line manager, a human resources director, a marketing manager, a sales manager, or a service manager want to become a project sponsor?
4. What is the difference between sponsoring a project and authorizing funds for it?
5. How does a sponsor determine that a project is feasible?
6. Who deals with project uncertainties that come from outside the project?
7. How does a project team know when they have completed a project?
8. When, in your career, can you expect to become a project manager?
9. When, in your career, might you expect to become a project sponsor?

3 PROJECT WORK BREAKDOWN STRUCTURE AND TEAM RECRUITMENT

INTRODUCTION

Once the specification is set with the sponsor, the project manager becomes responsible for the project and can begin work on the development of the project plan. Step One is to determine what work is required overall for the project, and who should do this work. Identifying the major jobs and the skills needed for them fulfills both of these objectives. When the skills become apparent, people with these skills then can be targeted for recruitment.

The major job groupings are called work packages, and a display of all work packages is called the work breakdown structure. As with all IPM steps, seeking advice from others inside or outside the organization who may have worked on similar projects must be done when developing the work breakdown structure.

THE PROJECT BEGINS

After the project manager and sponsor agree on the specification, the project manager takes full responsibility for the project. Choosing the right people for the project team then becomes job number one. Needed are specialists who can either lead skilled workgroups or execute jobs on their own. Each unit of work that the specialists will be working on is called a task. A task sometimes is small enough to be carried out by one person. Tasks that are larger require a group of workers. The lead worker from each workgroup serves on the project team. The project team then consists of a mix of specialists who will either work alone or lead a group of workers.

WORK BREAKDOWN STRUCTURE

The process of team selection begins with breaking down the project into major work packages, or bundles of jobs to be performed to accomplish one piece of work. For example, site preparation, foundation preparation, and erecting the steel for a building's framework are some of the work packages for a building construction project. To be sure that no work packages are left out, the project manager should query others who have "been there," or people familiar with this type of construction.

When every work package is known, the project manager should make a list of all the work packages. The entire process of identifying and listing work packages is known as "developing the work breakdown structure." *The work breakdown structure process is used for every project, regardless of its size or breadth.*

DETERMINATION OF THE SKILLS NEEDED FOR THE PROJECT

Having identified the work packages through the work breakdown structure, the project manager has a good idea of the skills required of the project workers.

The skills necessary for building a house, for example, are clearly implied. A house must have a foundation. Because installing a foundation is a work package that involves placing forms and pouring cement, it requires the skills of masons. Walls also are a necessary element of a house; construction of these walls is obviously a work package for skilled carpenters. A house must be wired for electrical services; wiring is a work package for electricians. Small workgroups of masons, carpenters, and electricians, headed by the lead specialist in each group, will work on the house. Installing window shades is yet another work package, but it is one that does not require a workgroup. A single specialist can do this type of work. This specialist also will serve on the project team, along with the lead mason, electrician, and carpenter.

Unless the project manager is an experienced contractor, discussing the work packages with actual contractors to ascertain that no packages have been left out, clearly is in order. The same is true of the electricians, masons, carpenters, and other workers on the project. Talking with them could unearth a work package that so far has been overlooked.

Erecting a larger building is another matter entirely. One level of breakdown will not produce enough details to expose the skills needed to build a skyscraper. The site preparation for a building of this magnitude may require a survey and an excavation. This adds another level of breakdown, which clearly reveals the need for survey and excavation crews. By pursuing this process of breaking down work packages into smaller and smaller groups, the project manager will eventually nail down all the workers needed to build the skyscraper.

However, there is no need to go it alone. Seeking the advice of knowledgeable and experienced project managers and skilled workers, called "subject matter experts," can greatly help identify the work packages. Such people are always around an organization. They have learned what to do and how to do it, and they may share their notes and documents, such as Gantt charts or resource tables. Because the project manager is not expert in all areas of project work, he or she must rely on the advice of those who are.

THERE IS NO SUCH THING AS A GENERIC PROJECT MANAGER

The work breakdown structure concept is generic: It fits all types of projects. The same cannot be said for the project manager. Background determines who should lead a project. The project manager of a house-building project could not be expected to lead the construction of a jet engine. A jet engine project manager must understand aerodynamics, thermodynamics, combustion, mechanical design, and other closely related specialties—things that are foreign to the house builder. This tells us that a marketing manager is obviously the logical person to manage a sales and marketing project, a software expert to manage a software development project, and so forth. Because the person who manages a project must have technical skills relevant to the project, there is no such thing as a generic project manager!

RECRUITMENT OF THE PROJECT TEAM

To begin recruitment, a project manager must meet with each of the supervisors of the potential recruits to solicit their recommendations for candidates. This meeting should be held even if the project manager has already chosen a particular individual, because it will smooth the way for the desired person's participation, or will lead to the supervisor identifying an alternate, as the case may be.

Sometimes circumstances are such that the project manager's boss chooses the project team. If this occurs, the project manager should review the work breakdown structure to ensure that all of the necessary skills are represented, and request additional help if necessary. Supervisors here also should be met with!

Once the desired team members have been identified, the project manager must meet individually with each one to request their commitment for the project, keeping in mind that they should be considered volunteers and treated as such. Some recruits may be over-committed for the foreseeable future and unavailable. When this happens, the recruit and the project manager should inform the recruit's supervisor and try to work out availability. However, if this proves impossible, the project manager must find an alternate person. If no one is available, it then becomes a problem for the project's sponsor. If the project could not be completed without this necessary person, the sponsor will quickly discover the need for more workers—temporary or permanent. The sponsor then has the responsibility to acquire new help or postpone the project.

When requesting a recruit's participation—unless IPM procedures are already familiar to the organization—the project manager must brief the person on what to expect. That is, that the project will be planned during a series of structured two-hour meetings, between which, team members will gather project data, and that meeting attendance is mandatory, with meetings scheduled collaboratively by the team to accommodate their other responsibilities.

When recruiting for the small basic project, as few as three or four team members may be all the workers needed. Tasks for the small basic project generally consist of work packages that can be completed without any further breakdown and performed by an individual. Therefore, explaining IPM procedures to a small group may be done all at once at an informal meeting.

THE TASK LEADER AND THE TASK WORK GROUP

Most tasks in a large basic project are performed by groups of workers. Each group is called a "task workgroup" and is headed by a lead member, who is called a "task leader." This task leader represents the group on the project team. A few tasks may be so small that they can be handled by one person. These individuals also are called "task leaders." In essence, each project team member is a task leader. Therefore, a team meeting can be described as an assemblage of task leaders.

One example of a task workgroup is that of an engineering group that is charged to design a part for a machine. The individuals in this group have experience working together. They are: 1) an engineer who does calculations and produces a design sketch, 2) a designer who converts the sketch to engineering drawings, 3) a pair of tool room operators who take prototype parts drawings and produce sample parts, 4) an inspector who verifies accuracy and manufacturability. In this setting, the engineer typically acts as the task leader and represents the workgroup at project meetings. The project manager acquaints the engineer with IPM processes, asking that he or she use them to lead the workers into full participation in the project.

A large basic project can require up to 30 task leaders, who sometimes represent up to 300 workgroup members. This type of project may consist of several hundred tasks and require several years to complete. It is developed like a smaller basic project; however, the project manager may need one or two assistants to help with team recruitment. These assistants should be drawn from within the project team, and they should hold the same basic qualifications as the project manager—the difference being that they also carry project task responsibilities. *Except for very small projects, a project manager should never carry project task responsibilities.*[1]

CONSIDERATIONS FOR RECRUITMENT

It is very important when recruiting team members to impress upon them the extent of their participation. They may not expect that they are being recruited to actively help plan and manage a project as well as execute tasks—yet, that is precisely what they will be doing! The project manager must emphasize that IPM will not be successful without their cooperation and hard work.

This is where trust and respect become tremendously important. Team members must believe in their project manager if they are going to produce the kind of work that IPM demands. If they feel otherwise, the project will have little chance for success.

With the work breakdown structure and recruitment completed, the project manager is ready to schedule the kickoff meeting. This meeting should be held as soon as possible but at a time convenient to all team members. It is better to delay the meeting a day or two to accommodate everyone, than leave someone out. The project manager should prepare the kickoff meeting agenda and project specification (or a condensed version), and distribute copies to each team member beforehand, along with an invitation to the kickoff meeting.

SUMMARY

The project must be broken down into work packages. The project manager accomplishes work breakdown with the help of every available resource. As the work packages are identified, the skills needed for them become apparent, and the

[1]From a personal letter written by John Ely, President, Surface Conditioning Division, FSI International, and used with his permission: "Never, ever have a design engineer with engineering responsibilities act as a project/program manager. We heard what you said, we under funded and tried it anyway, bombed!"

project manager can recruit team members with these skills—after first conferring with their supervisors for help in identifying the best prospects for the team. Recruitment is done on a person-to-person basis, with the project manager explaining the IPM process to each recruit.

DISCUSSION QUESTIONS

1. When is the project manager justified in developing a project work breakdown structure without any help?
2. Why does the work breakdown process go together with the job of identifying members for the project team?
3. What does the project manager do if several people chosen for the team cannot attend the kickoff meeting?
4. What can the project manager do if a supervisor reports that no one with the necessary skills is available any time in the near future?

4 THE KICKOFF MEETING

INTRODUCTION

The kickoff meeting is the first in a series of team meetings. It is critically important to team members because it provides a broad introduction to the project, and due to its importance, attendance is mandatory. Among the topics covered at the meeting are project planning, including the details of the Gantt chart used in project planning, and the methods used to plan and execute the IPM project. In addition, team members are put through a series of exercises and discussions. At this time, they learn what lays ahead for them throughout the project.

THE IMPORTANCE OF THE KICKOFF MEETING

Everything anyone ever wanted to know about the project is revealed at the kickoff meeting! It lays the groundwork for what lies ahead for the team. Working through the agenda, the project manager explains the IPM procedures to be used to execute the project. The team will learn that the project is a collaborative venture: They will all participate in project planning and share in achieving good communication within the project, and they will learn that their expertise will be needed in creating the project plan. They also will learn that in creating the plan, each team member can support the project by going beyond his or her personal knowledge to query subject matter experts within their organization, by asking for help in developing the information they bring to planning meetings. Because it is important that every team member fully understand these points at the beginning of the project, *everyone on the team must attend this meeting!*

To assure mandatory attendance, during team recruitment, the project manager must set a date when all team members are able to attend. Although it is always desirable to hold the kickoff meeting as soon as possible, it is more important to start with all team members present, even if this means delaying the meeting a day or two.

THE KICKOFF MEETING AGENDA

A. Explain why the project is being undertaken

B. Present the project specifications

C. Introduce the team members and state their technical specialty

D. Explain IPM team collaboration:

1. Communication
2. Development of team norms
3. Collaborative leadership
4. Conflict resolution and consensus decisions

E. Explain how an IPM project is planned, using a special Gantt chart that displays each planning step as a task and shows the linkage of project tasks with a tentative display of task dates

F. Explain the subject of the next meeting—the project task list

G. Set the next, and subsequent, meeting dates

AGENDA ITEM EXPLANATIONS

While walking the team through the agenda, the project manager should discuss the points that follows each agenda item, and encourage the team to raise questions if some points are confusing.

A. Explain why the project is being undertaken: The project manager should draw on discussions with project sponsors, recounting the ideas and concerns that led up to undertaking the project; explain the perceived need and the expected rewards following successful project completion; and point out the priority the project has within the organization. This explanation helps the team to recognize the importance that management places on the project and assures that management will support the resources committed to the project.

B. Present the project specification: The project manager should note that the specification explains exactly what the project's product is intended to be, and that the project's success is measured by how closely the finished product measures up to the specification. The project manager also explains the procedures for implementing changes to the specification. Experienced team members typically are accustomed to project objectives being changed during a project's execution. They will need assurance that these interruptions and intrusions are well recognized by the project manager and will be carefully monitored and controlled. (Change procedures are discussed later in detail in Chapter 13.)

C. Introduce the team members: The project manager should introduce the team members and explain how their expertise will be used in the project. He or she should introduce each person according to when they will participate, following the order the project will take from beginning to end. This order will demonstrate the flow of activities. Each person can speak for him- or herself with the smaller projects. However, with larger projects, the project manager should make the introductions to save meeting time. Team members may or may not know each other, but even if they are acquainted, it is important to foster good communication and cooperation by pointing out the specific role that each person is expected to play. In addition, it is useful for the project manager to handle the introductions so these important points are covered and be certain that the introduction period does not suffer from a long-winded team member.

D. Explain IPM team collaboration and lead exercises: (Note: Detailed explanations are found Chapter 1)

1. Communication: The project manager should explain good communication skills and how to give and receive feedback. He or she should stress that one reason IPM is successful is that the team—not the project manager—makes the critical project decisions, which are achieved through discussion during team meetings. It also should be noted that this only can be accomplished through effective team member communication. Feedback to insure good communications is covered in Chapter 1. It can never be overemphasized. Feedback examples must be cited during the kickoff meeting—one example is that of writing a textbook. In this example, the publisher's acquisitions editor asks the author when the book will be finished. The author replies, "September 1st," which could mean that he expects to get the last words down on paper by then. The editor, however, might interpret this to mean that the material will have been typed according to the specified format, hard copy will have been printed and diskettes made, and both mailed out by September 1st. Feedback, or querying each other, is essential between the editor and author so that they agree on the meaning of the term "finished." Getting this term correctly defined has great significance for the publishing house team who will copy edit the book and pass it along for composition and printing. It is relatively easy to neglect clarifying important terms and get the book-publishing project in trouble. This problem can become even more serious if the author and acquisitions editor do not talk to each other at all. If each is a task leader on the larger book publishing team and they do not communicate about the work, the rest of the team will be in limbo. A project manager must use examples of this type to urge task leaders to spontaneously communicate with each other often to assure that they agree on the message.

2. Development of team norms: The project manager should explain that the norms serve as guidelines for participation in team meetings. One thing that is learned through the operation of self-managing work teams is that norms (also called rules of procedure or engagement) play an important role in team meetings and in team collaboration. The project manager must explain the norms and conduct a norm-building exercise, using examples such as: "never let a meeting run over two hours," "arrive on time," "stick with the agenda," "come prepared," "do not interrupt each other during discussions," "focus disagreements on project outcomes, not personalities," and so on (refer to Chapter 1).

3. Collaborative leadership: The project manager also should discuss collaborative leadership, stressing that team members share in this leadership, and that this is done through spontaneous leadership role-playing (refer to Chapter 1).

4. Conflict resolution and consensus decisions: The project manager also should lead a discussion of the personal conflicts that can arise between team members during a project. It must be explained that if conflict does not become personalized, it can be channeled toward reaching good project decisions. The principles of reaching a consensus decision also should be explained (refer to Chapter 1).

E. Explain how an IPM project is planned, using the project planning Gantt chart: The project manager should pass out a copy of the project planning Gantt chart with tentative task dates, to each team member. The chart should look like Figure 4-1. The project manager should inform the team that they will be following a series of steps to complete the project. He or she should note that the output of one step serves as the starting point for the next step; the steps themselves are standard, but the procedure to execute each step is unique to IPM; and they will learn these procedures—not all at once—but as each step comes up. (Between meetings, each team member is to gather information to be used at the next meeting.) The project manager will pass out blank graph paper for a sample project planning Gantt chart to each team member. There are 13 steps on the Gantt chart that lead up to the time the project work is launched. Step 14 refers to the project manager's role of leading and managing the project's execution. Project planning task and task meeting dates are indicated on the Gantt chart. The project manager should note

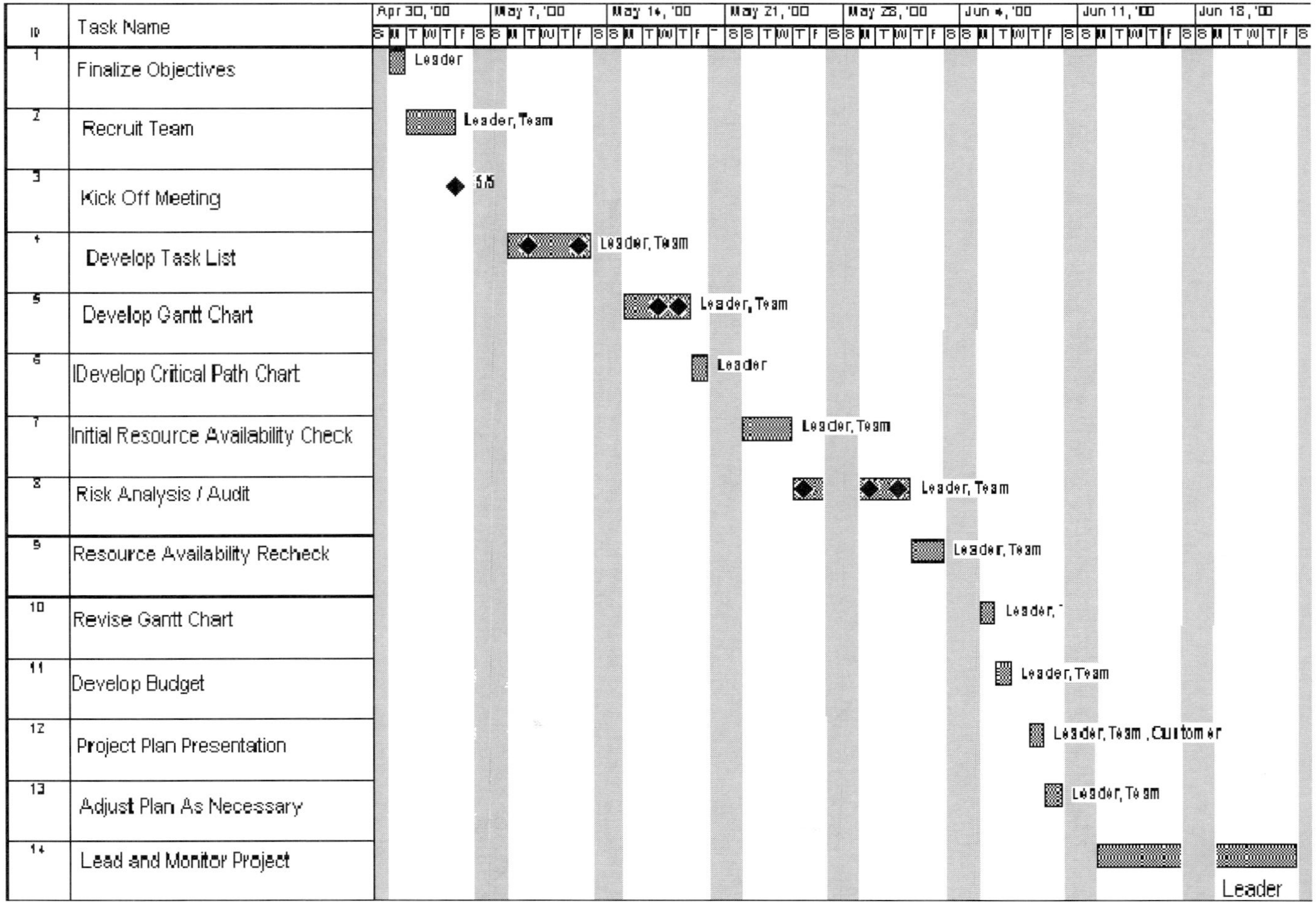
ID
Task Name
Apr 30, '00
May 7, '00
May 14, '00
May 21, '00
May 28, '00
Jun 4, '00
Jun 11, '00
Jun 18, '00
1
Finalize Objectives
Leader
2
Recruit Team
Leader, Team
3
Kick Off Meeting
5/5
4
Develop Task List
Leader, Team
5
Develop Gantt Chart
Leader, Team
6
Develop Critical Path Chart
Leader
7
Initial Resource Availability Check
Leader, Team
8
Risk Analysis / Audit
Leader, Team
9
Resource Availability Recheck
Leader, Team
10
Revise Gantt Chart
11
Develop Budget
Leader, Team
12
Project Plan Presentation
Leader, Team, Customer
13
Adjust Plan As Necessary
Leader, Team
14
Lead and Monitor Project
Leader

Figure 4-1

that the Gantt chart steps are not open to discussion! However, as planning progresses, the team will be able to decide on and revise the dates and the amount of time per step that will work best. This planning process must not drag out. Although team members should take their other responsibilities into consideration, they also must tend to the project. The priority given the project by their organization will help determine this project's priority. Should other work cause a planning delay of a week or more between steps, it is better to delay the whole planning process. Delays create loss of continuity, which is detrimental to good planning.

The first two tasks listed on the sample Gantt chart in Figure 4-1, "finalize objectives" and "recruit team," came prior to the kickoff meeting. The kickoff meeting date (8 a.m., Friday) was chosen earlier by the project team.

Reading across the chart, a diamond indicates the date of each two-hour meeting. (When more than one meeting per planning unit is required, additional diamonds will appear within a horizontal bar.) A horizontal bar represents the days that team members gather information for individual tasks, while simultaneously taking care of their other responsibilities.

The sample in Figure 4-1 shows the kickoff meeting held in one two-hour session on a Friday. At the meeting's conclusion, initial action items are assigned to team members who determine the date and time for the next meeting, which is based on the time required to complete the action items. By starting work on Monday, this hypothetical team expects to be finished with the data gathering for the task list by mid-Tuesday, and so they set the next meeting for 1 p.m., Tuesday.

At the two-hour Tuesday meeting, the team begins to collaboratively develop the task list. They also agree that they must reconvene to finish it, and set that date for 8 a.m., Friday.

At the Friday meeting, each team member takes responsibility for tasks on the task list. Friday action items call for the individual task leaders to decide who will work on each task as well as the amount of effort and time each require. They also must clearly identify their tasks' immediate predecessors. The team decides that two and a half days will be allowed to gather this information. A session to develop the *planning* Gantt chart is scheduled for 8 a.m. the following Wednesday, and a second at 3 p.m., Thursday. The team also will set other project planning dates in a similar fashion.

The planning meeting sequence, as outlined in the sample, must not be a long, drawn-out procedure. Even with large projects, individual planning units (such as creating the task list) should not take more than four days.

Each task leader will copy (on graph paper) the planning Gantt chart that the team collaboratively develops for the project. This chart is kept as a reference, and is revised as the team revises its planning process. The project manager should coach the team members as they complete this process. Doing so will give them a better understanding of the project execution Gantt chart that will be developed later at the Gantt chart meetings. This longhand process works best for the project planning Gantt chart. Software is, however, more effective for developing the full project Gantt chart.

F. Explain the product of the next meeting—the project task list: The project manager should describe the action item that each team member must complete for the next meeting: To identify all tasks within their area of expertise, as well as all other tasks they can think of that are necessary to the project. There will be much overlap between the lists. This overlapping assures that the team will not miss an item or omit anything.

G. Set the next and subsequent meeting dates: If it appears that the kick-off agenda is going to take longer than two hours, the project manager should plan to cut it off at two hours and reschedule a second meeting for completion. He or she should be respectful of the team members' other commitments when scheduling meetings.

TEAM MEMBER EXPECTATIONS

By the end of the kickoff meeting, team members realize that they have taken on an active role. Work is required of them both at and between meetings. The between-meeting work involves interviewing others not on the project team for advice and data. Although conducting these interviews (this is called an action item) is interspersed with the team members' efforts to meet other commitments, it must not be considered secondary to other commitments and be laid aside. The project manager should ask the team members to build project commitments into their day planners.

Everyone is expected to attend the next meeting, with their task list in hand.

Flexibility

The IPM model, as described at the kickoff meeting, sets forth specific directions on how to plan a project. If these directions are followed, the project can meet its specifications on time and within budget. However, the model should not be viewed as rigid. It can, and sometimes must, be used with flexibility.

For example, at one particular Caterpillar Corporation plant, planning meetings are limited to 90 minutes (instead of two hours). This, of course, necessitates a few more meetings, but nothing else is changed. (Note that forty-five minute meetings, would be too short.)

The IPM model prescribes that team members be encouraged to play shared leadership roles. A young engineer attending a workshop session reported that his team would laugh at this concept. He then suggested asking each individual to play one support leadership role, when appropriate.

Another workshop student had team members scattered all over the world. Her organization would not support bringing them together for project management meetings. Therefore, she devised a telecommunications network that supported virtual team meetings and got the job done!

Always use the IPM planning model with the necessary flexibility. Results, not method, are important. The project manager should do whatever it takes to make the model work.

SUMMARY

The Major IPM Steps: Project Meetings and Between-Meeting Activities

The following are the major IPM steps:

1. **Kickoff meeting:** As previously described. The project manager will schedule a second meeting if the first runs over two hours.
2. **Task list meeting:** The team creates a task list using the affinity diagram procedure. It may require two meetings to complete the list. The last meeting should produce the task list, which is organized under the work packages with the tasks listed in their expected sequence order.
3. **Task time sequence and resources meeting, Gantt chart meeting:** The team collaboratively creates the Gantt chart. It may take two or three meetings to do so. Capturing this Gantt chart requires assistance from a computer, using project management software.
4. **Critical path between-meeting activity:** The project manager uses the Gantt chart information to create a critical path arrow diagram.
5. **Time buffer analysis (risk analysis) first meeting:** The project manager explains risk analysis procedures to the team.

   Project team between-meeting activity: The team members individually gather risk factor contribution data, calculate task contributions, and submit their results to the project manager.

   Project manager between-meeting activity: The project manager compiles list of contributions and distributes it to the team.

   Second team meeting: Insertion points for the risk factors are selected and the duration of each risk factor is calculated.

   Third team meeting: A Gantt chart with the risk factors inserted is redrawn.

6. **Activity to assure team member availability as scheduled:** The team members meet with their respective supervisors to review their time commitments to the project to assure their availability.

7. **Team meeting to redraw the Gantt chart, reflecting team member availability:** It should generally be not more than a one-hour meeting.
8. **Customer review meeting:** The project manager, supported by the key project team members, presents the project plan to the customer(s) for their consideration.
9. **Meeting to revise the Gantt chart per customer input from customer review meeting:** This may take several meetings. It may even require going back to task listing and Gantt chart redevelopment if the customer requires major adjustments.
10. **Meet with customer for signoff:** This confirms a clear agreement between a customer and a project manager on the project goals.
11. **Project launch meeting:** The project manager and team review the Gantt chart. Task leaders whose tasks have no predecessors start today!
12. **Project manager walkabout management activity:** The project manager keeps in close touch with the active project teams, provides support when needed, and maintains an up-to-date project effort report in the form of an actual task time Gantt chart.
13. **Milestone meeting:** The project manager convenes the team at preselected progress points to review their accomplishments and to look ahead.
14. **Project achievement of objectives demonstration, customer acceptance meeting:** This brings closure to the effort to achieve project objectives.
15. **Share project report, and review achievements, discuss with team, "What did we learn?" team meeting.** It is very important to reinforce the learning that the project team members have experienced.
16. **Project closure celebration:** This is the closure of all project effort and a morale booster for future projects.

DISCUSSION QUESTIONS

1. What are the purposes of the kickoff meeting?
2. What other means might be used to achieve these outcomes?
3. What is unique about collaborative leadership?
4. What changes can the project team make on the project planning Gantt chart?
5. What are the characteristics of the action items following each meeting on the project planning Gantt chart?
6. What action is each team member expected to take immediately after the kickoff meeting?

5 THE PROJECT TASK LIST

INTRODUCTION

After moving a project from its scope statement to its specification, the project manager is ready to identify its major work packages, which provide the foundation for recruiting team members. Because the people who will be recruited for the team are specialists in each project job area and most familiar with the work, they are best suited to draw up the project task list. This project task list is a comprehensive listing of every individual job found within the project. This chapter explains how the team, working through a procedure called the affinity diagram exercise, creates the task list. The affinity diagram exercise is beneficial even beyond its original purpose, in that it builds team communication and cooperation.

PREPARATIONS FOR THE FIRST PROJECT TASK LIST MEETING

A task is an individual job within a project. The total number of required tasks is determined by the size and complexity of the project. There can be 40 or fewer tasks for a small basic project and 200 or more for a large basic project, with every one being important and necessary. The "master list" of all the tasks is called the project task list. Creating this project task list is the project team's first collaborative effort. The project manager covers the steps for creating this list at the kickoff meeting.

Because the project task list names every task in the project, it must be comprehensive. *Any job omitted from the task list will not get done.* To begin to pull together a comprehensive task list, each team member is instructed at the end of the kickoff meeting to prepare a list of tasks in his or her area of expertise, and to be thorough about it. Reaching beyond their area of expertise, each member must add tasks in other specialty areas. This action is to be done following the kickoff meeting, and the list must be brought to the next meeting.

Team members also are instructed to not include merely the obvious tasks from their specialty area in their list, but to seek task suggestions from those "who have been there," or persons in their firm with experience in a similar project.

In addition, they are asked to reach outside their area of expertise for tasks in other specialties so that the full extent of their collective imaginative effort will be utilized in the project and to assure that no task is left out. Often, an outsider's list will contain a task—or even an entire work package—another specialist forgot or assumed that would be included. If an entire work package is missed, it is necessary to enlarge the project team to include someone to cover the overlooked area.

The essence of IPM is to focus as much expertise as possible on the planning process and to do it as quickly as possible. Team members working independently and in parallel on an action item, as just described, fulfill both of these objectives.

While working on this action item (and others to come), team members usually have other job responsibilities. However, an action item must be considered a primary effort, having a prominent place in each team member's day planner, and not something to be fitted in haphazardly.

When the project team reconvenes at the next meeting, their individual task lists will be used to create a composite task list. Determining when to hold this meeting is based on the team's collaborative decision. Altogether, two meetings will be held to create the project task list in its entirety. Figure 5-1, which is lifted from the sample planning Gantt chart, depicts three days total time, or two 2-hour project task list meetings, with team members working on action items between meetings.

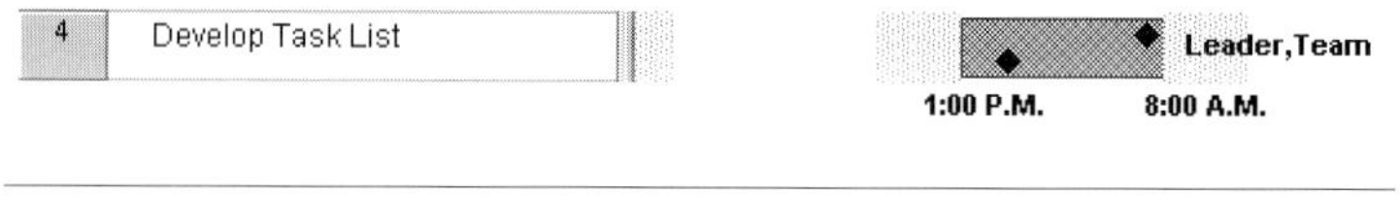

Figure 5-1

THE AFFINITY DIAGRAM

When a manager in any business setting tackles a problem or opportunity, input often is needed from a broad group of informed colleagues. Their combined experience and imagination can be a great contribution to the effort at hand; their ideas invaluable to the initial decision-making process. This situation often comes up in the area of process improvement and in the general area of improving quality. Leaders of the modern quality movement invented a device to help capture worker input and to systematically organize it. It is called the affinity diagram.

The process is simple. First, the workers are asked to each make a list of suggestions relevant to the decision-making process for the effort at hand, being as thorough as possible. This could be a listing of actions, components, or processes. Because everyone is doing this all at once, it proceeds quickly. The workers then are brought together in a conference room and asked to copy each suggestion from their list onto a small piece of note paper, writing one suggestion per note paper. Working together, they place their suggestions on a display table or tape them on a board—doing so without conversation. Next, they arrange the suggestions in clusters of like suggestions. At this point, the workers can freely talk and discuss the clusters, and organize them under headings. This process proceeds rapidly, and before long, a diagram has emerged with a heading for each cluster of suggestions. This diagram, with each grouping determined by affinity, can produce a good basis for the manager to decide on how to proceed.

This entire process is a fast way to gather a great deal of input from a large group of people, and to organize the input to provide a systematic and comprehensive approach to action.

THE FIRST PROJECT TASK LIST MEETING: USING THE AFFINITY DIAGRAM TO CREATE THE TASK LIST

The affinity diagram exercise has proven to be very useful in creating project task lists. It enables team members to individually identify every task they know of, and in a fast-moving process, to group all of them together. These groups then are defined either as major tasks or work packages. Using this method, a well-structured task list that has hundreds of tasks can be produced in a very short time. The team performs the affinity diagram exercise at the first project task list meeting, with the focus of the exercise being the team members' individual task lists.

The project manager must obtain a meeting room with a large blackboard or other large surface to which Post It Notes®[1] will adhere in order to carry out the affinity diagram exercise. Each team member is given a generous supply of these notes to use in this exercise. (Other methods can be used to display task suggestions, but Post It Notes® are ideal.)

When the meeting begins, the project manager instructs the team to do the following:

1. This is a silent exercise; there should be no talking during the exercise.
2. Copy each individual task from your list onto a separate Post It Note®, one task per note, and stick them on the wall. Place each task close to other related tasks posted by yourself and others to form a grouping. Throw away your note when one exactly like it is already posted.
3. Post all the tasks on your list. Add any new ones that come to mind as you work, and post them accordingly.
4. When you see a task that should be broken down into sub-tasks, write each sub-task on a separate note, and post them touching the task from which they are derived.
5. If you see a Post It Note® that you think belongs in a different group, go ahead and move it. (Someone else may move it back, if they wish.)

The first instruction, "This is a silent exercise. There should be no talking during the exercise," is a sleeper. No matter how strongly it is emphasized, team members will be talking to each other before long, organizing the tasks into groups, and, in general, proceeding to spontaneously organize the project. This is good. It builds team relations and stimulates creativity. Good processes of breaking down larger tasks into smaller packages will occur here. It is desirable, however, that the teams start the procedure working individually and silently. It is not productive to compare lists before posting them. Workers do not as thorough a job of listing tasks if they converse before the posting process. However, breaking into discussion later is inevitable, and it is very effective in the general pattern of collaborative planning. The project manager participates by encouraging the breakdown of tasks into smaller tasks, as appropriate, and by encouraging the grouping and ordering of these tasks.

Some large project teams will complete the listing and organizing in the allotted two hours. If it is not completed, the project manager and the team will have to schedule another two-hour meeting. These meetings should not be allowed to run over! People tire of this process after awhile and need a break.

[1]Post It Notes® is a registered trademark of the 3M Corporation.

As the posting and grouping progresses, work package and major task headings will emerge. The project leader should facilitate this organization. It is helpful to have an open area on the wall to hold any notes containing questions that surface during the exercise. These questions can be referenced when the project manager and the team proceed to organize and record the task list. Often, they will flag multiple interdependencies among tasks that will be important later when building the project Gantt chart.

When the list seems complete and has taken on structure, the project manager will help the team capture it on paper. This can be done manually, with sheets of paper laid out to jot down the information. Work package headings, with their tasks underneath, are copied down. The result resembles a project outline. Manual recording is tedious, however. A laptop computer loaded with project management software works well and is essential for large projects. The process of recording the list does not require the entire team. Assigning one person to operate the computer and one or two people to help the project manager pull the tasks from the board works well. Recording the list should be done immediately after the task list meeting, before the display has time to get cold.

If using Microsoft Project 2002® software, the data entry worker needs only to click the mouse pointer on the Microsoft Project icon and a blank Gantt chart form will display as the default screen. This screen has a task list column on the left-hand side, and it is ready for the first column entry. A work package heading that requires no predecessor tasks can be selected from the package headings on the board. The data entry worker should enter this heading on the first row of the task list column. Keying "entry" moves it to the next row. The project manager should pick the task in this group that should come first and have it entered. The "indent" icon on the tool bar is used to start the list, indented under the heading. (Note that the task's Post It Notes® should be saved for future reference.) Picking the task that seems to logically come next continues the entry process. Getting the tasks and work packages in the functionally correct order is not important. After each team member has reviewed the list and perhaps added some tasks, the project manager then can have the entry person adjust the list using the "delete" and "insert" commands.

The project manager should enter the work package headings in the order the work is to begin. The headings should be entered along with tasks, one after another, for the work beginning without predecessors. Successor work packages should be entered in the order expected predecessors would be completed. The sample task list shown in Fig. 5-2A, Fig. 5-2B, and Fig. 5-2C was created using Microsoft Project 2002® in this manner.

The project manager should get the completed list printed and distribute copies to the team members, asking them to review the list as soon as they receive it. They should look for tasks that have been omitted or overlooked. They also should break down tasks into subtasks, as appropriate. Team members now are asked to identify tasks that are their responsibility. They are to bring this information to the next—second or third—project task list meeting.

	Task Name
1	⊟ **DISK CLEANING MACHINE A**
2	Project Manager
3	⊟ **Prototype Design**
4	Component specs.
5	Component interface:
6	1st comp skchs
7	Select prfd skch
8	Mech dsn sketch
9	Fluid flow sktch
10	Elect dsn sktch
11	Software spec.
12	Revise comp skch
13	Design audit
14	Finalize dsn sktch
15	Milestone
16	⊟ **Fluid Flow Dsn**
17	Fluid candidates
18	⊟ **Dsn Fld Test Fac**
19	Spec fld pref
20	Sketch tst dsn

Figure 5-2A

	Task Name
21	Pick test pts
22	Lay out dsns
23	Mfg test parts
24	Assemble
25	Perf test fluids
26	Select fluids
27	Lay out fl path
28	Pick components
29	Order std parts
30	Design special parts
31	Mfg spec parts
32	⊟ **Mechanical Design**
33	Composite layout
34	Unit dsn frame
35	Unit dsn handling
36	Unit dsn housing
37	Parts design
38	⊟ **Work Order Make**
39	Parts1-7
40	Parts A, B, C

Figure 5-2B

	Task Name
41	Part X
42	⊟ **Purchase Std Pts**
43	Group W
44	Group Z
45	⊟ **Software developmen**
46	Write specs
47	Make or buy
48	Write
49	Purchase
50	Design tests
51	Purchase test hdw
52	Install hdw
53	Test and debug
54	⊟ **Electrical Design**
55	Configure
56	Purchase std pts
57	Purchase spcl pts
58	Milestone #2
59	⊟ **Lay Out 3D Design**
60	Lay out
61	Team Review

Figure 5-2C

A DISCUSSION OF WORK BREAKDOWN

At the beginning of the project, the project manager created the work breakdown structure (see Figure 5-3) to determine the skills needed for project work, by first identifying the major tasks to be performed and the specialty work areas that they entailed. This, in turn, guided the selection of the project team. One, or several, team members (who are specialists in each area) now represent each major project task. Each specialist will have already identified the work package that his or her major task should be broken into and have listed the individual tasks making up this work package. If a workgroup, rather than an individual, is required to complete a task, which is often the case, the workgroup leader must consult with the workers in order to develop the task list.

When Is a Task a Task? If the individual or workgroup is able to do a task without breaking it down into smaller discreet units of effort, the level of breakdown is sufficient. Each unit of work is designated as a task. If a work package consists of several discreet separable efforts, it should be broken down into these separable efforts. These separable efforts will be treated as "tasks" on the final task list and are shown in Figure 5-3 as subtasks.

For example, one work package for a project to build a house is to build the foundation. The "build the foundation" work package breaks down into these tasks: (1) survey the lot and determine corner locations, (2) excavate the site, (3) lay out the footings, (4) pour the footings, (5) establish the lot drainage, (6) construct the cinder block basement walls, (7) pour the basement floor, and (8) cap the basement. These tasks can be done by individual teams, and constitute sufficient breakdown to be designated as "tasks." However, providing for drainage requires two separable tasks: 1) install drain tile, and 2) install a sump pump. Each of these subtasks will be considered as a task.

Note that several different craftspeople involved in the "build the foundation" work package are on the project team. The masons will quite readily note their tasks of "pour the footings," "construct the cinder block basement walls," and "pour the basement floor." They also should have included in their task lists other like tasks that come to mind, in order to assure that nothing was left out.

The project task list does not necessarily describe task sequence, but the task leaders will often think in these terms. It is important for the project manager to keep in mind that these tasks must be broken down into smaller, discreet, independent work units, and that none are left out. Breakdown is satisfactory when individuals are identified who can determine exactly what has to be done, how long it will take, and who will do it. If, on one unit of effort, several groups are each working independently of each other, the unit needs even further breakdown. Each autonomous team should have its own task.

Projects that are more complex than building a house often break down into several levels between the "major task" level and the "task" level diagram (shown

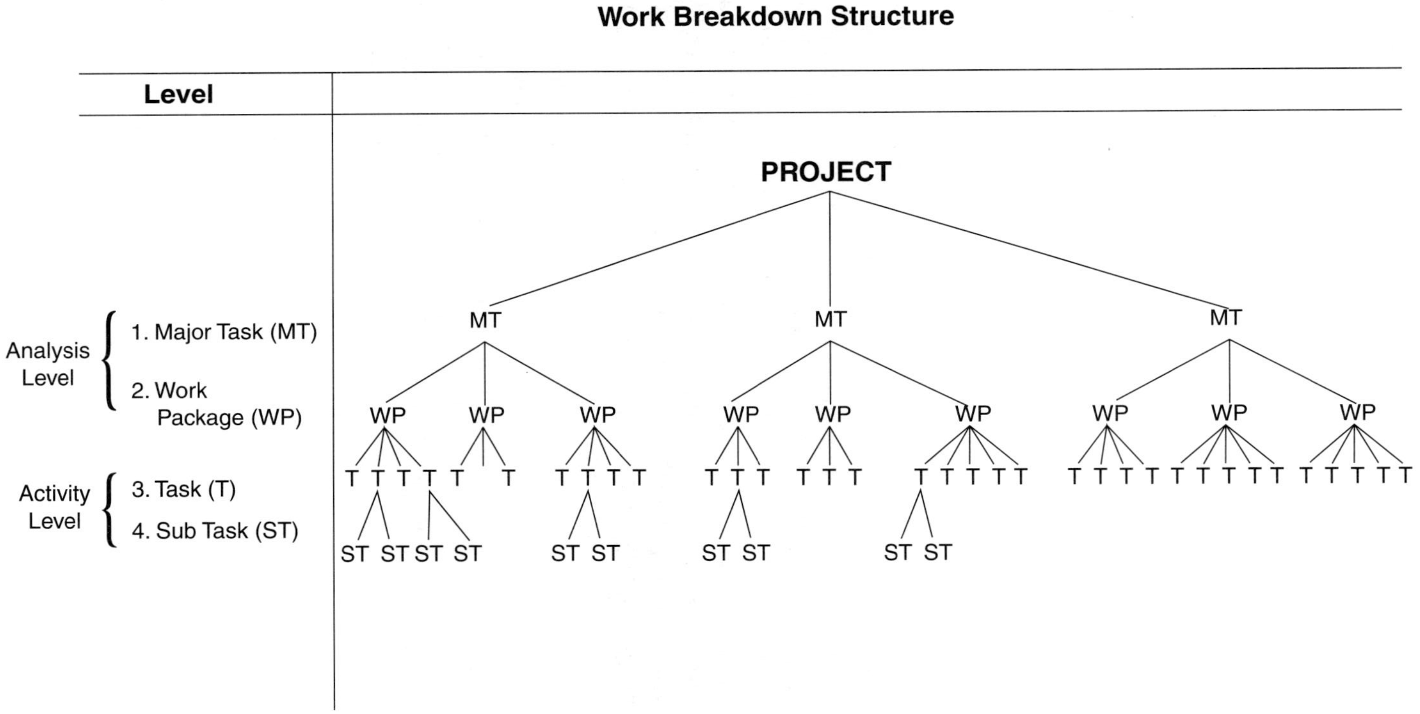
Work Breakdown Structure
Level
Analysis Level
1. Major Task (MT)
2. Work Package (WP)
Activity Level
3. Task (T)
4. Sub Task (ST)
PROJECT
MT
MT
MT
WP
T
ST

Figure 5-3

in Figure 5-3), but the process still remains the same. The team should continue the breakdown until all work units have been broken down to their task levels. To achieve this breakdown, team members should seek out information about similar and previously completed projects, examine the Gantt charts, and then perhaps talk to resource persons outside their organization. The team's goal is to always be clear and complete about what needs to be done.

The procedure used in IPM of having the task performers—not the project manager—provide the task list information results in a more complete list and also achieves a greater team member commitment to the project.

The sample task list in Figure 5-2A, B, and C is used for one basic project in a series of basic projects that comprise a major project. The major project is to construct a very sophisticated machine to be used in the computer chip industry.

The sample task list covers the design of the machine. Its major tasks are prototype design, fluid flow design, mechanical design, software development, electrical design, and layout 3D design. The prototype design major task breaks down into 11 tasks. Fluid flow design breaks down into nine components that are tasks, and one design fluid test facility, which is a work package broken down into six tasks. Mechanical design is a major task that breaks down into five tasks and two work packages, each of which break down into several tasks. Software development is a major task that breaks down into eight tasks. Electrical design breaks down into three tasks. Layout 3D design is a major task that does not break down at all but is simply one task.

The major project described here is real, and was completed several years ago. Its goal is to design, develop, manufacture, test, deliver, and install a unit ordered by a customer. The work package for the design basic project is done first. It is followed by the development basic project, the manufacturing basic project, and on down, with each requiring its own task list.

There are fewer than 30 members on each project team, and each team works efficiently in developing their task lists and subsequently executing their projects. The basic project managers comprise the major project team, which is led by a major project manager who coordinates all their basic projects.

REASONS FOR WORK BREAKDOWN

Some people ask why IPM insists that project work be broken down into small units. This questioning assumes that it is easy to look at a work package and say "we know how to do that." This idea can be very wrong. Those who look at a large work package with the confidence that they (or their work group) know all there is to know about doing the job, assume that the package can be broken down into smaller units as they go along. They think that when they start the first tasks, the subsequent tasks will become obvious. However, all projects have some unique characteristics, and therefore, some hidden traps and bottlenecks when approached at only the major task or work package levels. Breaking down the package into tasks and subtasks is an exercise in discovering if "we" really know how to do it. A project manager might assume, for example, that a software package output could be directly input into the next task user's equipment. Careful task breakdown may reveal that a conversion step is necessary before Task Number 1's output can be used with Task Number 2's equipment. However, more important is the real possibility that the work package team will unexpectedly reach a hurdle that they have not considered, one that cannot be surmounted without significant outside help.

Another reason for work breakdown is connected to the projected completion date for the project. The task time estimates, which are provided by work package leaders and add up to the project completion date, are always less accurate than those derived by adding the time estimates from the series of smaller tasks that comprise the work package.

The initial analysis provides the base information for the project's planning time buffer analysis. When the initial analysis and project plan are completed, the project manager will lead the team through the process of determining the appropriate time buffers, or "risk tasks," for the plan. The initial analysis, with these risk tasks added at strategic places, along the flow of project tasks, provides a finish date that can be used with confidence.

The breakdown process also may suggest that several trials may be necessary before reaching satisfactory task completion in some task areas. Information may surface that suggests two or more parallel work teams are needed to assure the timely completion of certain tasks. This is valuable data to keep for the Gantt chart.

AFFINITY DIAGRAM BONUSES

The affinity diagram exercise is beneficial to the project beyond its intended purpose. By learning whose work supports their work, each team member can develop a sense of "where I fit in the project" and "how I can support downstream tasks." This provides a basis for "internal customer" relations among team members for the duration of the project and also builds strong team ties.

Following the affinity diagram meeting, team members must allow themselves enough time to review the task list before scheduling the next project task list meeting(s). They must not let this process drag, however.

THE FINAL PROJECT TASK LIST MEETING

At this meeting, the project manager will ask each task leader to claim his or her individual task(s). Every task on the list must be someone's responsibility. If any of these tasks are unclaimed, additional people must be recruited to perform them and brought into the project team.

A very important set of action items will be assigned at this meeting. Each team member will be asked to determine 1) Which task(s) must be completed immediately before "my" task can start? 2) Who will do "my" task work? 3) How much effort, in terms of days or weeks, is required? 4) How long will the task take? and 5) What other resources will be needed?

The sample template shown in Table 5-1 is recommended to record this information, which is to be used at the next meeting. This sample identifies the tasks that one member of the team, Joe, is responsible for.

Task leaders must consult with their workgroups, asking each worker to put careful thought into estimating the amount of effort involved in their task (see column 3 on the task template in Figure 5-4).

Workers must be asked what percentage of time they can devote to the task, along with their other responsibilities. This may amount up to 50 percent of their time, or perhaps only 20 percent. Effort, divided by the percentage of time devoted to the task, determines the task's duration. A task that requires one week of effort from a group working only half of the time will have a two-week duration.

A project manager cannot expect absolute accuracy in effort and duration estimates. Asking task leaders for guaranteed duration times results in a somewhat padded time span, which is harmful to good project planning.

Workers must not buffer the estimates, but they provide estimates expected to be good "most of the time." The worker's past experience, or what is learned discussing the experiences of others, determines the "most of the time" estimate. "Most of the time" estimates will be good some percentage of the time when a like task is undertaken. With routine tasks, this percentage may be 95 percent of the time. Estimates for technical tasks, or those involving developmental efforts with few technical difficulties anticipated, may be considered good 80 percent of the time. "Most of the time" may mean only 70 percent if technical difficulties or resource availability is anticipated. For tasks where the workgroup has limited experience and only limited available input from outside sources, 60 percent may be the time estimate to use.

The project manager can suggest these guidelines to the task leaders, but he or she should not suggest which percentages to apply. The task workgroup must use their judgment and experience in providing a "most of the time" estimate at this planning stage. Some technical people are leery of task time estimates. To get around this problem, ask the question "How long does it take you to drive to work, most of the time?" This question may help explain to them the type of estimate that is needed.

This procedure also provides information for the initial time baseline. Some tasks are going to overrun estimates, which stretches out the project and must and will be accounted for in the Chapter 8 risk analysis and time buffer calculations. However, experience shows that "most of the time" estimates seldom overestimate the task time by much. When wrong, it is underestimated.

The chapters on risk analysis explain how to develop time buffers to take care of the time overruns of some project tasks. The team will work with the project

Table 5-1

(1) PREDECESSOR	(2) WHO WILL WORK ON THE TASK	(3) EFFORT IN DAYS OR WEEKS	(4) TIME COMMITMENT	(5) DURATION (EFFORT/COMMITMENT IN PERCENT)
Preliminary Sketch	Design Team/Joe, Mary, Tom	4 weeks	50%	8 weeks
Assembly Design	Joe and Mary	3 weeks	100%	3 weeks

manager on this analysis and will develop risk factors to insert in the plan timeline later in the project planning effort. What is needed at this time are good "most of the time" task time estimates.

IPM procedures eliminate task time estimate padding. Estimates used in developing the project Gantt chart are tight. All task leaders must recognize this fact and realize some tasks may overrun, but they must still work hard to meet their estimates. If, with conscientious commitment, a task does run over, the project manager must not criticize the task leader and the workgroup. The risk factor determined during risk analysis will absorb this overrun at the end of the task stream. Thus, all task leaders must understand that the risk factors are only required for unpredictable difficulties.

The meeting following the last task meeting is the first of the project Gantt chart meetings. Team members must allow enough time to gather task time and resources information for this meeting and should schedule it as soon as possible. Each team member must bring his or her completed task template (refer to Table 5–1) to the second Gantt chart meeting.

SUMMARY

A project is always executed task by task. The team members are chosen for the project because they have expertise in the major task areas identified in the development of the work breakdown structure. They, therefore, are well equipped to decompose the major tasks into work packages and the work packages into project tasks. Project tasks represent small units of work that the task team need not break down any further to execute the task.

Breaking down work packages into tasks does two important things. It assures that the task team fully understands what they need to do, and it provides a work unit with duration and resource requirements that are much easier to accurately estimate than composite work units.

The technique for compiling and organizing the project task list involves using the affinity diagram approach. This approach enables much planning work to be done in a short time period while building the project team's cooperation.

DISCUSSION QUESTIONS

1. Which project team members perform the project tasks?
2. Who tells the task leaders which tasks to perform?
3. What are the advantages of using the affinity diagram approach to creating a task list?
4. What is gained in the project when the task leaders know and talk to each other?
5. At the end of the task listing effort, what is the project team prepared to do?

6 CREATING THE PROJECT GANTT CHART

INTRODUCTION

Every basic project needs a project plan. Starting a basic project before the planning is completed does not produce the desired results. Each project needs a written description of what is to be done, task by task, when each task must be started, and how long each task is expected to take. Projects progress in a task-by-task order. A few tasks can be started simultaneously at the launch of a project, however most are dependent on predecessor tasks. These tasks are started when a prior task or several immediately prior tasks have produced the task outputs needed as their starting point.

The project Gantt chart was designed to display, on graph paper, the flow of tasks, predecessors and successors, that describe the execution of the project. It is a basic document that enables the project manager to keep track of a project's progress and to anticipate when preparations must be made to start successor tasks during the project's execution. When risk analysis and risk factors are added to the Gantt chart, the project completion date will be identified. (Note: IPM uses a different Gantt chart to plan the planning of a project).

As the Gantt chart is developed and task bars are created to indicate task duration, the names or titles of task leaders and workgroup members can be added to each task bar along with the amount of effort each workgroup member will contribute to each task. This charting provides the project manager with the basis for project resource management. As hourly, daily, or monthly work rates are added to the resource information, the project budget is defined (see Figures 6-1A through 6-1D). The Gantt chart, therefore, provides the basis for project time management, resource management, and cost management.

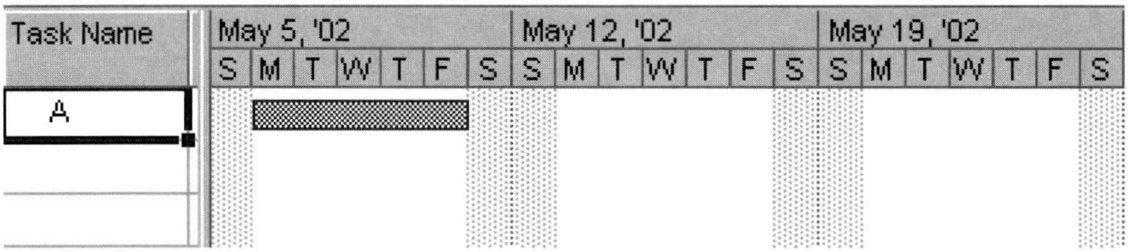

Figure 6-1A

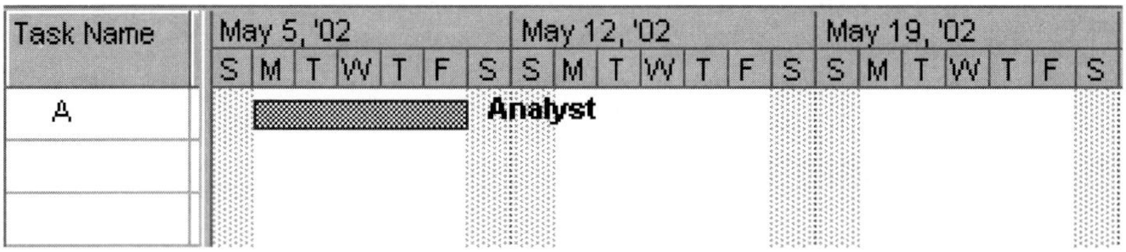

Figure 6-1B

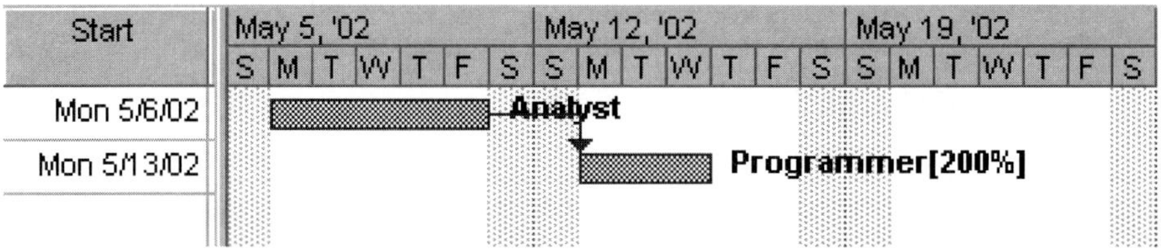

Figure 6-1C

	i	Resource Name	Type	Max. Units	Std. Rate	Ovt. Rate	Cost/Use	Accrue At	Base Calendar
1		Analyst	Work	100%	$4,000.00/mon	$0.00/hr	$0.00	Prorated	Standard
2		Programmer	Work	200%	$30.00/hr	$0.00/hr	$0.00	Prorated	Standard

Figure 6-1D

GANTT CHART BASICS

The Gantt chart concept goes back to the days of World War I. Yet, only since the 1980s have most new project management students become familiar with it. This late familiarity may be due to the recent and more widely accepted use of project management software and the use of the Gantt chart as a principal tool in software applications. Software applications are used to chart project tasks. Before the advent of software, the Gantt chart was done manually using graph paper.

A project manager and project team have completed planning a project when they have determined what needs to be done when, in what sequence, by whom, over what period of time, and using what non-human resources.

The project task list defines what needs to be done. When the task sequence and dependencies, and the required time estimated for each task has been determined, the outline can be converted to a flowchart that shows the project's timeline. If you identify who will execute each task, what effort each worker will devote to each task, along with what non-human resources are needed, you can establish the basis for defining the project's budget. When you have determined the time and effort buffers that must be added to the flowchart to allow for overrunning the original estimates and have determined where these buffers should be placed on the flowchart, you will have completed the work of project planning.

We display the plan in the form of a Gantt chart. This small project Gantt chart is repeated here to aid the discussion of time, resources, and cost planning (see Fig. 6-2).

In Figure 6-2, the outline of the task list is displayed under the heading Task Name on the left-hand column of this chart. Bars laid out paralleling the calendar line and following each task name display each task's duration. The thin black lines ending in arrowheads indicate the task dependencies and sequences. The names beside the boxes indicate who will perform the task. If a worker will be busy full time executing the task, just his or her name or title is displayed. If he or she will only work part time, the percentage of time that he or she will work during the task effort is displayed in decimal form and in brackets, after his or her name. If two (or more) people in the same work category will work on the task, the number of those people in % (100% = 1) will be displayed inside the brackets (project task workers can be identified by their name or title). At this point in the project planning, non-human resources and time buffers are not displayed. They can be easily added.

For each project, the knowledge required to fill in all of this information is distributed among the members of the project team. It is fundamental to IPM that the team members supply this information for the project plan. The problem that you may face is how to get from the point where the knowledge is scattered among team members to the point where you have a composite project Gantt chart. This situation is not unique to IPM. The method that we use in IPM is one where the team, under the project manager's leadership, cooperatively creates the Gantt chart.

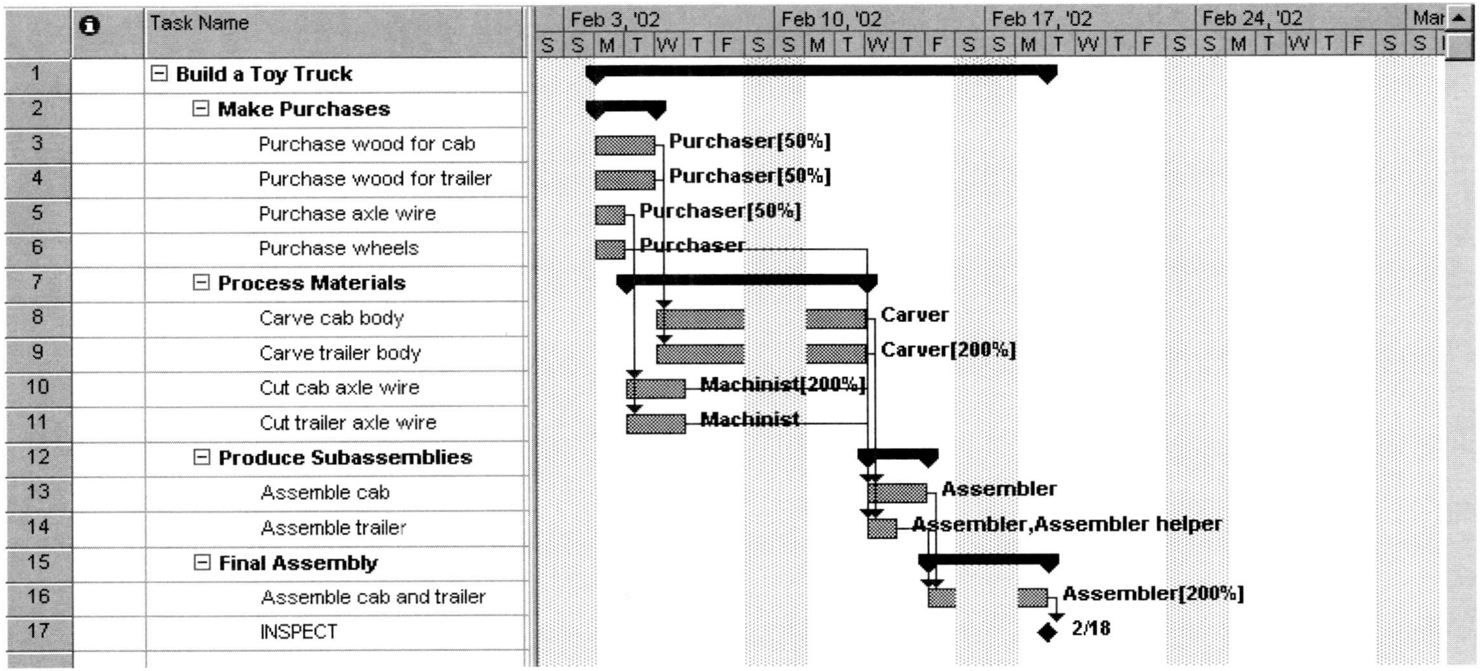

Task Name
Feb 3, '02
Feb 10, '02
Feb 17, '02
Feb 24, '02
Mar
1 Build a Toy Truck
2 Make Purchases
3 Purchase wood for cab
4 Purchase wood for trailer
5 Purchase axle wire
6 Purchase wheels
7 Process Materials
8 Carve cab body
9 Carve trailer body
10 Cut cab axle wire
11 Cut trailer axle wire
12 Produce Subassemblies
13 Assemble cab
14 Assemble trailer
15 Final Assembly
16 Assemble cab and trailer
17 INSPECT
Purchaser[50%]
Purchaser[50%]
Purchaser[50%]
Purchaser
Carver
Carver[200%]
Machinist[200%]
Machinist
Assembler
Assembler,Assembler helper
Assembler[200%]
2/18

Figure 6-2

The Gantt chart not only displays the project plan, but it also will be the primary tool that a project manager uses to monitor, manage, and display progress when the project is being executed. These details are explained later in Chapter 12.

PREPARATION FOR CREATING THE GANTT CHART

In preparation for cooperatively creating the Gantt chart, each project team member has prepared a task template (refer back to Table 5–1) that identifies the task name, task predecessor(s), taskgroup members, member effort (member time commitment during task), and task duration for each project team member's task. Each project team member brings this task template to the meeting following the last project task meeting. The action item from the last project task meeting was for each member to go out and prepare a task template, using all the help he or she can get. This first Gantt chart meeting is scheduled by the team to allow each member just enough time to gather up this important data.

GOOD PROJECT TASK ESTIMATES

To get good task estimates, a project manager should discuss the following issues with the task leaders:

1. Explain how an inaccurate estimate can impact planning and project management. It not only clouds the accuracy of the finish date, it also distorts the task start date anticipated later on by other task leaders.
2. Ensure that the task workgroup member with the most task knowledge participates in making the estimate. Discuss each of the following factors for developing an accurate estimate:
   - The task leader's experience with similar tasks from other projects
   - Other worker's task experiences
   - Expert opinions (subject matter experts)
   - Support needs and availability
   - Time availability of the task workers
   - Management support
3. For a new or experimental task, consider having two or more experts help make the estimate. A task estimate can include time for two or three tries if experience suggests they will be necessary to get it right. (If time is more critical than cost, it sometimes is desirable for some technical tasks that two, or even three, task workgroups work on the task at the same time.)

Earl Hall worked on a project to design of a hydro-mechanical device that was unique enough to result in a patent. In this project, time estimates were based on his experience with similar efforts. Each task in this prior similar creative experience invariably involved a series of tries. Each try was a learning experience on which to base the next try. Three tries in succession typically produced the desired task result. Experience taught Earl what it takes to "worry" a problem from recognition to "Eureka!" The time duration he predicted for the task was the time it took to make three tries. Thus, it is reasonable to ask creative people to give time estimates!

Motivating and empowering a team often begins by the project manager providing some help. A task leader may become uneasy when asked to produce reliable task time and effort estimates. The project manager can assist this task leader by helping to review past projects or by identifying knowledgeable people for the task leader to query. Such help empowers the task leader to make a good call.

Gathering data for the project Gantt chart must be taken very seriously! The project team must allow enough time for this process; yet, the process must not drag. It may take more than a one- or two-hour meeting. Be prepared to schedule two or three Gantt chart meetings in close succession to complete the chart's development.

Some people who perceive their tasks to be very creative may insist that they have no idea how long a task is going to take and that they cannot do anything about it. This attitude torpedoes project planning. The creative person with experience does have the knowledge for stating how long tasks typically take, but he or she just has never kept track of the time. A project manager may have to patiently lead this person back through his or her work history to arrive at the task estimates. This person will be somewhat comforted by knowing that he or she does not have to be exactly right with the estimate.

UTILIZATION OF A COMPUTER AND PROJECT MANAGEMENT SOFTWARE TO HELP COMPLETE THE GANTT CHART

Work on the project's Gantt chart begins once the construction method is determined. This chart can be constructed in longhand on graph paper or by using a computer and project management software.

Fifty years ago, Earl's project team got down on their hands and knees and rolled long sheets of newsprint across 100 feet of floor. They then nailed down a surveyor's tape at one end and stretched it the length of the room for the timeline. Using large wooden triangles, T-squares, and straight edges, they laid out jet engine projects. *Give thanks for software!*

A large sheet of graph paper is still reasonable, however, for very small projects.

When using project management software to help develop a Gantt chart, the necessary tools must be set up in advance. One configuration is set up so that a data entry person faces the computer keyboard, the monitor, and the team. A projector then is positioned to capture the monitor's image and to project it onto a large screen over the data entry person's head, enabling the team to watch the Gantt chart develop. A printer also should be hooked up to the computer (see Figure 6-3).

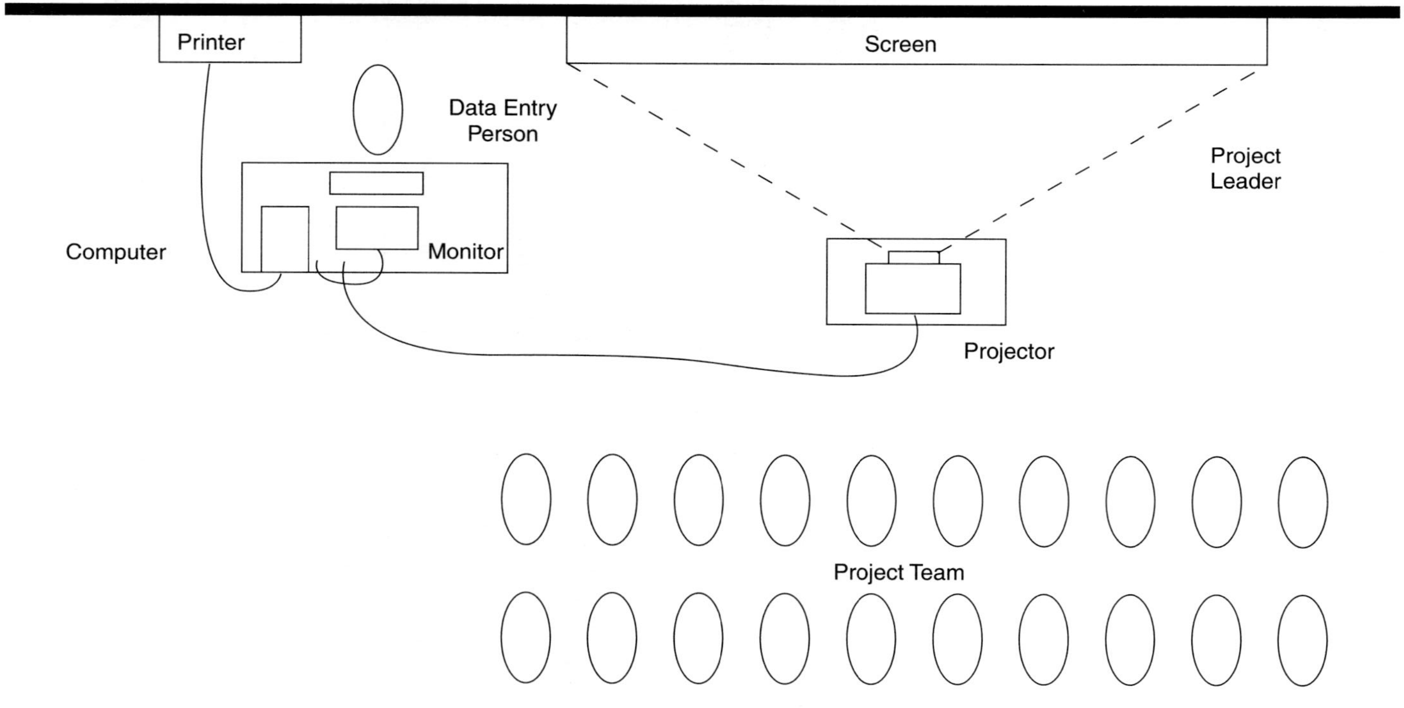

Room Layout

Figure 6-3

Other configurations can serve this purpose. A laptop computer combines the monitor and keyboard with its disadvantage being its small screen. (We prefer a large monitor screen.) In another configuration, the project manager, standing up, works the keyboard and watches the monitor, while leading the team through the Gantt chart development. Combining the two jobs (data entry and facilitating team input) is difficult unless the project manager is particularly well versed in the software and is a fast typist.

THE PROJECT GANTT CHART TASKS

Referring to the task list, the project manager requests that the team identify the tasks with no predecessors (that is, those ready to be tackled at the project launch meeting.)

The project manager asks, "Which task should be entered first?" The owner of this task then reports the length of time that the task will take. The data entry person enters the task name in the Task Name column and, using the computer, lays out a bar horizontally along the row named by this task. It extends the number of days (or weeks) from project launch to task completion. (Using Microsoft Project 2002®, the data entry person enters a number in a duration column beside the task name column and the computer draws the bar.) The duration of time can be discussed by the team. Some project team members may have experience that makes them think the duration is too long or too short. *In the end, it is the task leader's call.* Giving the task leader the final authority over the task time duration goes a long way toward having the task happen the way it is predicted. It assures each task leader that his or her judgment is respected and that his or her input is important.

In the matter of time divisions, hour or month time divisions can be used with project software (rather than days or weeks), but neither is particularly functional for Integrated Project Management. Using hour divisions leads a planner to pretend that each worker will be actively involved every hour of the working day and knows exactly at what hour he or she will work on a task. No one reaches this level of productivity, and few tasks can be realistically estimated in this way. Rather, you should estimate a half-day task duration and a part-time commitment for that half day (2 hours). Sometime during this half day, the task worker will get the task done but not necessarily between 8 and 10 A.M. Using months also is not a precise enough measure. It generally means that the work packages have not been sufficiently broken down into tasks. A task may be estimated to require six or six and a half weeks. This is a useful estimate. (One and a half months is not a precise enough.)

The time duration estimated to complete a task is represented by a bar in the Gantt chart. Each task will have a bar. Each bar begins immediately after the task's necessary predecessor is completed. Some tasks have more than one predecessor. These tasks begin when the predecessor extending furthest along the timeline is completed. (All dependencies on prior tasks are shown by connecting lines.) With Microsoft Project 2002® software, the data entry person uses the mouse pointer and indicates a predecessor task name. Then, this person indicates the successor task name while pressing the control (ctrl) key. Next he or she puts the mouse indicator on the "chain" icon on the computer's tool bar and the computer moves the successor task bar to start just after the predecessor ends.

Once the time duration is determined, the task leader names the person(s) who will work on the task, the period of time in percentages (working full time on the tasks equals 100 percent) to be spent, and the other necessary resources. This information then is entered on the line following the task bar by the data entry person. With Microsoft Project 2002®, the resources icon on the tool bar is turned on with the mouse pointer and a resource box will display on a corner of the Gantt chart screen. The task then is designated with the mouse pointer, the resource name is entered with the percent commitment on the resource screen, and "assign" is indicated. The name of the resource then appears beside the bar.

After the initial task entry, entries will follow on lower lines for each other task that has no predecessor. Some vertical spread (that is, gaps in the task column) can be allowed on the Gantt chart for major task and work package headings—or adjustments can be made later. Software procedures are friendly to "Input" and "Delete" and it handles adjustments nicely.

When all "no predecessor" tasks are entered, the project manager identifies the initial task with the shortest duration, and requests that the team provide data on tasks that only depend upon this shortest start-up task. These tasks begin the day after their predecessor is completed. Their bars are entered according to the task duration, which the task leader defines. Microsoft Project 2002® software will draw a vertical arrow from the end of the predecessor bar to the beginning of the successor bar to show dependency. This new task bar begins the day after the predecessor ends (see Figure 6-1C).

The project manager and team then will move on to the next task and repeat this process until all project tasks are placed on the Gantt chart. The basic principle here is to start each task as soon as its longest running predecessor is finished.

As team members report task information, the data entry person enters it into the computer. The project management software package processes this information, and the Gantt chart begins to take shape on the monitor and on the screen in front of the project team. If the data entry person misunderstands any information or makes a mistake, a task leader will notice it on the screen and immediately ask him to correct it.

When resource availability causes a time delay, a vertical start line is dropped down from the predecessor and a single horizontal line is extended to the right until the task's start date is reached if Microsoft Project 2002® is the software package being used. The task's bar then will begin at that point.

Using this method, a Gantt chart showing hundreds of tasks can be constructed quickly—but hundreds of tasks cannot be recorded in two hours. The project manager can estimate what can be accomplished in a two-hour meeting, and he or she can suggest that those task leaders not involved skip the first meeting. They should, however, attend the second meeting, which is scheduled soon after the first. In a few cases, a third meeting may be necessary. It also should be similarly planned. No one should be denied the opportunity to attend any meeting—some team leader overlap is desirable at successive meetings. Everyone also should attend the final meeting to review a display of the completed Gantt chart.

In addition to showing the project timeline, the Gantt chart displays the resource usage on a task-by-task basis. Following the bar on the task row are the actual name(s) of the person or the occupation of the worker who will perform the task. Because many tasks are completed by a person only working part time, the assigned person's name is followed by a percentage. Non-human resources are similarly represented if the resource is billed by the day or week. If the resource is a one-time charge, such as purchased raw materials, it is represented by the name of the material. Consequently, the Gantt chart not only describes the timeline, but it also spells out, day by day or task by task, the project resource needs.

If Microsoft Project 2002® software is used, a "Resources Table" is developed as each resource name is entered on the Gantt chart. The resource screen that takes up a small portion of the Gantt chart screen during the chart's development not only is the mechanism for entering a resource name on the Gantt chart, it also enters this name on a resource table that is not displayed at this time (see Figure 6-1D). This table can be "referred to" by selecting the resource table view from the software's View menu. On this resource table, the project manager can enter the pay rate of each resource (hourly, daily, or monthly, as appropriate). The software prorates costs according to this rate information and the time commitment of the resource person to the task. This also provides information for calculating cost, task by task, as the Gantt chart is being developed. After using the resource task view, a person doing data entry can "turn back" to the Gantt chart view.

Once the first draft of the Gantt chart is completed, the critical path is identified (see Figure 6-4). It is the sequence of tasks through the project that follow one after the other, with no break in time. Only the tasks on the critical path must be started as soon as their predecessors are completed (see Chapter 7 for details.) The first draft will reveal "slack" for non-critical path tasks. Slack is the lag time between a task's completion and when its successor can start (see Figure 6-5). Critical path and slack situations are discovered after the completion of the Gantt chart. Assumptions must not be made about them until the first draft of the Gantt chart is completed.

Computer Disadvantage

Using a computer to create a Gantt chart has many advantages, but there is one disadvantage. The Gantt chart fills up the entire screen, and soon the finished part has

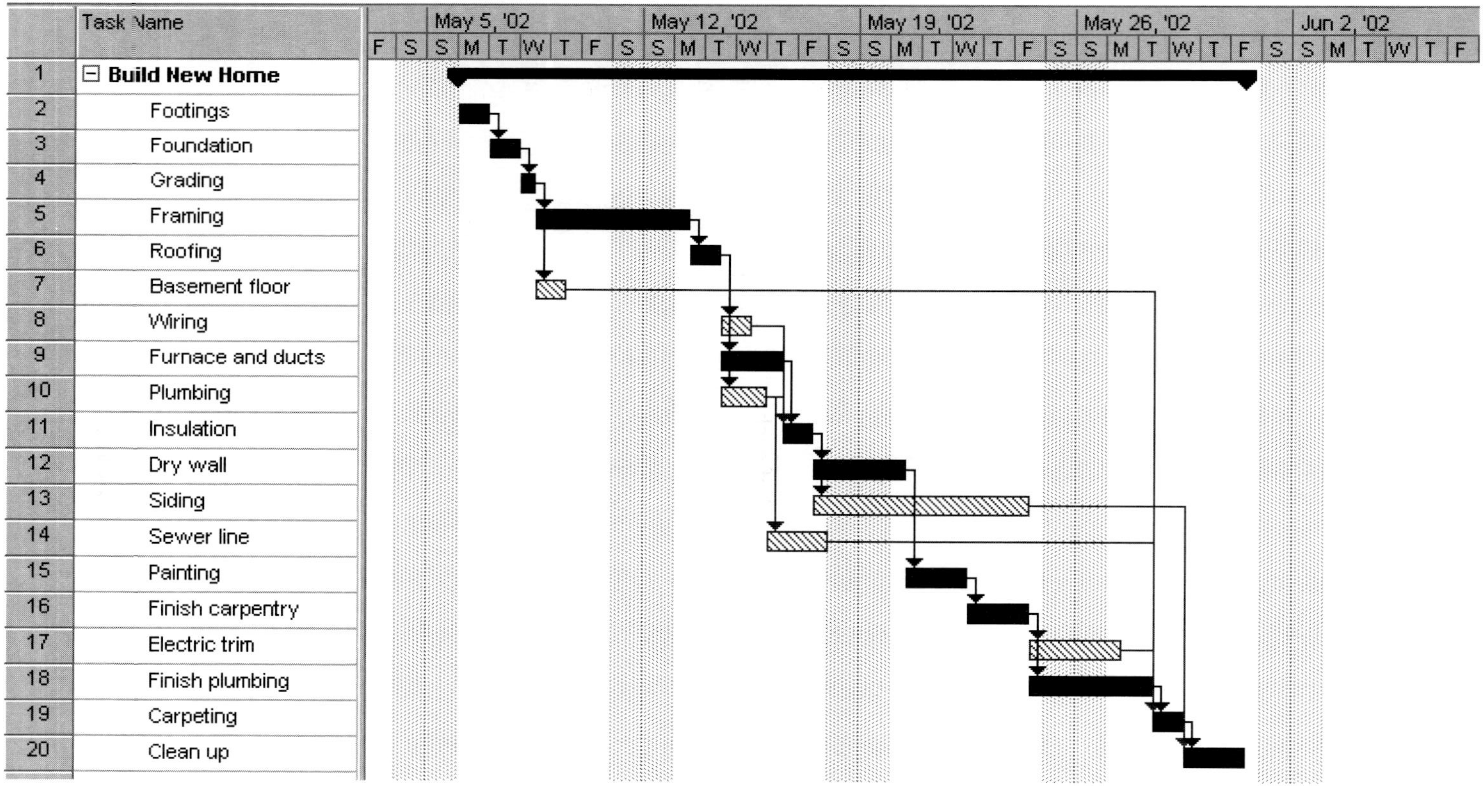
Task Name
May 5, '02
May 12, '02
May 19, '02
May 26, '02
Jun 2, '02
F S S M T W T F S S M T W T F S S M T W T F S S M T W T F S S M T W T F
1 Build New Home
2 Footings
3 Foundation
4 Grading
5 Framing
6 Roofing
7 Basement floor
8 Wiring
9 Furnace and ducts
10 Plumbing
11 Insulation
12 Dry wall
13 Siding
14 Sewer line
15 Painting
16 Finish carpentry
17 Electric trim
18 Finish plumbing
19 Carpeting
20 Clean up

Figure 6-4

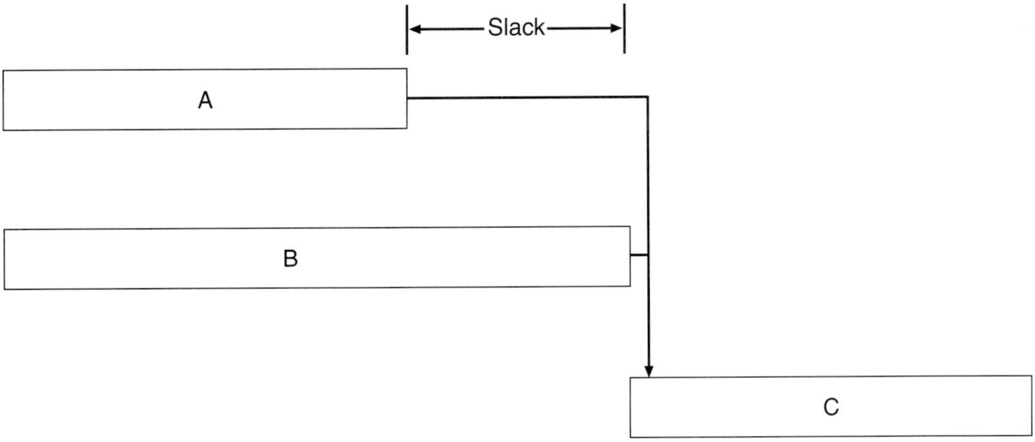

Figure 6-5

to be "scrolled" into memory to make room for new entries. Although it is possible to scroll back the chart for review, it soon becomes impossible to display the entire chart all at once. Hooking a printer (the bigger, the better) to the computer helps to reduce this problem.

Periodically and at the end of each two-hour session, the finished portion of the Gantt chart should be printed and copies distributed to the team. When a very large printer is not available and portions of the Gantt chart are printed on 8 1/2 by 11 paper, the pages will have to be pasted together to show the complete Gantt chart. This completed portion of the chart should always be immediately displayed on a large wall.

Cutting and pasting is a project skill. Lots of cutting and pasting is necessary with 8 1/2 by 11 printouts. It works best to trim one edge of the page with a paper cutter and tape it at the working edge of the prior page. One must not shrink the scale to reduce the number of pages—large scale is necessary to make the task relationships clear. We have previously taped together dozens of pages to display a large project Gantt chart. A wall in a large conference room or hallway works well for this display.

Team members can review the Gantt chart on their computers wherever a good Local Area Network (LAN) is available. Entries must always be password protected! They can be viewed, but only the project manager can add information or make changes! (Put the project in a data file and protect it from data entry. Allow "read only" access to the file.)

A VERY SIMPLE GANTT CHART EXAMPLE

We use the very simple immaginary Toy Truck example several times because it is both complete and easy to explain.

Build a Toy Truck and Semi-Trailer Set Specification

The project is to build a carved, wooden toy truck and semi-trailer set that is four feet long with a 10 inch wheelbase. This set will role on its own wheels. The wood pieces must be carved as realistically as possible, which is indicated in the attached parts and assembly drawings.

First, the project manager discusses the project with people who have experience building toy trucks, and concludes that the major tasks will be purchasing materials, processing materials, sub-assembly, and assembly. (This is the project's work breakdown structure.) See Figure 6-2 for the project's complete Gantt chart.

The project manager recruits representatives from purchasing, two carvers, one machinist, and two assemblers to serve on the project team. This team develops a task list named "Build a Toy Truck" as follows:

Make Purchases

- Purchase wood for cab body
- Purchase wood for trailer body
- Purchase axle wire
- Purchase wheels

Process Materials

- Carve cab body
- Carve trailer body
- Cut cab axle wire
- Cut trailer axle wire

Produce Sub-Assemblies

- Assemble cab
- Assemble trailer

Final Assembly

- Assemble unit

The worker's schedules, as defined by each task leader, are as follows:

1. The purchasing manager informs the project manager that the purchasing tasks can start immediately, "next Monday."

2. Purchasers report:

It will take two days for the wood for the cab and trailer to be delivered: One purchaser will work half of the time for two days for each of these tasks.

It will take one day to get the axle wire delivered: One purchaser will work full time.

One day is needed to get the wheels delivered: One purchaser will work half of the time on this day.

3. Carvers report:

One carver will start work as soon as the cab wood is delivered. The carver's task will take five days. The carver will not work Saturday or Sunday.

Two other carvers can start work as soon as the wood for the trailer is delivered. It will take them five days. They also will not work Saturday or Sunday.

4. Machinists report:

Two machinists can start cutting the cab axle wire when it is delivered. It will take them two days. It also will take the second machinist the same amount of time for the trailer axle wire.

5. Assemblers report:

One assembler can start assembling the cab on Wednesday if the carved cab and cab axles are finished and the wheels have been delivered. This job will take two days.

Another assembler and a helper can begin assembling the trailer as soon as the carved trailer body, axles, and wheels are available. Both assemblers can start assembling the complete unit as soon as the cab and trailer are assembled. This job will take two days.

Printouts from a software product may look like the Gantt chart shown in Figure 6-2.

Proceeding this way, the project manager has accomplished several important things. Under his or her leadership, workers have taken ownership of their tasks and the project as a whole. By demonstrating recognition of workers' needs to attend to other responsibilities, the project manager has established a basis for gaining support from their resource managers. In this context, it becomes reasonable and workable to negotiate with the resource managers for the appropriate availability of the workgroup personnel. In such negotiations, it is very helpful to show a resource manager that the project dates are realistic. Using a Gantt chart will accomplish this task.

ACQUISITION OF THE SUPPORT OF THE RESOURCE MANAGERS

Once the Gantt chart has been created, the project manager takes a day to print copies of it and auxiliary reports showing each of the workers' project commitments. He or she then distributes them to every person working on the project.

The auxiliary report is an individual's schedule worksheet. It sequentially lists the tasks for which that person is responsible, the calendar period during which he or she anticipates doing the work, and their expected effort in days or half days (sometimes weeks), as shown in Figure 6-6.

PERSONS NAME: ____

TASK	DURATION START DATE	END DATE	EFFORT: DAYS
____________	____________	____________	____________
____________	____________	____________	____________
____________	____________	____________	____________

Figure 6-6

Armed with this Gantt chart and the auxiliary reports, the project manager and the team take two days to visit the team's various resource managers. (Resource managers are the persons that the team members report to on a permanent basis.) This visit is done to ensure that each resource manager is fully informed of and concurs with the time his or her worker(s) will spend on the project.

It is critical that this visit is not the first time that the resource manager has heard of the project. In order to create a favorable climate, a project manager must communicate with the resource managers early on. Communicating early and often (especially face-to-face) with those whose support is needed, is a basic responsibility of a project manager.

An individual's schedule worksheet is easily derived from the Gantt chart. This form may look like the form shown in Figure 6-6.

RESOURCE NEGOTIATIONS: A COMMUNICATION SCENARIO

A project manager (P) and/or appropriate task leader(s) meet with a resource manager (R). They negotiate the availability of skilled persons who are managed by R and are necessary in the execution of Project X.

STEP 1: P familiarizes R with Project X and with P's perception of its significance and priority with in the company.

STEP 2: P seeks to understand the various activities/commitments of R's staff during the life of Project X.

STEP 3: P shares with R the project Gantt chart (with persons from R's group who are participating) and identifies the ideal time commitment, both duration and effort, for persons on R's staff.

STEP 4: P and R discuss the necessary tradeoffs that will enable R's people to commit by date and effort level. P shares with R the risk/contingency considerations that could shift the commitment date. P and R finally reach agreement on the commitment of R's staff.

After the project manager and task leaders have checked with the resource managers on task participant availability, they may need to reconvene the project team to revise the Gantt chart to take into consideration some member availability delays. The project manager then may reasonably decide to not complete these adjustments until the risk analysis has been completed and the Gantt chart including the risk factors has been developed.

PREPARATION FOR RISK ANALYSIS

At the final Gantt chart meeting, the project manager begins the explanation of risk analysis. To prepare the action items for the next meeting, each task leader must search out information that determines what the longest time requirement (worst case) for his or her task might be, and what the likelihood of the task overrunning at all might be. (Note that these are two separate items. The worst case may occur very rarely—perhaps less than 1 percent of the time a task of this type is undertaken. The likelihood of the task overrunning at all was initially considered when the task times were estimated. It could be up to 40 percent.) The project leader asks team members to reconsider these estimates, state them in terms of percent likelihood of overrun, and confirm or correct them. There is no set number for them to shoot for; they just need to report as accurately as they can on what they determine is realistic. If, upon review, the overrun likelihood runs as high as 30 or even 40 percent, the project manager and the team need to know this now. (Originally, project leaders were asked for "most of the time" task time estimates, and they were asked to considered the probability—estimated, not statistical—that tasks would overrun, expressing it in a percentage. They are now asked to revisit these considerations. The *likelihood of overrun* is the difference between the most-of-the-time probability and 100 percent).

Another part of the action items to be prepared for the next meeting is to ask task leaders to consider where there are risks and what they might do to mitigate their impacts. Examples are adding task team members, working overtime, outsourcing task elements, bringing in experts, and authorizing special payments for parts or services to get early delivery. Discussing these risks and their impacts helps the task leader to be prepared to reduce and manage risks if he or she sees task delays creeping into the task. Risk Analysis is explained later in Chapters 8 and 9.

The risk analysis used in IPM plays a very significant role in supporting manager and team confidence that they can finish to specifications, and be on time and within budget. When task leaders learn about the process for the first time, it will need some detailed explanation. Unless the project team is made up of members who are familiar with IPM risk analysis and risk management, it is advisable for the project manager to schedule a special discussion meeting as the next meeting. This meeting—the first in the risk analysis sequence—should be scheduled as soon as possible after the wrap-up Gantt chart meeting. Note that the task leaders are not required to complete their assigned risk analysis actions for this meeting. In addition, this first risk analysis meeting will not take place before the project manager has completed and distributed the critical path chart.

PRE-ORGANIZATION OF COMPUTER DATA FOR THE PROJECT GANTT CHART

When using software to create the project Gantt chart, the project manager should pre-enter the basic project data into the software package prior to the first Gantt chart meeting. One entry is the estimated project launch date, which should be the day after the team expects to complete the plan review. This entry sets the computer's calendar, which can be adjusted after the Gantt chart development is completed. In addition to entering this date, company nonworking days also should be entered.

Another important entry is the resource cost information. The project manager should have a fairly good idea about the people and other resources needed for the project. All task leaders will work on the project and can be entered by name or category on the resource table. (Software packages come with a resource cost-entry table to be used for the cost rates of all identified resources.) It is helpful to log in this information as soon as possible. Additional entries can be made as the Gantt chart is being created. Figure 6-1D shows an example of a resource entry cost sheet from Microsoft Project 2002®.

THE LARGE BASIC PROJECT GANTT CHART

The toy truck example used earlier is very simple. It represents the basic Gantt chart characteristics. The Gantt chart shown in Figures. 6-7A, 6-7B and 6-7C is taken from the real world. Although it does not take us through the whole "Build a New Style Disk Cleaning Machine" project, it does take us four and one half months into the project and takes us to a major checkpoint—"Lay out 3D design."

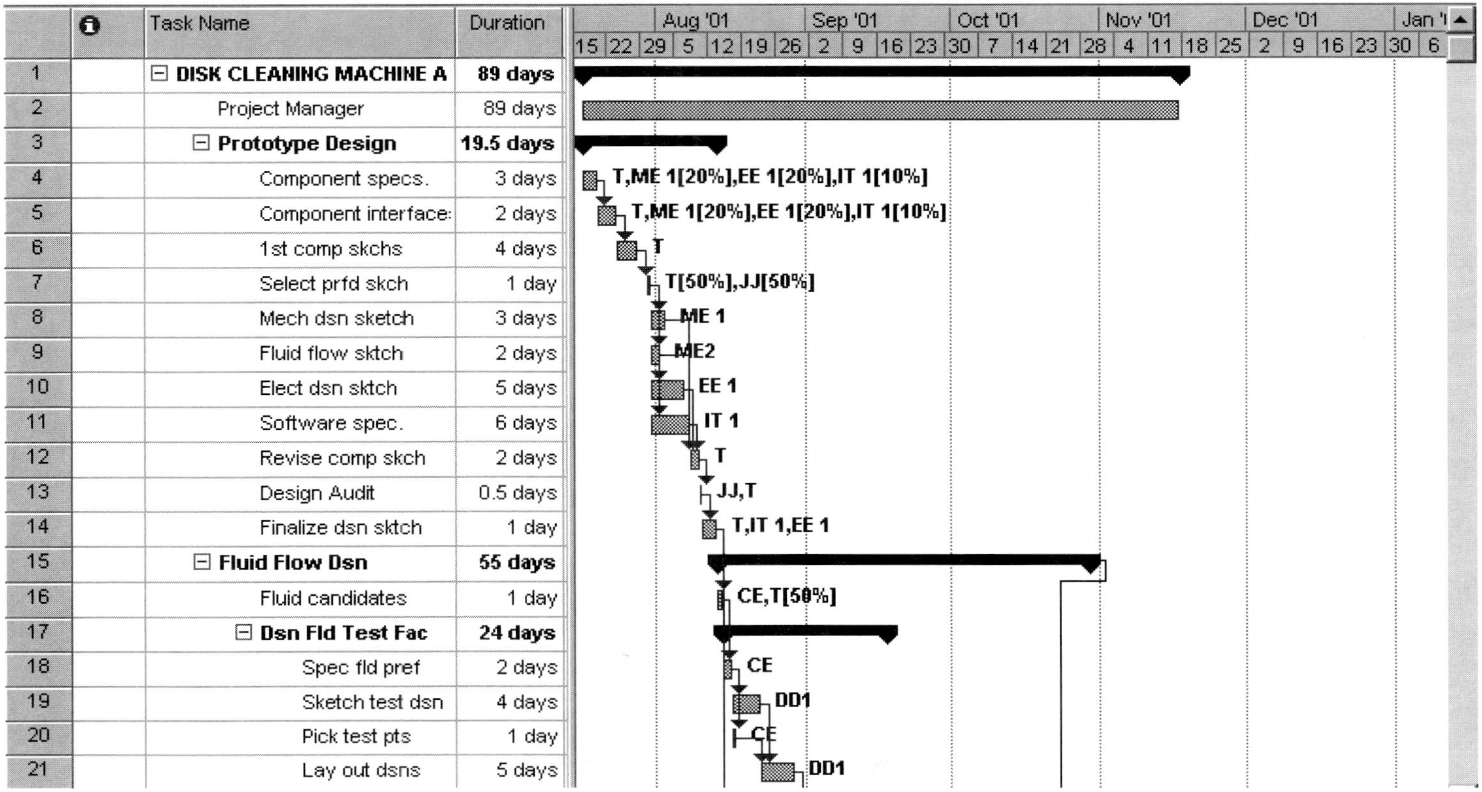

Task Name
Duration
Aug '01
Sep '01
Oct '01
Nov '01
Dec '01
Jan '
15 22 29 5 12 19 26 2 9 16 23 30 7 14 21 28 4 11 18 25 2 9 16 23 30 6
1 DISK CLEANING MACHINE A 89 days
2 Project Manager 89 days
3 Prototype Design 19.5 days
4 Component specs. 3 days
5 Component interface: 2 days
6 1st comp skchs 4 days
7 Select prfd skch 1 day
8 Mech dsn sketch 3 days
9 Fluid flow sktch 2 days
10 Elect dsn sktch 5 days
11 Software spec. 6 days
12 Revise comp skch 2 days
13 Design Audit 0.5 days
14 Finalize dsn sktch 1 day
15 Fluid Flow Dsn 55 days
16 Fluid candidates 1 day
17 Dsn Fld Test Fac 24 days
18 Spec fld pref 2 days
19 Sketch test dsn 4 days
20 Pick test pts 1 day
21 Lay out dsns 5 days
T,ME 1[20%],EE 1[20%],IT 1[10%]
T,ME 1[20%],EE 1[20%],IT 1[10%]
T
T[50%],JJ[50%]
ME 1
ME2
EE 1
IT 1
T
JJ,T
T,IT 1,EE 1
CE,T[50%]
CE
DD1
CE
DD1

Figure 6-7A

		Task Name	Duration
22		Mfg test parts	10 days
23		Assemble	3 days
24		Perf test fluids	5 days
25		Select fluids	1 day
26		Lay out fl path	4 days
27		Pick components	1 day
28		Order std parts	10 days
29		Design special parts	11 days
30		Mfg spec parts	8 days
31		⊟ **Mechanical Design**	**36 days**
32		Composite layout	6 days
33		Unit dsn frame	5 days
34		Unit dsn handling	7 days
35		Unit dsn housing	4 days
36		Parts design	10 days
37		⊟ **Work Order Make**	**13 days**
38		Parts1-7	13 days
39		Parts A, B, C	7 days
40		Part X	5 days
41		⊟ **Purchase Std Pts**	**5 days**
42		Group W	5 days

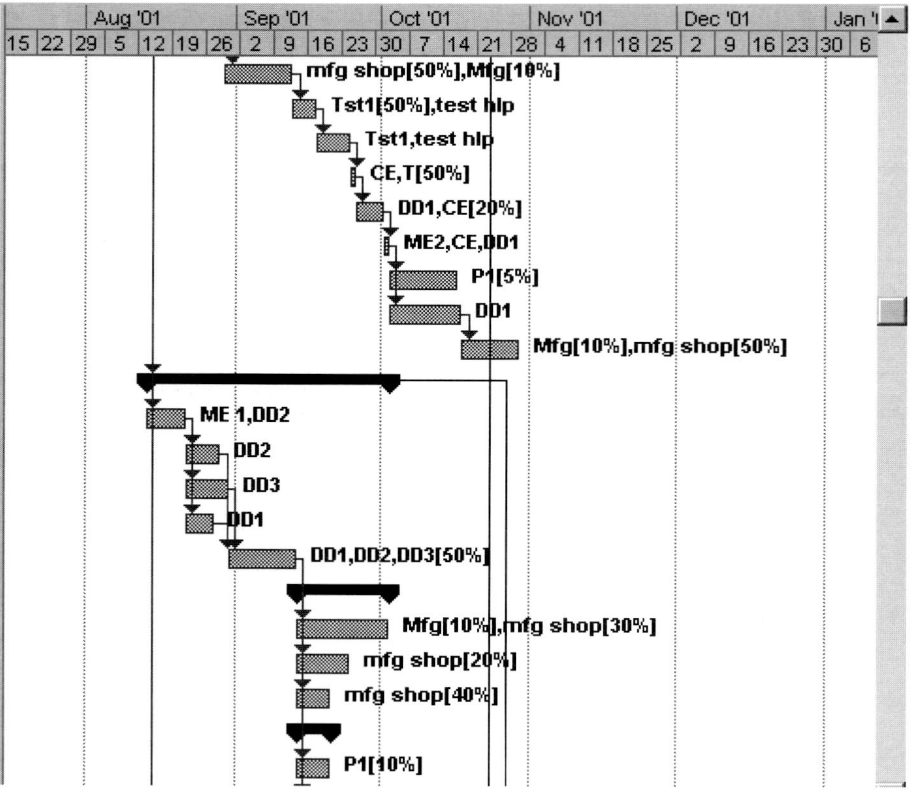

Figure 6-7B

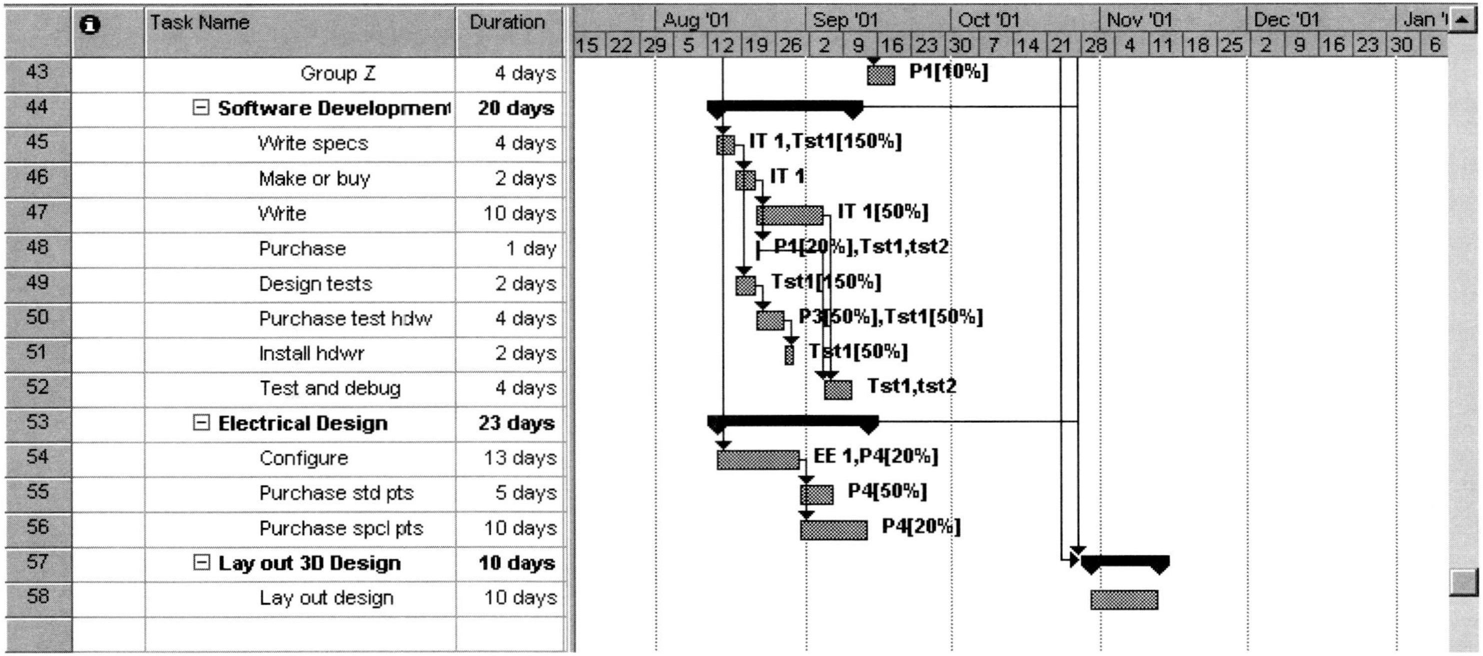
Task Name
Duration
Aug '01
Sep '01
Oct '01
Nov '01
Dec '01
15 22 29 5 12 19 26 2 9 16 23 30 7 14 21 28 4 11 18 25 2 9 16 23 30 6
43 Group Z 4 days
44 Software Developmen 20 days
45 Write specs 4 days
46 Make or buy 2 days
47 Write 10 days
48 Purchase 1 day
49 Design tests 2 days
50 Purchase test hdw 4 days
51 Install hdwr 2 days
52 Test and debug 4 days
53 Electrical Design 23 days
54 Configure 13 days
55 Purchase std pts 5 days
56 Purchase spcl pts 10 days
57 Lay out 3D Design 10 days
58 Lay out design 10 days
P1[10%]
IT 1,Tst1[150%]
IT 1
IT 1[50%]
P1[20%],Tst1,tst2
Tst1[150%]
P3[50%],Tst1[50%]
Tst1[50%]
Tst1,tst2
EE 1,P4[20%]
P4[50%]
P4[20%]

Figure 6-7C

There are 15 task leaders on the project team at this point. The names of the workers who will execute the project are identified by a code. There is one work team, "Mfg shop," that is represented on the project team by the manufacturing supervisor of the tool room—the facility providing the manufactured parts for this part of the project. The manufacturing supervisor is designated as "Mfg" on the Gantt chart. He or she is responsible for discussing tasks with the machinist in the tool room when he or she develops task estimates for their work. In the case of "work order make," the work will take up 30 percent of the effort of the tool room machinist over thirteen days, 20 percent over seven days, and 40 percent over 5 days. The tool room is budgeted on a cost-per-day basis. For budgeting purposes, the project cost for this task will be calculated as tool room cost-per-day times days needed times the percentage of tool room effort needed each day.

On the project team, the Test Foreman, "Tst1," speaks for the test helper, "Ttst hlp."

There are five major work packages that lead up to the 3D design layout, and there are 46 tasks within these work packages. One of the five major work packages, the prototype design work package, must be completed before the other work packages can start. (a milestone review is scheduled at the end of the prototype's design.) The four other work packages can each begin when the last task of the Prototype Design package—finalize design sketch—is completed. These four work packages proceed in parallel—there are no task dependencies in any of these work packages that depend on a predecessor in another work package.

This project was planned exactly the way the toy truck project was planned. There were 36 task leaders on the full project team (this is a *very* large team). The project manager invited all of them to the task list meeting where all the tasks for the project were identified. Because the team used an affinity diagram to form the task list, the groupings of tasks easily emerged in work package clusters. This formation of groups confirmed the work packages identified in the original work breakdown structure analysis. The entire affinity diagram exercise was completed in two hours.

The project manager invited only the 15 task leaders dealing with the portion of the Gantt chart shown to attend the first Gantt chart meeting. The rest of the team and many of the original 15, who had continuing task responsibilities, came to the second and third Gantt chart meetings.

As one looks at the Gantt chart, one sees that there is a stair-step characteristic to the task sequences, and that some tasks and the last four work packages are proceeding in parallel. Note that the project manager is assigned full time to the project and has no task team responsibilities!

Tasks that proceed in parallel like the "mech dsn sketch," "fluid flow sketch," "electrical," and the "software specification" task do not require the same amount of time. They all are predecessors for the "revise comp sketch" task. The "revise comp sketch" task cannot start until the longest of its predecessors—the "software specs" task—is completed. Note that there is a time lapse between the ending of each of the other tasks and the beginning of the "revise comp sketch" task. We call this time lapse slack. These characteristics are important as we determine the critical task path through the project. (The critical path is the subject of the Chapter 7.)

GANTT CHART UTILITIES

The time scale that is used in the displayed Cleaning Machine Gantt chart is one with the major division as months and the subdivision of weeks. It is a scale that enables us to get the chart into this book. It also is a good scale to use when explaining the project to stakeholders outside the project. When building the Gantt chart in the project team meeting, you should use a scale in weeks with the subdivision in days. This arrangement works the best for task discussion purposes. We use this weeks-divided-into-days scale for the Gantt charts that we post on our office walls or in a conference room or hallway for monitoring a project after its launch. Either scale, however, will support good project monitoring. (Note: Project management software will enable you to print out your Gantt chart both ways.)

When this Gantt chart was first developed, two project team members over-scheduled themselves without noticing it. The data entry person only periodically checked the resource table. However, the Resource Table view of the Microsoft Project 2002® software package caught it immediately. Thus, they quickly rescheduled to avoid a commitment of over 100 percent on two days.

SPECIAL USES FOR GANTT CHARTS

Beyond the use as a project planning and monitoring tool for IPM, there are other ways a Gantt Chart can serve project management.

The Stretch Gantt Chart

The project manager who does not have sufficient control over the project people to be able to develop a dependable bar chart can create one with all the help he or she can muster by creating a "wish list." The wish list helps to communicate when and why task team help is needed. Although not a desirable form of project management, it is better than having no planning or management at all.

The Template Gantt Chart

Some organizations will repeat a certain type of project over and over. Here, a project manager can apply project-planning principles to a sample project and create a bar chart template for the repeated projects. These Gantt charts thus will provide valuable reference material for future projects. Disk cleaning Machine A is a Template used in a large specialty shop. You will see it again in this book with different particulars entered for different but similar projects.

How Long—the Gantt Chart Answer

The major question that a project manager is always asked is, "How long is this project going to take?" Sometimes the project manager is told when the project must be finished and he or she is faced with the following question, "Can the project be finished as required?" Sometimes he or she is faced with the same problem a wife had when her husband ordered her to deliver her baby in six months so that they could get a "this year" income tax deduction. She expects to deliver in nine months. The husband and his financial problems cannot change that fact. Projects always have a minimum, best effort duration. This may not be as obvious to a manager/sponsor as it should be to a husband. The device for defining the necessary time required for a project is the project Gantt chart. When we specify that a project will be finished on time, we are referring to the completion date indicated by the project Gantt chart, not the date ordered by the sponsor.

There are ways for shortening up projects. (These are discussed in Chapter 11). There is always a minimum, best effort time requirement. Project time planning begins with the Gantt chart. Project resource requirements and project cost also are derived from the Gantt chart.

One story from World War II is about building a pontoon bridge on the Marne River, in France. A U.S. Army Engineer company was preparing to build a pontoon bridge to get tanks and other motorized vehicles across to support the infantry who had crossed earlier.

The engineer company commander stood on a bluff overlooking the river. Almost out of nowhere, an officer wearing riding boots and britches, an "Ike" jacket, an enameled helmet, and two revolvers strapped to his side appeared. This officer said, "Captain, I want that bridge across by noon and if you can't do it I will get somebody up here who can." The young captain (22-years old and a veteran of the Normandy landing) said, "General, our site is still under German 88 sporadic fire. I have called for an airstrike. The P-47s will clear out the 88 in the next forty-five minutes. My near shore abutment crew is ready to go to work. They will cross to the far shore to put in that abutment as soon as they finish here. We have the pontoons and treads ready to launch and are establishing an upstream site. We will get them in the water, one unit at a time as soon as the abutment is ready to receive the first unit. The river is deep and running very fast. We can get in three units an hour. It will be nine o'clock tonight before we can open the bridge."

General George S. Patton did not say a word. He just turned and walked away and the engineers got the bridge in by 9:00 P.M.

General Patton had the good sense to recognize competence with a well thought-out project plan and realistic time estimates. He left the young captain to do his job. Many project sponsors are not as wise as George Patton and will insist on the impossible. The Gantt chart defines what is possible.

SUMMARY

A successful project requires a specification and a plan. The task list is the beginning of the plan. The core of a project plan describes the task sequence needed to complete the project, the task's timing, and the people and other resources needed for each task. The Gantt chart has been proven a very useful format for displaying a complete project plan.

There are several approaches that project managers can take when planning a project. The major difference in these approaches is whether the project manager plans the project or whether the project manager leads and facilitates the workers, who will execute the tasks, in creating the plan. The IPM approach opts for the participation of each task leader when creating the project's plan. This participation centers around a series of team meetings where each team member reports his or her task data for the Gantt chart. A procedure using project management software with a data entry specialist and a viewing screen is recommended. The Gantt chart, which can be created using this project management software, provides a detailed task breakdown, resource management, and budgeting in one operation.

DISCUSSION QUESTIONS

1. What are the advantages of creating a project Gantt chart over planning a project as an outline with task time requirements noted beside each task on the outline?
2. What are the advantages of collaboratively developing the Gantt chart?
3. Why is it important that the task leader have final say over how long his or her task will take?
4. When does a project get to big to be described using a Gantt chart?
5. What disadvantages are associated with laying out a project plan using a computer and a computer screen?
6. What advantages does project management software bring to project planning?
7. What do we mean when we say that using the modern Gantt chart enables the project manager to combine time planning, resource planning, and cost planning?

7 CRITICAL PATH

INTRODUCTION

The completed project Gantt chart, laid out by hand on graph paper or, more likely, laid out using project management software, displays a sequence of tasks that have the characteristics of stair steps descending from start to finish. Within this display is a sequence of tasks where each successive task depends upon its immediate predecessor and starts as soon as this longest predecessor is completed. There is no time break in this sequence.

This sequence is called the critical path. It is a string of dependent tasks that have the longest duration. Generally, there is only one critical path through a project. Occasionally, there is more than one, however. The critical path identifies the amount of time that is required to complete the project. If any task on the critical path overruns, the project completion date then will be moved out by the period of time that the task overran.

A critical path is not a sequence that the project manager chooses. It is a product of the project plan development. The project manager and the team do not know which tasks comprise a critical path until the Gantt chart is completed. Sometimes individuals inside and outside the project speak of one task or several tasks as being critical. These tasks may be critical for any number of reasons. They may be very important to the quality of the project output; they may be long tasks; they may require many task team members. In the sense that "critical" is used in project management, they are not critical unless they are on the critical path or have a predecessor character for tasks on the critical path and have very little slack to use before they become critical.

Project managers and project teams need to know which tasks comprise the critical path in order to do risk analysis. The critical path also becomes a very useful management tool for the project manager after the project is launched. The project manager will need to know which tasks are on the critical path, and how much slack the other tasks have that can protect them from overruns which would impact the critical path. You can refer to the critical path chart when considering start delays for non-critical tasks.

Slack, for a task—Task A—is the time between the scheduled task completion date and the scheduled start date of Task A's successor—Task C. Task C's start is delayed because it has another predecessor—Task B—that parallels Task A and has a later completion date. See Figure 7-1.

There are several ways of representing the critical path and task slack graphically. Project management software can identify the critical path tasks and slack on the Gantt chart. This representation is not as obvious as an arrow diagram critical path chart. The IPM method recommends that the project manager always create and use an arrow diagram critical path for both guiding risk analysis and for managing the project.

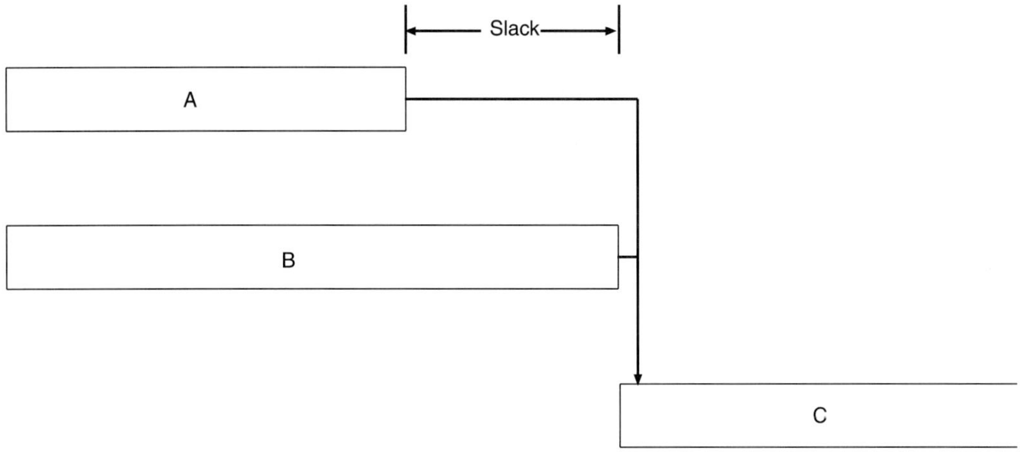

Figure 7-1

CRITICAL PATH DETAILS

With every project, at least one stream of tasks has no slack between any of the sequenced tasks. Each task, except the first, depends upon completion of a predecessor before it can commence. Many tasks have more than one predecessor. The last completed predecessor determines the successor task's start date.

Predecessors that finish earlier leave some slack time before the critical task successor begins. Therefore, if non-critical tasks finish late but do not utilize all their slack time, the project timeline is not affected. Also, if there is plenty of slack (that is, slack is greater than the possible time over run of the non critical path task), these tasks do not have to start as soon as possible. It is important, however, that they finish well before the critical path task is scheduled to start.

A project manager must take care not to delay a non-critical task start for so long that no slack remains. Where there is a cushion, keep some cushion. Otherwise, this task will have to be defined as a critical path task and included in risk analysis. Some discretionary flexibility is always desirable. However, if the project effort is proceeding and the task leader and the project manager determine that a start delay for one task must be allowed that uses up all the slack, downstream task leaders must be warned of any increased risk.

Gantt chart software can identify critical path tasks. Microsoft Project 2002® can depict them with bars that are shaded or colored differently from other tasks (see Figure 7-2A and B). It also can print critical path task names in a different color or typeface, when instructed to do so. One Microsoft Project 2002® special report lists critical path tasks and their characteristics. This report is available through computer commands.

When a critical path is displayed on the Gantt chart, the line connecting a non-critical path task to its successor will extend horizontally until the critical path task start date is reached (as shown in Figure 7-1). This line represents slack. Slack lines do not stand out on a large complex project. This is particularly true when a series of connected tasks end with the last task showing slack before a critical path task can start.

The critical path arrow diagram is a tool that we find very useful for monitoring and managing resources. It is currently not found in many project management software packages. Preparing it longhand is easy, once the Gantt chart is finished. It is a management tool that is intended for project managers. You can, of course, create one for your own use.

The critical path is essential to IPM because risk analysis is performed for all tasks on and closely related to the critical path tasks. Before risk analysis is undertaken, all team members must know the critical path task names.

Using graph paper, the project manager (or an assistant) can construct longhand an arrow diagram critical path display. The technique is simple. The necessary information can be found in the Gantt chart. (Although software can display

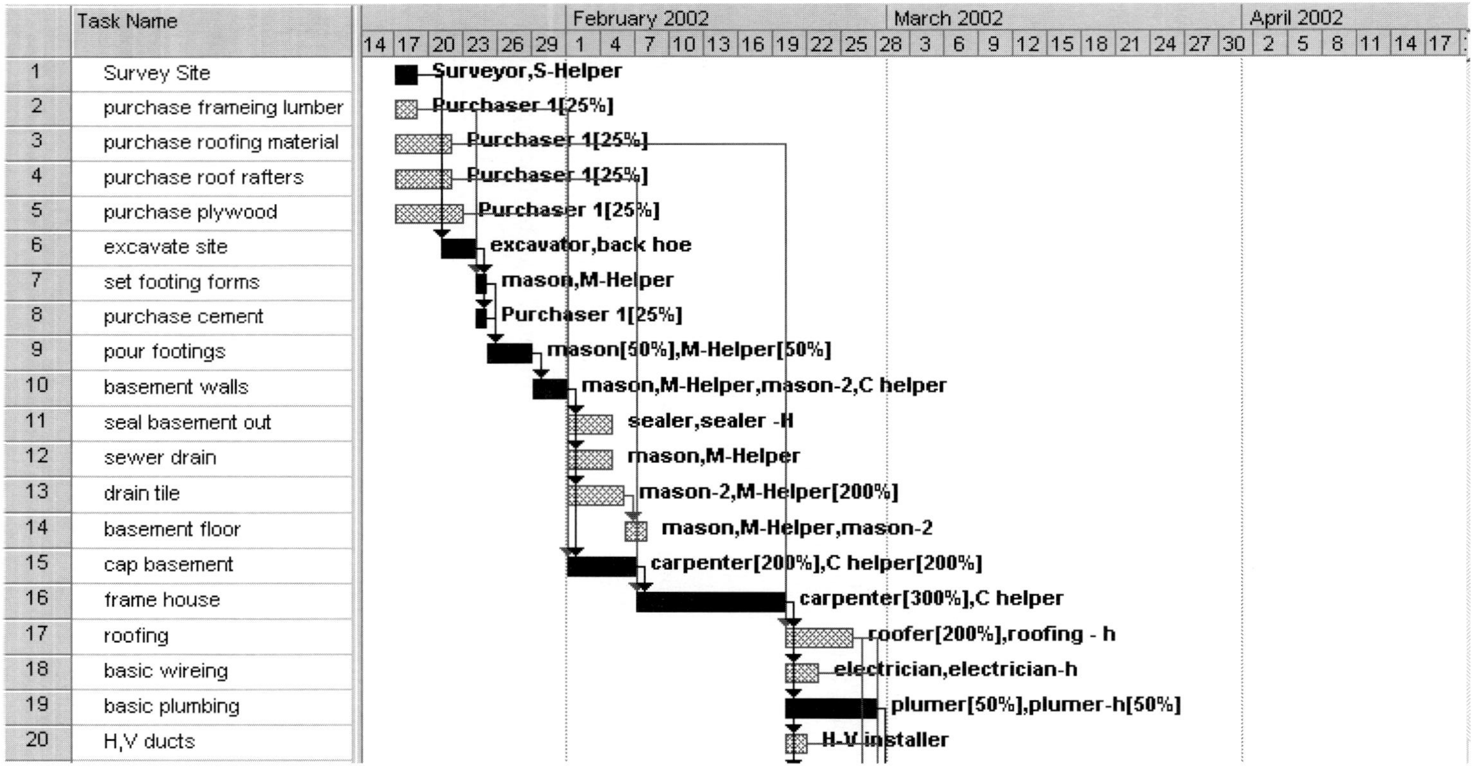
Task Name
1 Survey Site
2 purchase frameing lumber
3 purchase roofing material
4 purchase roof rafters
5 purchase plywood
6 excavate site
7 set footing forms
8 purchase cement
9 pour footings
10 basement walls
11 seal basement out
12 sewer drain
13 drain tile
14 basement floor
15 cap basement
16 frame house
17 roofing
18 basic wireing
19 basic plumbing
20 H,V ducts
February 2002
March 2002
April 2002
14 17 20 23 26 29 1 4 7 10 13 16 19 22 25 28 3 6 9 12 15 18 21 24 27 30 2 5 8 11 14 17
Surveyor,S-Helper
Purchaser 1[25%]
Purchaser 1[25%]
Purchaser 1[25%]
Purchaser 1[25%]
excavator,back hoe
mason,M-Helper
Purchaser 1[25%]
mason[50%],M-Helper[50%]
mason,M-Helper,mason-2,C helper
sealer,sealer -H
mason,M-Helper
mason-2,M-Helper[200%]
mason,M-Helper,mason-2
carpenter[200%],C helper[200%]
carpenter[300%],C helper
roofer[200%],roofing - h
electrician,electrician-h
plumer[50%],plumer-h[50%]
H-V installer

Figure 7-2A

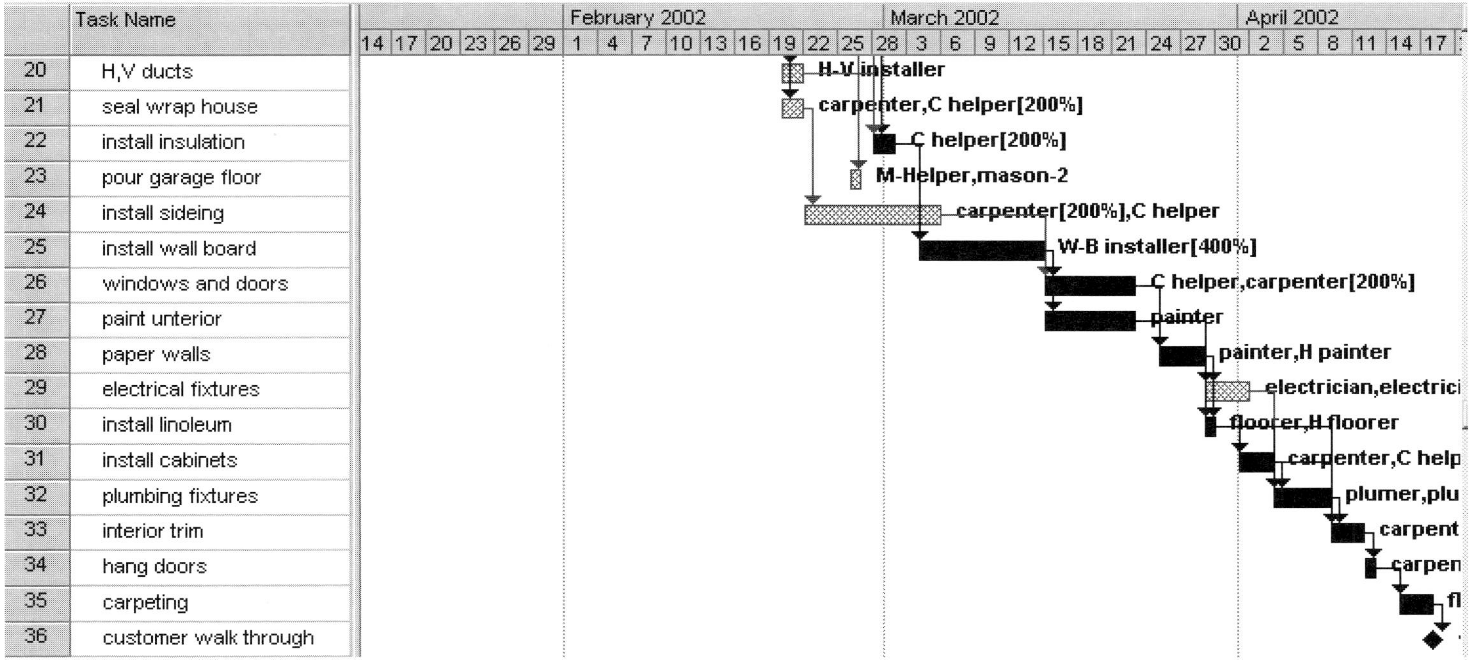
Task Name
February 2002
March 2002
April 2002
14 17 20 23 26 29 1 4 7 10 13 16 19 22 25 28 3 6 9 12 15 18 21 24 27 30 2 5 8 11 14 17
20 H,V ducts
21 seal wrap house
22 install insulation
23 pour garage floor
24 install sideing
25 install wall board
26 windows and doors
27 paint unterior
28 paper walls
29 electrical fixtures
30 install linoleum
31 install cabinets
32 plumbing fixtures
33 interior trim
34 hang doors
35 carpeting
36 customer walk through
H-V installer
carpenter,C helper[200%]
C helper[200%]
M-Helper,mason-2
carpenter[200%],C helper
W-B installer[400%]
C helper,carpenter[200%]
painter
painter,H painter
electrician,electrici
floorer,H floorer
carpenter,C help
plumer,plu
carpent
carpen
fl

Figure 7-2B

the critical path on the Gantt chart [refer to Figure 7-2], the arrow diagram works better for managing larger complex projects because slack may be hard to find on a Gantt chart visually and because the entire project plan cannot be displayed on one screen for very large projects.)

The project manager creates the critical path arrow diagram as soon as the Gantt chart is completed. The chart should be printed and distributed to every team member before the risk analysis discussion meeting. Remind each task leader that they will need to give special attention to the critical path arrow diagram for risk analysis.

CREATION OF THE CRITICAL PATH ARROW DIAGRAM

The only dimension used in the arrow diagram is task time. As with the Gantt chart, days or weeks are measured horizontally. Reading from the Gantt chart, you should identify each task with no predecessor. Lay a line for each one, beginning at Day zero, extending it to the right for the required number of days. The arrow does not need to be horizontal. Its *horizontal component*, however, must equal the task duration of the represented task.

The first task(s) should be laid out beginning about halfway up the vertical side of the page: One may extend diagonally upward, another diagonally downward (see Figure 7-3). Others will follow. This layout spreads out the arrow diagram, which is visually useful as a managing tool.

Task X has no predecessor and requires seven days. Note: seven days is the horizontal component.

Task Y has no predecessor and takes four days. Note: four days is the horizontal component attributable to Task Y.

Task Z has no predecessors and takes 10 days.

Tasks X, Y, and Z are the only tasks shown on the Gantt chart that have no predecessors. After completing the layout of tasks with no predecessor, you should pick the one with the shortest time duration—Task Y—and beginning at its endpoint, lay out a line for Task C, which is the next task. Note that Task C is a two-day task.

Next, look at the task endpoints on the chart and identify the closest endpoint to the project's start date. This endpoint is at the completion of Task C. It is six days from the start. Identify any tasks that are dependent upon the completion of Task C. Task D is dependent upon the completion of Task C and also is dependent upon the completion of Task X.

Task D will start as soon as Task X is finished. A dotted line from the end of Task C to the end of Task X, where Task D starts, shows the dependence of Task

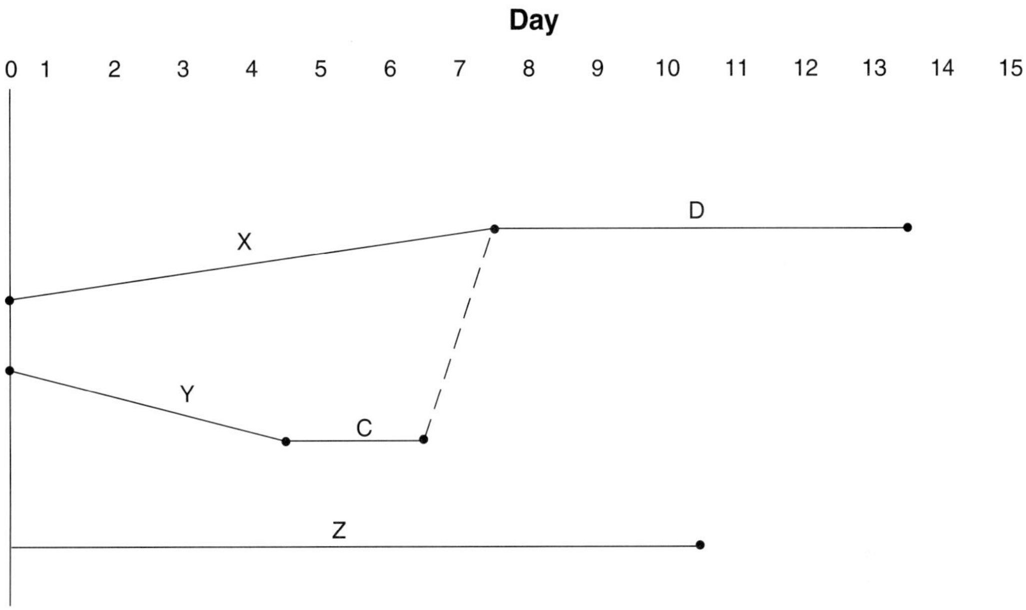

Figure 7-3

D upon Task C. It is shown as a dotted line, which represents slack. The slack applies to the Task String Y-C. It is slack that can protect either task or both from overruns that could impact the critical path.

Task D's endpoint occurs beyond Task Z's endpoint. Therefore, the next task you need to consider is any task that depends upon Task Z as its predecessor.

At a task terminal point, its successor task begins and is laid out. With several predecessors, this task starts at the end of the one extending farthest to the right. Other tasks then are connected to this starting point by dotted lines, indicating dependence. (The dotted lines also represent slack.)

EXAMPLE

The project to be planned is to build a custom three-bedroom home according to specifications determined in a detailed set of architectural drawings. A good construction superintendent has reviewed these plans with the carpenter, mason, plumber, roofer, and construction foreman, and has listed tasks that need to be performed, their necessary sequence relationship, and the amount of time each task is expected to take (see Table 7-1). To be able to focus supervisory attention on tasks that are on the critical path, the superintendent laid out a critical path chart. This original rough charting and the final critical path chart are shown in Figures 7-4 and 7-5.

Table 7-1

TASK	NECESSARY PRECEDING TASK(S)	TIME REQUIRED ESTIMATE IN DAYS
1. Concrete Footer		1
2. Foundation	#1	1
3. Grading	#2	.5
4. Framing	#3	2.6
5. Roofing	#4	1
6. Concrete Basement Floor	#2	1
7. Wiring	#4	1
8. Furnace & Ducts	#5	2.25
9. Plumbing	#5	2.5
10. Insulation	#7,8,9	2.25
11. Dry Wall	#10	1
12. Siding	#10	5.5
13. Sewer Lines	#9	2
14. Painting	#11	1.5
15. Finish Carpentry	#14	2.5
16. Tile	#14	5
17. Electrical Trim	#14	1.5
18. Finish Plumbing	#15	3.5
19. Heating Trim	#14	2.5
20. Carpeting	#6, 12, 13, 16, 17, 18, 19	2
21. Clean up	#20	2

The shaded line on the first draft chart represents the critical path. The construction superintendent chose to lay out the "concrete footer" and "foundation" tasks horizontally. When these tasks are completed, both "grading" and "concrete" then can begin.

"Grading" is laid out horizontally and "concrete" angles upward. Continuing like this, "framing" and "roofing" are laid out horizontally and "wiring" is laid out angled upward. Once the tasks of "roofing is completed, "furnace and ducts" and "plumbing" then can be started.

When laying out the critical path, you should either angle each of several Day 1 start tasks up or down, or start them at different vertical points on the Day 0 line.

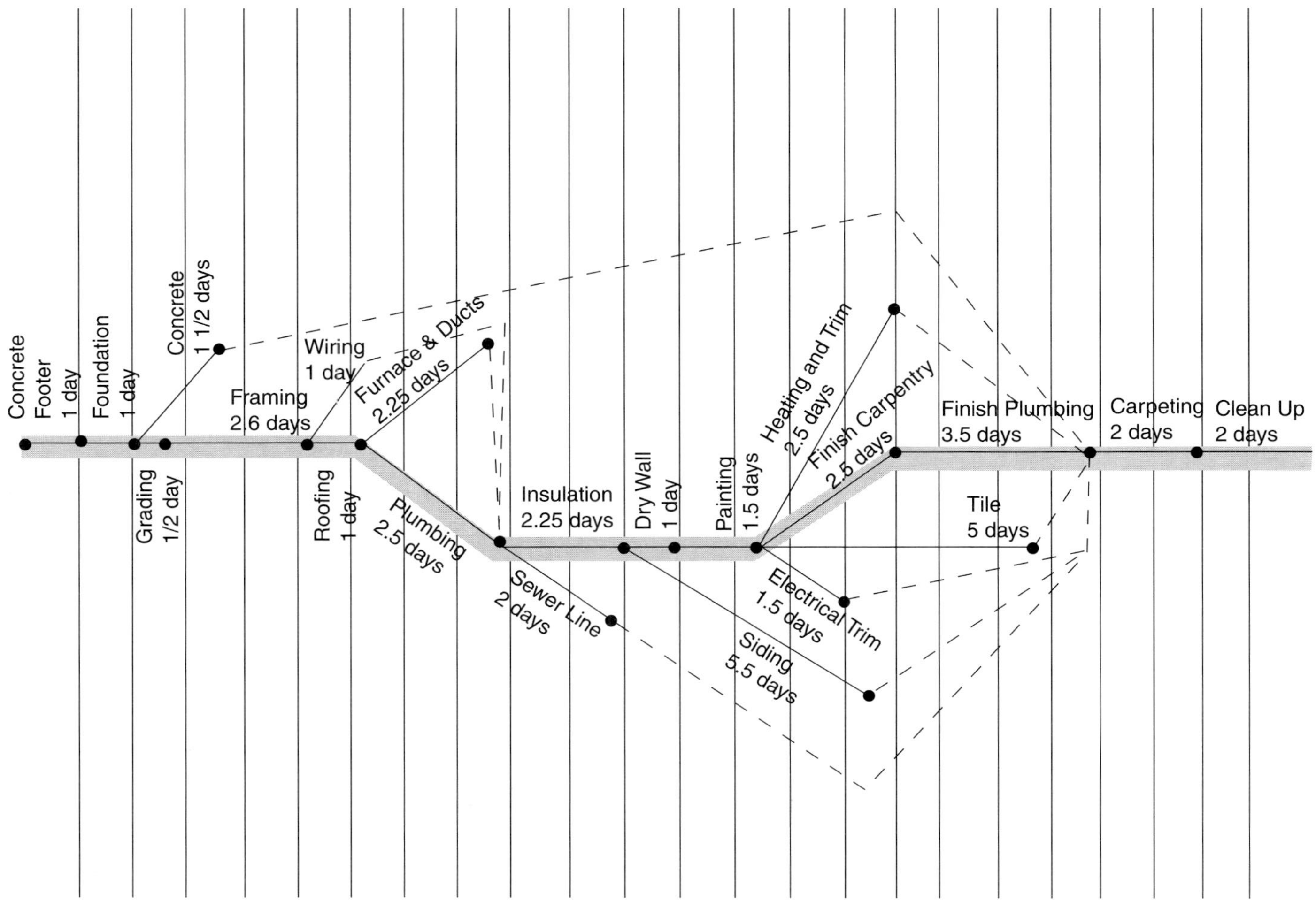

Concrete Footer 1 day
Foundation 1 day
Grading 1/2 day
Concrete 1 1/2 days
Framing 2.6 days
Wiring 1 day
Roofing 1 day
Furnace & Ducts 2.25 days
Plumbing 2.5 days
Sewer Line 2 days
Insulation 2.25 days
Dry Wall 1 day
Siding 5.5 days
Painting 1.5 days
Heating and Trim 2.5 days
Electrical Trim 1.5 days
Finish Carpentry 2.5 days
Tile 5 days
Finish Plumbing 3.5 days
Carpeting 2 days
Clean Up 2 days

Figure 7-4

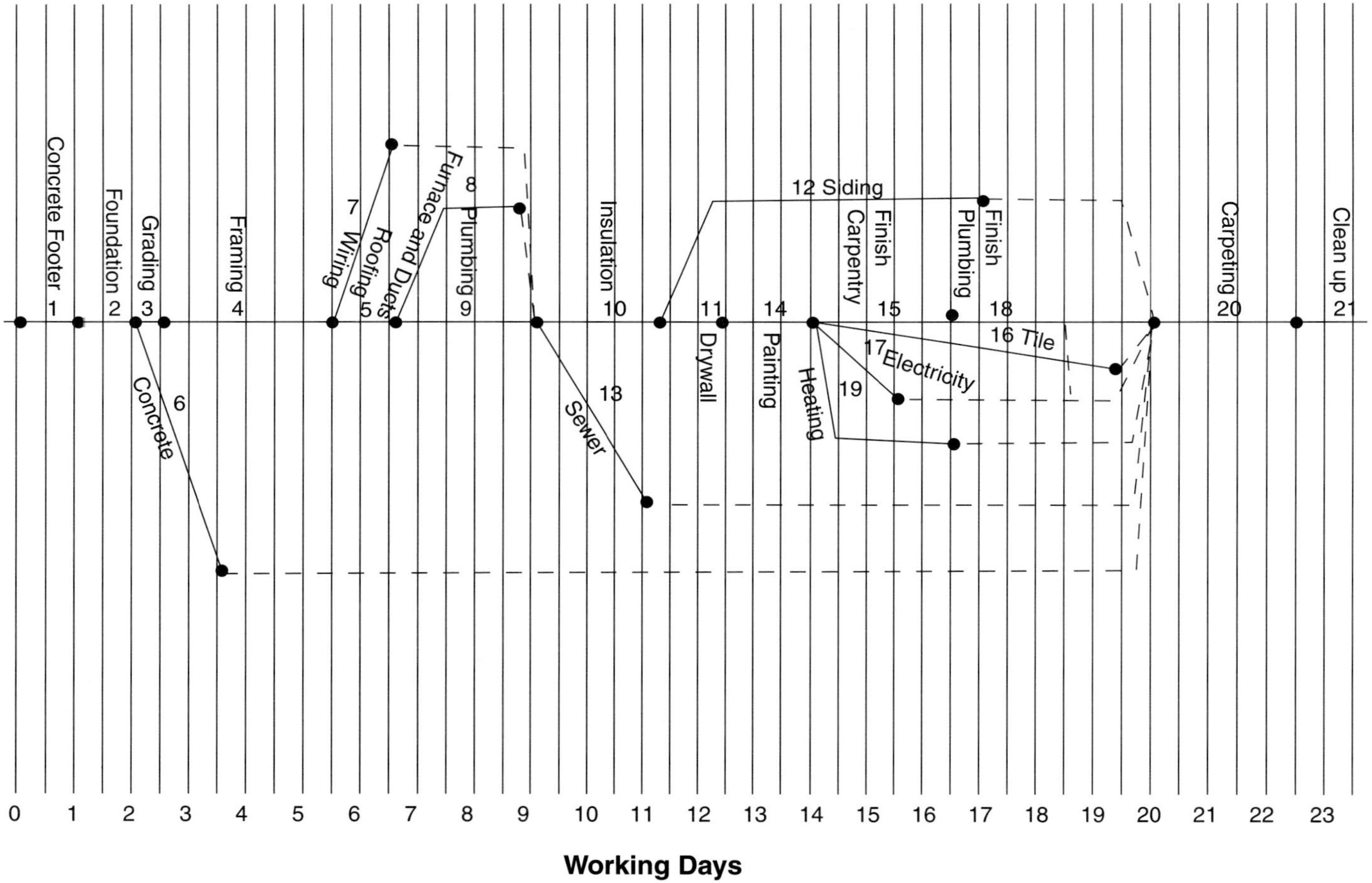
Concrete Footer 1
Foundation 2
Grading 3
Framing 4
6 Concrete
7 Wiring
Roofing 5
8 Furnace and Ducts
Plumbing 9
Insulation 10
13 Sewer
11 Drywall
14 Painting
12 Siding
Finish Carpentry 15
Finish Plumbing 18
16 Tile
17 Electricity
19 Heating
Carpeting 20
Clean up 21
0 1 2 3 4 5 6 7 8 9 10 11 12 13 14 15 16 17 18 19 20 21 22 23
Working Days

Figure 7-5

The superintendent can redraw the chart, which becomes the second critical path chart draft. He or she shows each critical path task laid out horizontally. The slack, depicted by dots, is very easy to see on this chart. (These dots connect necessary predecessors to their successors, when another predecessor takes more time.)

Slack is selectively utilized to make the most efficient use of the resources. It may be advantageous, for example, to delay starting the wiring task by one day. This might be doable without delaying the overall project. The superintendent will not agree to use up all the slack on one task unless there is a serious necessity. Remember, using up the entire slack for a task makes the task critical.

We find the critical path arrow diagram extremely useful during a project's execution. We each prepare one for every project we lead, particularly the large ones.

Figures 7-2A and B show a Gantt chart representation of the "Build a House Project" using Microsoft Project 2002®. In these figures, the critical path tasks are represented with solid bars. Non-critical path tasks are shown with shaded bars.

EXAMPLE

The following example illustrates a project in which several strings of tasks ending with slack parallel the critical paths. When using only the Gantt chart critical path, this relationship is hard to track and to utilize for managing a project's execution.

A National Marketing and Sales Project

A company that manufactures machinery for light metal fabrication has developed a new piece of machinery and has planned a marketing/sales campaign to push the sale of this product. The major tasks are sales, marketing, advertising, and printing. The detail tasks and the scheduled duration of each task and interdependencies are shown in Table 7-2 and Figure 7-6.[1] (Note: There are some interdependencies of sub-tasks among the four major work packages.)

This is an unusual case. There are two critical paths through the project. Also, several sequences of tasks parallel the critical paths, and they have an accumulation of slack at the end of their sequence. This accumulated slack can be used to adjust resources for any task in the sequence, not just the last task. This feature makes the arrow diagram critical path chart particularly useful.

Note the sequence tasks L, M, and N end with slack. This means the start date of L, or all the start dates for L, M, and N can be delayed successively if the delay does not use up all available slack between N and U. Even if all the slack was used up, there is more slack after Task U to protect the timeline.

[1]William K. Holstein and Walter H. Warrek, Arrow Diagram Exercise. Boston: Harvard Business School. 1995. Copyright 1965 by the President and Fellows at Harvard College. Reprinted by permission.

Table 7-2

SALES TASK	DAYS	DEPENDENCY
A. Prepare Phase 1 of training	(8)	None
B. Sales managers select trainees	(2)	None
C. Sales personnel relieved of duty and sent to home office	(4)	B
D. Train sales personnel in Phase 1	(10)	A & C
E. Prepare Phase 2 of sales training (Approval of Phase 2 training after general marketing approach is completed as required)	(9)	A
F. Conduct Phase 2 sales of training	(12)	D & E & I
G. Sales trainees become familiar with customer instruction manual	(5)	BB & F
H. Sales trainees return to territory	(1)	G
MARKETING TASK	**DAYS**	**DEPENDENCY**
I. Determine general marketing approach	(10)	None
J. Select marketing personnel	(4)	I
K. Bring marketing personnel to home office	(2)	J
L. Consolidate training plans for marketing personnel	(2)	I
M. Design a familiarization course for marketing personnel	(8)	L
N. Train marketing personnel	(8)	M & K
ADVERTISING	**DAYS**	**DEPENDENCY**
O. Firm up advertising plans	(6)	I
P. Prepare a paper	(6)	O
Q. Get paper printed in a professional journal	(8)	P
R. Prepare national advertising approval	(4)	O
S. Get national advertising approved	(4)	R
T. Distribute advertising to media	(2)	S
U. Release national advertising	(2)	N & Q & T

Table 7-2 (*Continued*)

PRINTING	DAYS	DEPENDENCY
V. Draft and approve a general brochure	(4)	O
W. Layout of brochure	(5)	V
X. Print a brochure	(3)	W
Y. Prepare a customer instructional manual	(3)	V
Z. Approve a customer instructional manual	(1)	Y
AA. Print an instructional manual	(2)	Z
BB. Send a customer manual to sales training center	(1)	AA
CC. Package brochure and manual and deliver them to marketing for general distribution	(8)	X & AA
Implement Campaign		

If L–M–N runs out past the designated start time for Task U, there is still slack time between the end of Task U and the end of the project identified by the completion of Tasks H and CC.

The project manager may note that many tasks in the project can overrun or start late without affecting the project's completion date. Slack that is identifiable at the end of Task Q can be used to enable Task P to start a half-day late. Slack identifiable at the end of Tasks AA and BB will protect the project if Task Y overruns by one day.

The diagram in Figure 7-6 reveals many ways the project can be adjusted without affecting its end date. These characteristics are not as obvious on a computer-created Gantt chart. The computer software generates a Pert chart that has arrow diagram characteristics and is somewhat more helpful for these purposes than the Gantt chart, but it is not as useful as the arrow diagram. It is this type of clear and complete arrow diagram (showing that the A–D–F–G–H sequence and the I–O–V–W–X–CC sequence are both critical) that the project manager provides for each team member prior to the risk analysis discussion meeting.

Figure 7-6 shows the "National Marketing and Sales" project arrow diagram laid out with each of the critical paths on a parallel straight line. The slack represented between Task I and F is not useful slack. As a predecessor to Task F, Task I is completed long before Task D and has plenty of slack. However, Task I is on the second critical path as a predecessor to Task O and has no slack there. The slack between Tasks BB and G is likewise not useful slack. The slack between Tasks BB and CC is useful for the Y–Z–AA–BB sequence. Because of Tasks BB's relationship to the second critical path, the slack between Tasks BB and G is not usable.

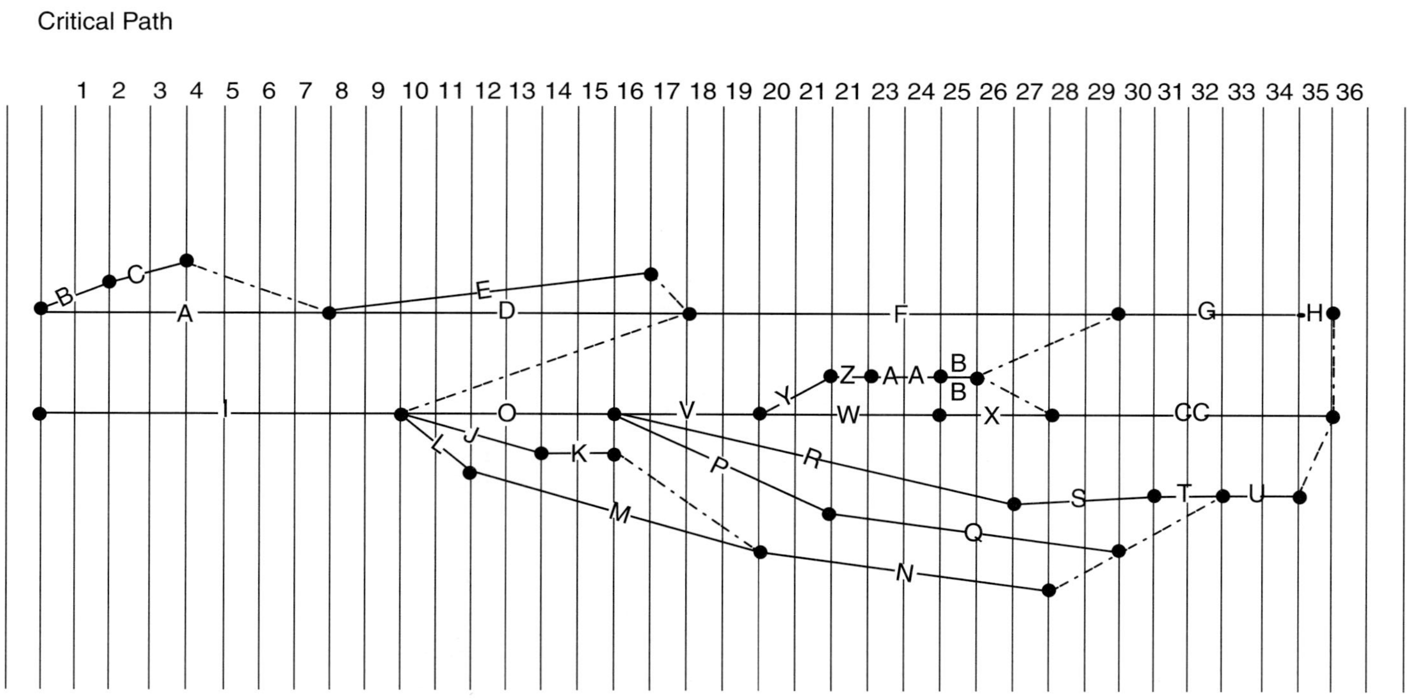
Critical Path
1 2 3 4 5 6 7 8 9 10 11 12 13 14 15 16 17 18 19 20 21 21 23 24 25 26 27 28 29 30 31 32 33 34 35 36
B
C
A
E
D
F
G
H
I
O
V
Y
Z
A A
B
B
W
X
CC
J
L
K
M
P
R
S
T
U
Q
N

Figure 7-6

SUMMARY

The critical path shows the task sequence through the project where any task delay becomes a project delay. It is important that project team members know if their task is on or close to the critical path when they contribute to risk analysis. The critical path and task slack information is crucial knowledge for the project manager to have while managing a project's execution.

Project software will display a project's critical path, but an easily constructed arrow diagram that the project management can prepare is a much more useful tool.

DISCUSSION QUESTIONS

1. Who defines a project's critical path?
2. Who creates a critical path arrow diagram?
3. What does a critical path consist of?
4. What is slack?
5. How can a project manager make use of his or her knowledge of slack in managing a project?

8 RISK ANALYSIS BASICS—TIME BUFFER CALCULATIONS

INTRODUCTION

The risk analysis used in IPM makes it possible for a project manager to expect to consistently finish a project to specifications, and be on time and within budget. This chapter focuses on the risk that some tasks on the Gantt chart will take longer and need more resources than were anticipated and how to extend the project completion date to account for this adjustment.

The development of a reliable project time buffer is one of the biggest problems that project managers face. It is discussed at most meetings of the local chapters of the Project Management Institute. Papers are presented at every national and international meeting. A basic question managers and customers ask is, "When will the work be completed?" It is worth some sophisticated effort to get the completion date right.

The IPM method of risk analysis grew out of struggles with probability theory and years of experimentation. Eventually, we developed a method that works. It involves project team members performing some data gathering and decision making that is unfamiliar to them. This means that a project manager has a good deal of explaining to do at the first risk analysis meeting.

PROJECT TEAM MEETINGS

There will be two, three, or sometimes four, two-hour meetings devoted to creating the Gantt chart. After it is completed, the project manager makes sure each team member has a copy. The project manager then explains to the team that the next step is creating the critical path chart and that he or she will do this for the team and distribute the chart as soon as it is finished. With the team's input at the final Gantt chart meeting and allowing just enough time to create and distribute the critical path chart, the project manager will schedule the first risk analysis meeting.

The only team member action items that follow the last Gantt chart meeting are: 1) review the critical path chart when you get it and be sure that you identify the tasks you—the task leader—are responsible for, and 2) make plans and be very sure that you can attend the next meeting—the initial risk analysis meeting. This meeting is particularly important because the project manager will explain to all of the team members what is needed from them for risk analysis, how they can best gather the data that they must bring to these meetings, how this data will be used, and why risk analysis is so very important.

WHY RISK ANALYSIS IS NECESSARY

When the project team has completed the Gantt chart development described in Chapter 6, they have a working Gantt chart with a precisely identified completion date. This chart is built up with "most of the time" time estimates for each task. We refer to this chart as a working Gantt chart because the completion date is not one to which a project manager can commit. "Most of the time" means not all of the time; a few tasks will take a little less time than estimated and some will take longer than estimated. Therefore, there is still work to be done to arrive at a completion date to which the project manager can commit.

THE HISTORY OF RISK ANALYSIS

The problem recognized early in IPM development was to discover how to set up a procedure so risk factors could be added to the project's critical path that would cover task overruns and not pad the project. The objective was to finish the project—not early or late—but at the planned time! In other words, how could one add a risk factor, or series of risk factors, to the Gantt chart that allowed for some overruns but not overstate the overruns?

This problem was approached theoretically and experimentally. We decided that risk analysis should be based on a task-by-task analysis. We recognized that by going into detail, we could improve accuracy. We asked ourselves, "What additional information do task leaders have or have access to that can help with risk analysis?" Discussion of this topic led to focusing on data items. Experienced task leaders generally know or can find out the longest time a task like my task for the project has taken or might take under unusual circumstances. They also can review past experiences and determine what percentage of the time a task like my task for the project over runs its estimated duration.

These are educated estimates that are based on experience. They provide data to use in developing risk factors that can be inserted along the critical path.

Using the risk analysis method a life insurance actuary might use, it was recognized that task facts present a random distribution of overrun possibilities that somewhat resemble the random age distribution at death for a general population. There is an average age expectancy for a population. No one knows in advance which individuals will overrun this expectancy rate, but they know that some will. Annuity life policies must pay monthly annuities to people in the overrun group for as long as each one lives.

How much money should the insurance company set aside to cover these payments? How much additional time should the project manager and the team set aside as a risk factor to cover the overruns from some of the tasks? Insurance actuaries solve these problems by applying statistical analysis to the insurance company's massive body of data. The project manager and the team have only limited data on a project task overrun, which is not nearly enough to justify a statistical analysis.

Could, then, a rule of thumb be developed, based on actuarial philosophy, that would functionally solve this problem? The answer—following some creative trial and error attempts—is yes! Risk analysis as it is presented here is the outcome.

RISK ANALYSIS

Risk analysis is conducted so that a project team can accurately predict the project completion date. It is based on task-by-task analysis. We discovered that we can identify each task's duration expectation that will be good most of the time—over 50 percent of the time if the task were repeated over and over. And, we can identify the likely worst case over run for each task. We discovered a way to use this information to average out task overruns to create a project time buffer similar to that an insurance actuary creates. He tells his company how much money to set aside to pay claims of clients who achieve longer than average longevity. We create a time buffer for the Gantt chart to protect our completion date estimate from the tasks that over run their most of the time forecast.

TASK DURATION BASICS

Task leaders provide the raw data for risk analysis. They are chosen for a project because they have knowledge and experience that they can use when doing the necessary task work to complete a project. Their knowledge and experience also gives them a good foundation for speaking with other experienced people about task duration. All of these task leaders do not necessarily have the same experiences, but they each have done very similar things. Carpenters have built frames for other houses, engineers have calculated the air flow through other ducts, programmers have written lines of code for other similar information systems projects, technical writers have written published papers describing similar products, and so on.

After he or she has helped identify the project tasks and has taken ownership of "my" task(s), the project manager will ask each task leader to report on how long his or her task will take most of the time. Most of the time, represented in this discussion by M, will be the time duration assigned to the task. (It is represented by a bar on the working Gantt chart.) It is absolutely necessary that each task leader supply this most-of-the-time information if a usable Gantt chart is to be created. It is equally important that this information not be padded. It must be an honest estimate of how long the task leader expects the task to take "most of the time."

The project manager must point out to the team members that there is a difference between "most of the time" and "all of the time". It is acknowledged that each task is likely to run over some of the time if the task is repeated over and over. It also is acknowledged by the project manager and the team members that a particular task may overrun its estimated time on "our" project. With dozens to hundreds of tasks, some will overrun their estimated time. The team members do not know in advance which of these tasks will overrun, but they do expect that some will. In addition, they do not wish to be in an embarrassing or threatening situation if one of the tasks that overruns is "mine." Risk Analysis protects team members who execute their task with due diligence from censure if their task overruns.

AN IMAGINARY EXPERIMENT

Consider that one task leader might execute a task like his or her project task 100 times. Experience discloses that once or twice everything falls together, and that the task is completed in an unexpectedly short time. The same experience guides the task leader to recognize that many of the 100 tasks being undertaken will finish a little later, but not much later. There will be little variation in the finish times for a large number of the 100 tasks. This is because experienced people are doing what they know how to do, thus their outcomes are not going to vary.

There will be a large number of tasks within the hypothetical 100 that finish in about the same amount of time. There also will be some that take longer and, generally, one or two worst cases that take the longest. If our imaginary task leader records the finish time for each task, he or she can number the tasks according to their finish time. The shortest task is named number one. The longest task is named number 100. If the task leader plots the task durations on a vertical scale against the task number on a horizontal scale, the plot will look like the Figure 8-1.

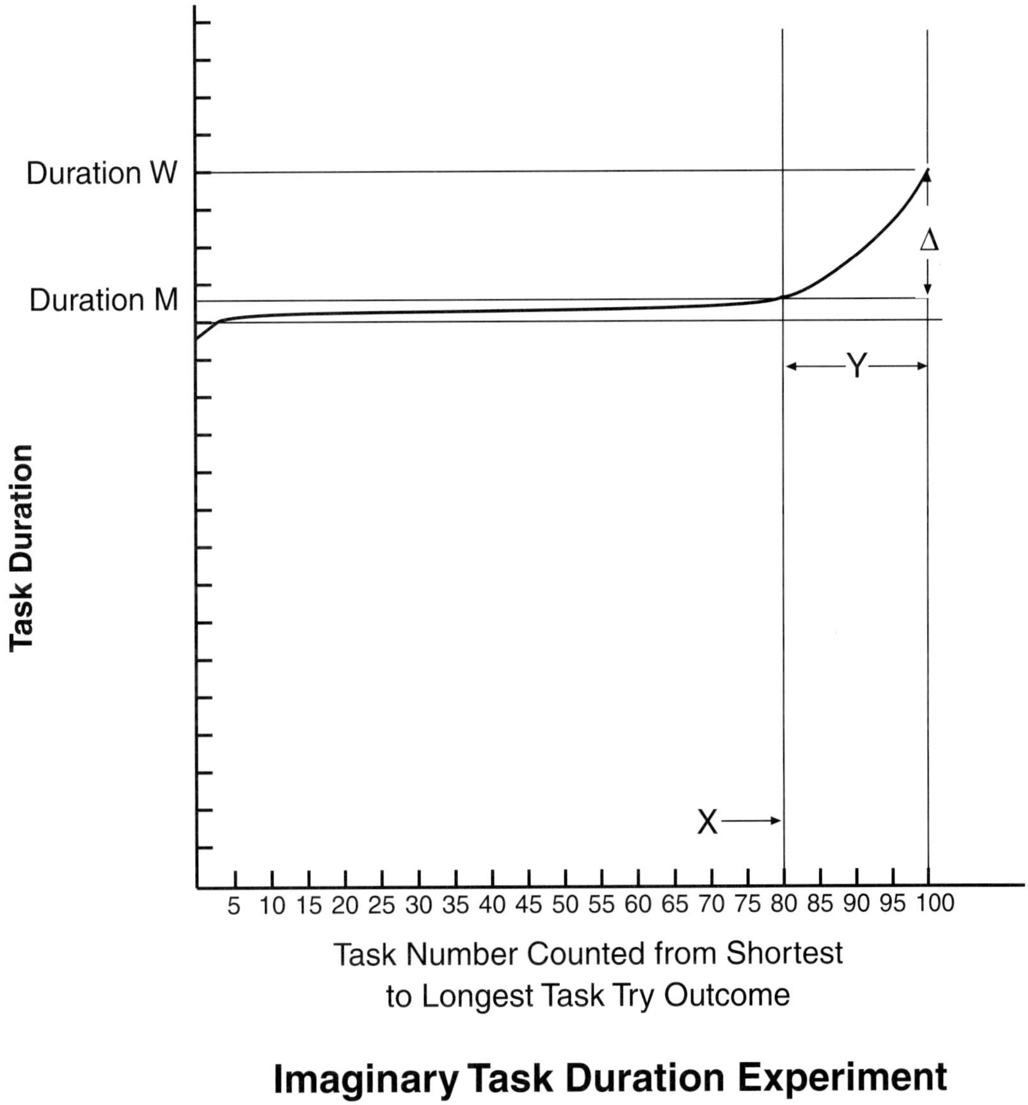

Figure 8-1

There is a general pattern for task duration distributions for tasks that are repeatedly performed by knowledgeable and experienced people. In Figure 8-1, break points where task duration exceeds it and the magnitude of Δ, vary from task type to task type. (W represents the worst case duration.) For a routine task, the break point is likely to occur at Task 95—it is possible that one task leader will insist that this is a very familiar task and it can always be finished on time. For a familiar task that is not technically challenging but involves some judgmental decisions, the break point—the point where the task's duration exceeds M—may be expected to occur at Task 85. Fifteen out of 100 tasks can require some extra effort, and one or two will require an effort equal to W. For tasks involving some experimentation to get it right or some uncertainty about the availability of a key workgroup member, the break point may occur at Task 75. For tasks that are particularly challenging or where resource availability is uncertain, the break point may be at Task 60. We expect experienced people to contribute an M estimate that is achievable at least 50 percent of the time (that is, for tasks 1–50). If this is not possible, the task leaders then are involved in a research effort, not a plannable project completion effort.

DATA FOR RISK ANALYSIS

An imaginary experiment is created to help the project manager communicate to team members what data is needed for risk analysis. At this time, each team member is asked to provide a likelihood of task time overrunning the M estimate, which is represented in Figure 8-1 by the number where the durations begin to exceed M, subtracted from $100(100 - 80 = 20)$ this number is called Y; and the size of the worst case overruning $W - M = \Delta$.

A project manager does not have to discuss the imaginary experiment with the project team. However, the project manager does ask each team member for three data points: M, Y, and Δ. He or she also leaves it up to the team members to determine when his or her task will be completed "most of the time," what the likelihood is of the task overrunning the M estimate, and what the worst case of overrun might be. These are the numbers that task leaders can be expected to estimate closely, based on past experience and discussions with other experienced people.

CASE EXAMPLE

The task time estimates experienced workers provide for IPM Gantt chart development for a familiar task will be accurate "most of the time." This estimate is not an average from a task time that fluctuates broadly. It is how long the task will take, within narrow time limits, or "most of the time." For example, we can tell you with confidence that "most of the time" in summer, it will take us between 22 and 25 minutes to drive to work. We cannot ever expect to get there in under 20 minutes! Occasionally, when it rains very hard, when there is a big convention in town, or when there is an accident on the highway, we may need up to 45 minutes to get to work. It does not happen often, and 45 minutes travel time is the worst case that we have ever experienced.

When we do experience a delay, it will vary from a few minutes, which is generally caused by heavy rain, to the maximum of 20 minutes, which is caused by an accident on the highway. "*Most of the time,*" (M), we can make it to work in 25 minutes.

APPLICATION OF THE RISK DATA

The project Gantt chart has been completed and shows when the project would be completed if there were no uncertainties about the task durations. Because there are uncertainties about the task durations and experience tells us that the sum of most of the task time estimates is going to be inaccurate due to overruns (overestimates are rare and small, and do not impact overrun risks), it is clear that the working Gantt chart finish date is an underestimation. To provide a reliable project completion date, it is necessary to have 1) some way to add a time buffer to the end of the project, or 2) several smaller time buffers placed at intervals along the critical path that adequately allow for the amount of time some tasks overrun. Determining the time buffer is made particularly difficult because there is no way of knowing which tasks will overrun and by how much in each case. It is known, however, that most tasks in the project will not significantly overrun. The method for choosing "most of the time" estimates (M:) assures this is the case.

A very simple way to calculate the project's necessary time buffer overrun would be to add up all the Δs for tasks on the critical path and to insert this duration at the end of the project. The project completion date then would be protected from overrun, but it would be greatly overprotected. It is desirable that each task with an overrun potential contribute some number measured in days to the project overrun buffer. However, letting every task contribute the Δ derived from its worst case is always going to be unacceptable to sponsors and customers.

There is a method of calculating a useful project overrun buffer that works. Take the overrun for the worst case for a task, Δ, and multiply it by the likelihood that overrun of M might occur, Y, which is expressed as a decimal. Then add it with each other "contribution" calculated in this way to determine a realistic project time buffer. The project will not overrun this buffer—it will finish close to the time predicted by adding the buffer.

There is an added advantage to determining the buffer this way. We called the buffer the risk factor when introduced it as a task bar on the Gantt chart. It is derived from summing together the risk contributions from a string of tasks. The critical path can be divided up into units, and a risk factor can be calculated for each unit. This risk factor is entered at the end of the string instead of at the end of the whole project. Doing so enables the Gantt chart representation to more accurately identify crucial task start dates. If the overruns were accounted for at the end of the project, the start dates would not be accurately identified.

Because a task will not overrun at all over 50 percent of the time, this type of task is executed—there is a better than 50 percent chance it will not overrun for our project. However, if we have five tasks on our project, each with a 40 percent chance of overrun, we can be reasonably certain that from these five tasks there will be some time overrun. When we have between 20 and 30 tasks in the mix, and have an appropriate "most of the time" estimation and the likelihood of overrun and worst case data for each task, the method of calculating the contribution creates a good risk factor. The 20 or 30 tasks used in the calculation averages out the overrun.

A project manager explains "most of the time," Δ and Y to the team members at the initial risk analysis meeting. Discussion of Figure 8-1 and the "drive to work" example often help. When discussing Figure 8-1, it is important to point out that Y and Δ vary from task to task.

The action items for each task leader at the end of the initial risk analysis meeting are to determine the Y and Δ that go with his or her "most of the time" estimate, to multiply them together (Y times Δ), and to report the product to the project manager.

There is an other item of information that is needed from each task team leader so that the project manager and team can complete the risk analysis. As the task leader analyzes the possibilities of task overrun, he or she will note that overrun task instances between X and 100 percent produce different amounts of overrun, reaching Δ in only a small percentage of cases. The data from the overruns creeps up to the Δ figure as the percentage of task completion increases. For example, a task may overrun because a key task team member is unavailable. This particular team member may have a history of illness that makes him or her unavailable from time-to-time, however, the number of days he or she is unavailable can vary from one day to 10 days, with 10 days being a very infrequent occurrence. Therefore, the magnitude of task overrun caused by this task team member's unavailability varies from one day to (occasionally) up to ten days (which rarely occurs). The upward curve on the timeline in the chart in Figure 8-1 displays this type of relationship. We call this a creeping or "creep" overrun. We can assume that most overruns have this characteristic.

There are, however some overruns that do not have this creeping characteristic. When one factor causes delay, it causes a significant delay and this delay amount occurs every time this factor creates a problem. For example, in a manufacturing process a task may require creating a specific part that is somewhat hard to make. A machinist will get it right a few times on the first attempt. Most often it will take two attempts. The "most of the time" task time number used is the time

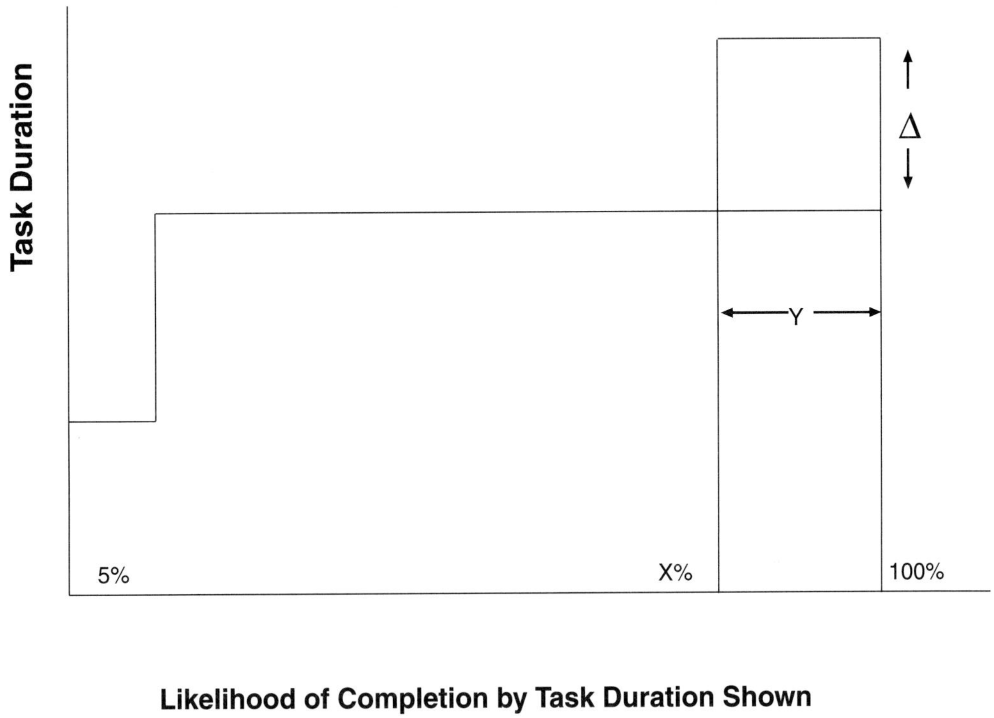

Figure 8-2

required for two attempts. On the infrequent occasions that a third attempt is required, the delay increases to the full time required for one more attempt. There is no creeping characteristic between the two and three attempts. The time delay rises immediately for any overruns to the full duration of a third attempt. We call this a step-function overrun. Figure 8-2 illustrates this characteristic.

Tasks that have this "step function" characteristic occasionally turn up. It is important to the calculation of a risk factor that the task team leader, whose task can have this step-function characteristic, report the Y and Δ for the step-function case along with the task contribution to the risk factor to the project leader. When there is one or more tasks that have a step-function risk, it is necessary to consider this risk as a special case when calculating a risk factor.

The method for calculating a contribution number for each task is laid out here. The principle that is used to determine the risk factor to be inserted on the Gantt chart timeline, which determines a realistic project completion date, is to add up the contributions from all tasks on the critical path and to use this sum as the risk factor.

This procedure yields a Gantt chart that looks like the one shown in Figure 8-3.

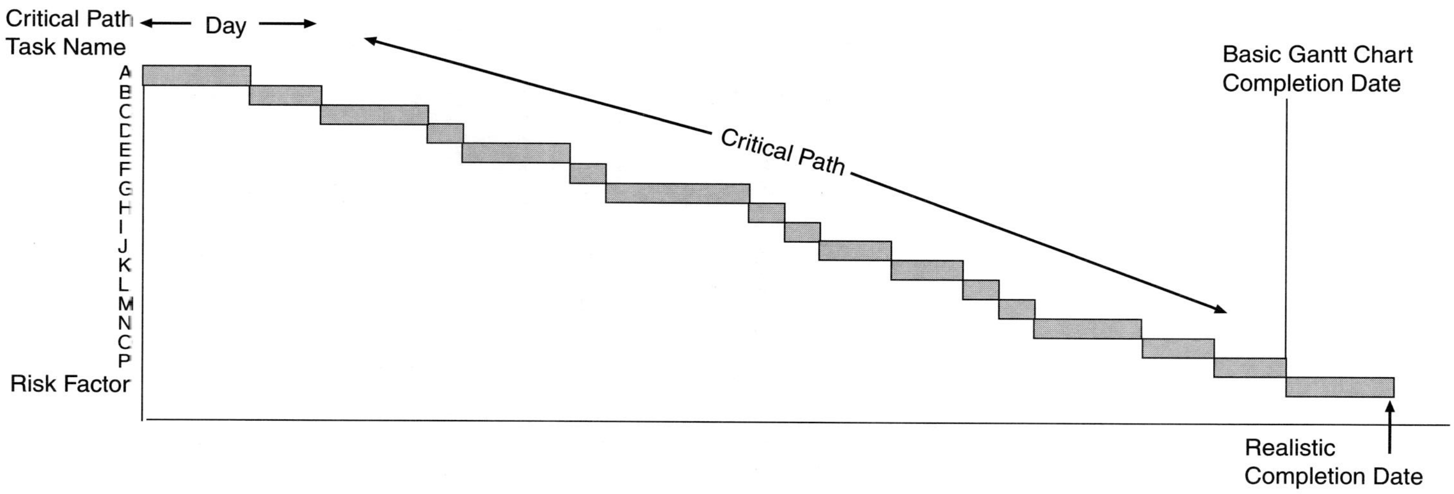
Critical Path
Task Name
Day
A
B
C
D
E
F
G
H
I
J
K
L
M
N
O
P
Risk Factor
Critical Path
Basic Gantt Chart
Completion Date
Realistic
Completion Date

Figure 8-3

THE PSYCHOLOGICAL IMPACT OF RISK ANALYSIS

Without risk analysis, a project manager and a team never develop a realistic project plan. If the team members are asked for task time estimates and they know that their estimates will be a matter of record, this is considered when they estimate the task duration; if they are even a little uneasy about the tasks, they can be expected to give padded time estimates. Knowledge of the worst case estimate in past experiences will drive up the estimate. In fact the worst case estimate provides for the most comfortable time buffer.

It would seem that if the task time estimates for all tasks are buffered, the actual project would always finish early. However, the opposite seems to be the case. Task leaders who know they have a padded finish date seem to feel free to start the task late, give their task effort a low priority, and lack the determination to get on with it in a world of conflicting demands. This behavior results in all of the padding in each task time effort being used up before the task is completed. Thus, the project finishes very late. Survey data that shows projects typically overrun in time by 100 percent or more seems to be, in part, a product of this particular situation.

Risk analysis raises to task leader's consciousness the difference between "most of the time" completion data and worst case completion data. When the project manager asks for both estimates and a report of how much difference there is between them (Δ), the task leader must rethink a padded time estimate. When he or she knows that a risk factor will be developed to protect him or her from being blamed for project delay, he or she is more willing to give serious consideration to both estimates. The task leader feels that he or she can be comfortable with the "most of the time" estimate because, "I told you that it might take longer."

The risk factor used for a string of tasks is the sum of the Δ times likelihood, (Y) for each task.

The risk factor, added to the working Gantt chart, provides a finish date. The project manager can expect the actual finish date to be close to, but not later than, the date derived from this analysis.

When the task team has a date to finish the project and it is the date that they have determined collectively, they are very highly motivated to meet that date. They take great pride in their accomplishment when they do hit that date. Being able to hit the projected finish date provides strong motivation for the team members. Workers like to work with a project manager who knows how to hit a team's completion date.

DOCUMENTATION OF THE RISK DATA

Overrun likelihood (Y), worst case overrun duration (Δ), and the creep or step-overrun characteristic function cannot be casually approached! As with other information gathered throughout IPM project planning, task leaders again must: 1) review past projects, 2) talk to other experienced people, 3) review the baseline and actual Gantt charts from other similar projects, and 4) confer with all task team members in their quest for contribution data (this may take several days, given their other responsibilities). The project manager must be available during this time. A manager's advice and help, especially to people new to the procedure, is essential.

Each task leader will report this gathered information to the project leader as soon as possible. The project manager then will accumulate this data as shown in Table 8-1.

Only critical path tasks will be used in the analysis. However, some tasks that have very little slack and high Δs can impact the critical path (This explanation of dealing with non-critical path task overruns is left for Chapter 9). The left vertical column of the table follows the sequence of the critical path. (This analysis is not completed until the various causes of contribution are analyzed, which is discussed in Chapter 9.)

Worksheet

The characteristics of Table 8-1 are discussed in the following paragraphs.

The # column identifies the task by number in accordance with its place in the Gantt chart task column. Breaks in the numerical sequence reflect the Gantt chart tasks that are not on the critical path.

The "Task" column should give the task's name (letters have been substituted for task names).

The next column gives the "most of the time" (M) estimate. This is the estimate that appears as a bar on the project Gantt chart.

The "Longest Time" (W) column gives the worst case estimate.

The "Delta" (Δ) column indicates the difference between the longest time estimate and the "most of the time" estimate. (On a spreadsheet, an equation can be entered for this column that will calculate the difference of W - M.)

The "% of time task overruns likelihood" column (Y) gives the likelihood in a percentage that the task will overrun its original estimate. (This is the likelihood that the task will overrun at all, not the likelihood that the overrun will be the worst case estimate.)

The "Contribution" column is the duration of the overrun in the worst case situation times the likelihood that the task will overrun. This is Δ times Y, and the equation can be entered in a spreadsheet column. It is the value you seek in doing the risk analysis and it represents the contribution the task makes to the determination of the risk factor for this sequence of tasks.

Table 8-1

#	Task	"Most of the Time" Estimate (M) (Days)	Longest Time Estimate (W) (Days)	Delta W-M Δ	% of Time the Task will Overrun Likelihood Y	Contribution Δ Times Y	Risk Type
1	A	2	3	1	0.10	0.1	C
3	C	5	5.5	.5	0.40	0.2	SF
4	D	1	3	2	0.30	0.6	C
6	F	2	2	0	0	0	—
7	G	5	6	1	0.20	0.2	C
9	H	4	5	1	0.20	0.2	SF
11	J	2	2.5	.5	0.10	0.05	C
13	M	7	7.5	.5	0.30	0.15	SF
14	N	6	6	0	0	0	—
15	O	8	11	3	0.20	0.6	C
16	P	10	15	5	0.10	0.5	C
17	Q	20	27	7	0.15	1.05	SF
19	S	3	4	1	0.40	0.4	C
23	W	5	7	2	0.30	0.6	C
25	Y	7	10	3	0.10	0.3	C
29	CC	19	28	9	0.10	0.9	C
30	DD	6	8	2	0.20	0.4	C
33	GG	10	14	4	0.15	0.6	C
34	HH	4	5	1	0.10	0.1	SF
36	SS	6	9	3	0.20	0.6	C
	Totals	132	178.5	46.5		7.55	

The last notation column on the risk calculation worksheet is for disclosing the "risk type"—creep (C) or step function (SF). In certain cases, a task with a large step function Δ will require special consideration in calculating the risk factor.

This worksheet is the essence of IPM risk analysis. The system has been developed through both analysis and trial and error. Likelihood is an estimate. It takes some discussion to help task leaders arrive at a good likelihood estimate. Everyone must realize that it is an estimate, a very useful estimate, but by no means is it mathematically precise. Experience has taught that task leaders can and will make good likelihood estimates if they understand why they are needed. (Likelihood is not probability. Probability is a technical term from statistics that is based on the analysis of a mass of data. This mass of data does not exist for project time buffer analysis.)

The delta figure (Δ) also is the result of estimates. It is the difference between the longest case *estimate* and the most-of-the-time *estimate*. Much of the experimentation that leads up to IPM time buffer analysis centered on how to choose Δ. One experiment was using the average overrun duration for the Y period instead of the longest overrun duration. Although it seemed reasonable, it did not work as well in practice as the Δ based on longest overrun estimate. (It was also harder to determine).

The IPM risk analysis methodology only works if task leaders take it seriously. However, the project manager first must understand it and explain it well at the risk factor discussion meeting. The project manager also must be available to help team members as they seek out the risk analysis data. (The details of determining a task's risk factor contribution are spelled out in the next chapter. Details are separated from fundamentals here because experience has demonstrated that this separation makes the total concept easier to understand.)

APPLICATION OF THE RISK ANALYSIS

The spreadsheet displayed in Table 8-1 provides all the information needed to determine the size of a risk factor to be inserted. The task overrun possibilities totaling 46.5 days are balanced against the likelihood that the tasks will not overrun by using the Δ times Y formula. The result of the calculation of contributions and adding them together is 7.55 days. Rounding up to eight days, this would be the risk factor to use for this string of tasks if there is no need for step-function adjustments.

There are five tasks in the list that have step-function characteristics. In four cases (3, 9, 13, and 34), the step functions (Δs) are small when compared to the risk factor. Their occurrences will average out just as the tasks with creep characteristics average out. No special adjustments are called for. Task 17 is a different case, however: There is a 15 percent likelihood that a problem causing overrun will occur here, and wherever the problem occurs there will be a seven-day delay. This is different from Task 29 where there is a 10 percent likelihood of a problem causing overrun to occur, but this problem does not instantly cause a nine-day delay; 29 is a creep overrun task, only in a very few cases will this delay (which has only a 10 percent chance of occurring at all) reach nine days. The likelihood of this happening is very, very small. It is not realistic or economical to try to protect a project from it. But for Task 17, there is a full 15 percent likelihood that the seven-day delay will impact the project and use of seven of the days provided for overrun by the risk factors. If this happens, the project time buffer represented by the risk factor has only one day to protect the project from all other sources of overrun. (We have used some elaborate calculations to try to determine a satisfactory time buffer size for the risk factor in this case. We have found that a simple rule of thumb works well.)

If the step function Δ is larger than half of the risk factor as calculated, subtract half of the original risk factor from the step function Δ, and add the difference to the original risk factor. In the situation being examined: 1/2 of $8 = 4, 7 - 4 = 3$, and the new risk factor is $8 + 3 = 11$, or eleven days is the revised risk factor. This is a conservative approach.

The project may finish a little earlier than predicted this way, but it will not be heavily buffered and it will not overrun the predicted finish date. Such is the condition that you can look forward to in all cases of IPM time buffer calculations.

Basically, risk analysis is a process that helps the project leader and the team make a good judgment call. Judgment is called for because project planners always know more about tasks than simple numbers can describe.

Note: Two tasks are at "0" risk in Table 8-1. Project managers are warned to beware of such estimates. Nevertheless, some jobs are successfully and repeatedly accomplished and additional resources are easily procured should problems arise. If history supports no more than a 1 or 2 percent likelihood of overrun, treat it as a "0" contribution. Note: It is impossible to run a business successfully trying to cover all apparent 1 or 2 percent risks.

The string of tasks used in Table 8-1 reflects a Gantt chart timeline of 132 days with no risks considered. It produces a 178.5-day sequence if every task runs over to its worst case amount; that is, the sum of the overrun possibilities is 46.5 days.

Risk analysis of the data described in the table shows that an 11-day risk factor inserted after Task SS will cover all the overruns that can reasonably be expected to take place during this sequence. The next task on the critical path—the one that begins the next task sequence of the project—can be confidently scheduled to start immediately after the risk factor task.

Here is a general question for all task leaders: If a delay is foreseeable during the early period of the task, is it possible to plan overtime and recruit more help or seek expert input, and thus avoid or reduce the delay? If yes, this piece of information should be included in the task notes of the project manager's diary, written into the notes recorded in the software, and introduced into the consideration of the task delta and likelihood.

THE RISK FACTOR

Generally 20 to 30 tasks along the critical path are used to create a risk factor. Such calculations, tempered with considerations of step-function contributions, are highly reliable. The risk factor will be added as a task bar on the Gantt chart at the end of the string of critical tasks, before the first task in the next task string is started (see Figures 8-4A and 8-4B).

The reason for using no more than 30 critical path tasks when calculating a risk factor is related to the good results that come from calculating and inserting risk factors periodically along the project's timeline. In practice, a few of the 20 or 30 tasks will run over, and for each overrun the project leader will have to inform downstream task leaders and help them adjust their start dates.

Most, but seldom all, of the cushion provided by the risk factor will be used. For a 30-task critical path string, the leader of Task 29 does not expect to start work as originally planned. Instead, the Task 29's start date will be delayed by almost the full amount of the risk factor. Thus, most task leaders will have a realistic, narrow band of startup dates and can adjust them accordingly. Task 31's task leader knows exactly when to expect to begin work. The prior risk factor has absorbed all upstream task delays. Therefore, he or she can start the day after the risk factor ends.

The risk factor will be largely used up by the task overruns. Generally, a small percentage is not used. It is not effective to try to start tasks by half of a day or day early, simply because conditions are ready for a startup. Efficiency is gained when task leaders know their startups will not be hurried.

Occasionally, one critical path task finishes sooner than predicted. If no risk factor time has been used, it will not impact downstream start dates. However, if some of the risk factor has been used, the amount of time saved will automatically be added back to the risk factor to cover overruns further down the critical path string of tasks. Project management software with the risk factor entered on the Gantt chart will automatically enter this time amount as the actual task times are entered during the project's execution.

If there are fewer than 20 tasks on a critical path, the procedure for calculating contributions and adding them together to determine a risk factor becomes less reliable. The averaging out of overruns and timely finishes of tasks achieved by the procedure is less certain with a few number of tasks. To protect from having the project overrun its estimated completion date when the critical path is between 10 and 20 tasks long, add 20 percent to the risk factor.

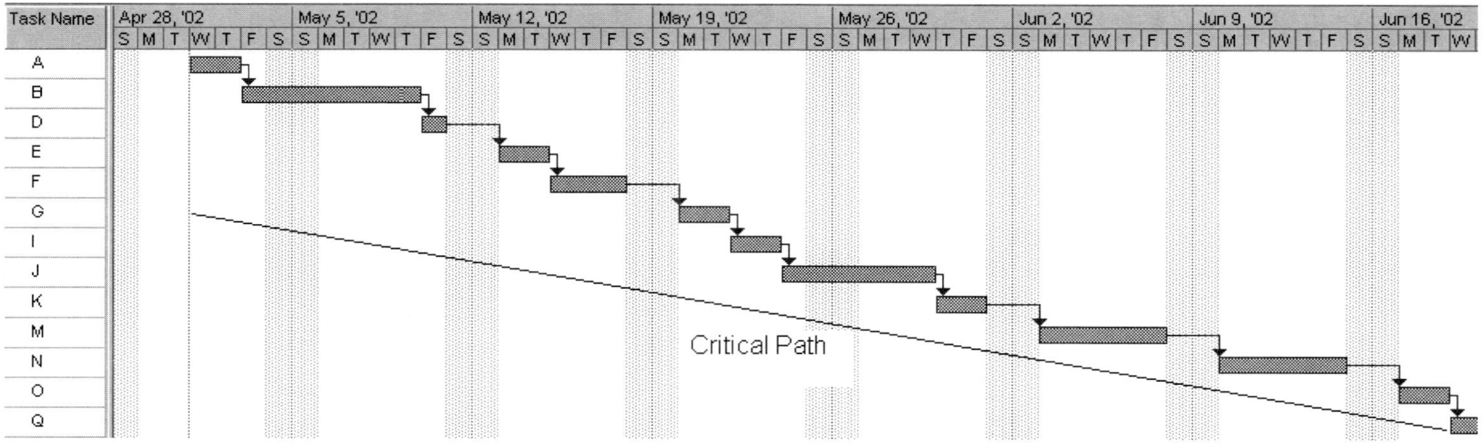
Task Name
Apr 28, '02
May 5, '02
May 12, '02
May 19, '02
May 26, '02
Jun 2, '02
Jun 9, '02
Jun 16, '02
A
B
D
E
F
G
I
J
K
M
N
O
Q
Critical Path

Figure 8-4A

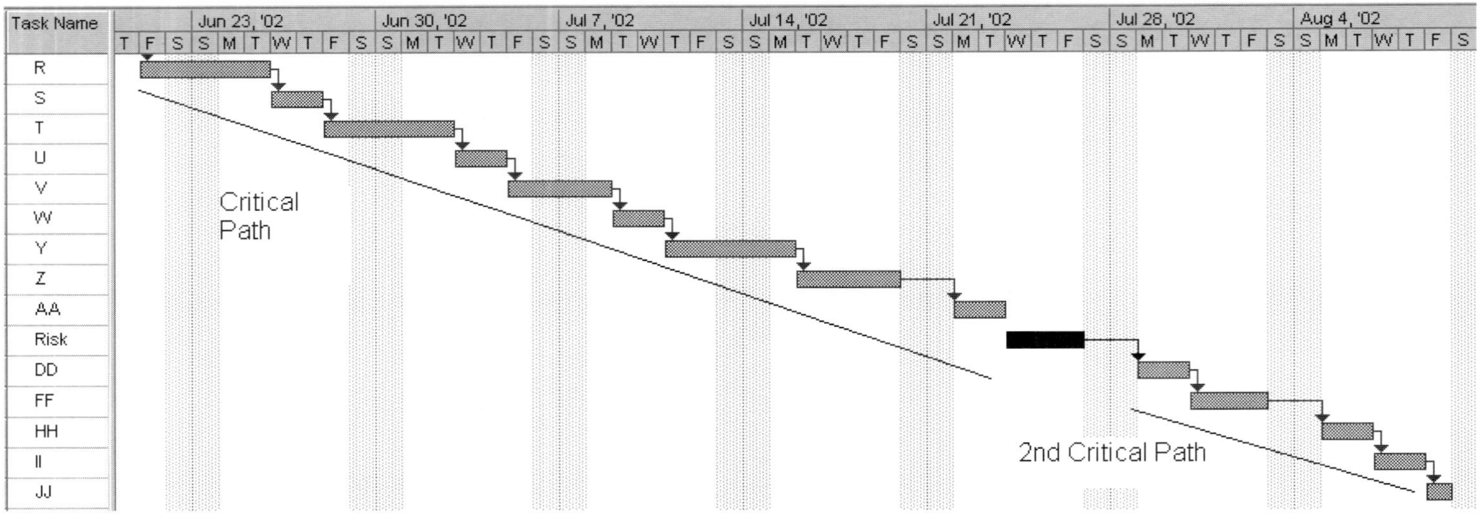
Task Name
Jun 23, '02
Jun 30, '02
Jul 7, '02
Jul 14, '02
Jul 21, '02
Jul 28, '02
Aug 4, '02
R
S
T
U
V
W
Y
Z
AA
Risk
DD
FF
HH
II
JJ
Critical Path
2nd Critical Path

Figure 8-4B

If the critical path is less than 10 tasks long, lay out each task's task overrun–Δ versus. "Likelihood of completion overrun–Y timechart as best you can with the task leader's help. Estimate the risk factor based on the characteristics of this task group. If all of the tasks have an overrun characteristic (Y) of 20 percent or less, determine a risk factor in the conventional way and double it. If the likelihood runs above 20 percent, you will probably want to triple the risk factor. If one task has a large Δ and an overrun likelihood of over 20 percent or a step-function overrun characteristic, use that task's Δ as your risk factor. Using these rules of thumb and if the decision is tempered by good judgment, your project may end up finishing early, but it will be protected from overrun.

SUMMARY

Good risk analysis is central to predicting how long a project will take. Task leaders supply estimates on how long the task will take most of the time, how long the task might take in the worst case, and what the likelihood is that the task will overrun the most-of-the-time estimate. The project manager will explain the what, why, and how of risk analysis at a team meeting scheduled at the start of the project's risk analysis meeting sequence. Each critical path task provides a "contribution" to the risk factor. Step-function risk tasks get special consideration—the risk factor is inserted after the last of the string of tasks that contributed to its calculation. The next task on the overall project's critical path is scheduled to start after the risk factor. This task leader will know exactly when he or she can plan to start his her task.

Risk analysis is discussed in more detail in Chapter 9.

DISCUSSION QUESTIONS

1. What happens in project execution if risk analysis is not done?
2. If we know that some tasks are going to overrun, why do we not simply provide buffers for each?
3. How does risk analysis average out the risks of task overruns in a project?
4. What makes step-function risks special?
5. What is the mentor role of a project manager in helping team members contribute to risk analysis?

9 RISK ANALYSIS DETAILS

INTRODUCTION

The discussion in Chapter 8 focused on asking task leaders how often they could expect, in the worst case, that their task would overrun their "most of the time" estimates. In developing the details of risk analysis, task leaders are asked to consider why their task could overrun. Asking *why* the task could overrun yields better task time overrun estimates and provides a basis for planning mitigation strategies to store in the task's notes and to use when an overrun seems to be developing during a task's execution. There is always more than one reason that a task might overrun. Each task leader is asked to list all the significant potential overrun causes and to analyze each one separately. The cause that produces the greatest contribution to the risk factor ($\Delta \times Y$) yields the contribution that is provided by the task leader in the determining of the risk factor.

In Chapter 8, the discussion of the risk factor was focused on critical path tasks. However, noncritical path tasks can sometimes cause a greater overrun impact than their parallel critical path tasks. The task leader of a noncritical path task must determine his or her tasks Δ and Y just as the critical path task leaders do. If the noncritical path has a Δ that is greater than the slack between it and the next critical path task, its potential for contributing to project overrun must be examined.

The project manager will ask each task leader to determine the worst case task time overrun duration (Δ) and the likelihood that the task will overrun (Y) to provide data for risk analysis. In the preceding chapter, this was discussed in general terms so that the basic concept could be explained. In practice, a project manager will ask each team member to go beyond a general analysis and look at each significant factor that could cause the task leader's task to overrun. For one task, problem sources such as uncertainty about a team member's availability, technical complications, and late delivery of ordered parts could each cause a delay. The project manager then asks each task leader to separately calculate the potential risk factor contribution for each possible problem source and to report the largest as his or her task's risk contribution. The project manager leads the team in a review of all their contributions from critical path tasks to determine good risk factor insertion points along the critical path. In addition, the project manager leads the team to consider possible project delays from tasks not on the critical path.

Although the work is detailed and may seem a little tedious, it is very important. The magnitude of the required effort is manageable because each team member only has to do a small part of it.

MULTIPLE CONTRIBUTIONS FROM ONE TASK

For every task, there is more than one potential cause of a time overrun. When the project manager asks a team leader to give an estimate of the likelihood (Y) and the largest overrun time (Δ) for his or her task, the project manager reminds the team leader to consider as many potential overrun causes as possible. There is a tendency for a team leader to focus on one obvious potential overrun cause and not to consider others. The project manager will ask the team leader to begin by making a list of all potential causes of task time overrun that he or she can come up with. The team leader should ask task workgroup members and subject matter experts for help. Each potential task time overrun source will have its own unique overrun likelihood (Y) and its overrun duration (Δ). Experience has taught that the cause that produces the largest product of $Y \times \Delta$ is the one that provides the contribution that best represents the task for the risk factor calculation.

As the task leader reviews the various sources of potential time overrun, he or she also can easily consider what actions to take to mitigate this overrun problem if it is seen developing. As project manager, you should ask each team leader to make notes of the ways to mitigate time overrun problems and to be prepared to refer to them if necessary. Microsoft Project Management 2002® software and other software packages provide for a "Notes" record for each Gantt chart task. This record is a good place to store a task team leader's notes about what to do when problems arise. This type of thinking ahead is particularly valuable in long duration projects.

The following is a sample list of frequently encountered task overrun causes:

1. A team member is unavailable when needed.
2. Some team members know less about performing their task than is expected.
3. The equipment does not perform as expected.
4. Resources are not available when needed.
5. The supplier(s) does not deliver the necessary materials on time.
6. Workgroup members have conflicts while working together and personalize them to the detriment of the task's progress.
7. The task's output does not pass a performance test and must be reworked.

There are many potential causes of task time overrun for every task. Most are particular to the type of task being considered. Purchasing tasks, for example, are particularly sensitive to having a supplier deliver a product of an inferior quality. A task leader, when reminded to do so, can create a good list of overrun causes for his or her task.

After the task leader completes this list, he or she estimates the Y and Δ for each overrun cause. If unavailability of a key task team member is a potential problem, the task leader must consider why this might happen. Is there a significant likelihood that a key team member will become ill? Is there a significant likelihood that a team member will be transferred or leave the company? If one of these things happens, what can the team leader do about it and how much delay will be caused by making adjustments? Careful consideration of this potential overrun cause might lead to the conclusion that there is a 20 percent likelihood (Y) of this problem emerging and a five-day worst case delay (Δ) associated with this cause. This same analysis may lead the task leader to decide that he or she needs a substitute list to back up his or her team members and to make such a list to include in the task "notes."

Another potential cause of task delay for this same task might be that some task members do not have the expected skills. Many projects involve tasks that are familiar to some team members but are new to others. Because estimates tend to be based on the capabilities of experienced workers, it is important to focus on the limits of those who are inexperienced. Making estimates of a possible overrun for such a situation is a challenge for a task workgroup leader. He or she should discuss it with subject matter experts whenever possible. If several members of his or her task workgroup are inexperienced, he or she probably will be generous in estimating the likelihood of task time overrun. In considering what to do about it, he or she probably will include obtaining coaching help from specialists outside the task workgroup and record in the notes the names of specialists that can be approached for help. The amount of time it could take to help inexperienced workers get their job done may cause the task leader to use a generous amount of Δ.

Facility availability may be easier to estimate because it generally has a long history. The facilities manager can help the task leader with this estimate.

This style of analysis must be conducted for every condition that the task leader considers as a potential source of overrun. To select the proper contribution from his or her task to the risk task, a task leader should use the worksheet illustrated in Figure 9-1.

In this figure, the unavailability of a task member has a 20 percent likelihood of impacting the task and, as a worst case, could cause a five-day delay. This is a creep type of delay because there is a much greater likelihood that a team member would become sick and cause a one- or two-day delay than a team member would leave the company and cause a five-day delay while he or she is being replaced. The contribution that this delay would make to the risk factor calculates as $0.2 \times 5 = 1.0$, or one day.

Lack of knowledge and skills among team members is considered to have a 30 percent chance of impacting the project because one team member has a limited background in the type of work he or she will be doing. Although he or she is conscientious and bright, and the project leader expects the worker to work well with the team, there is still a possibility that an outside subject matter expert will need to be brought in to coach this worker. This may delay task completion, in the worst case, for four days. It is a creep type of risk, and the contribution from this cause is $0.3 \times 4 = 1.2$ days.

Another potential source of task delay might be the unavailability of a test facility. This happens about 20 percent of the time. When it does happen, the team must wait one day to complete its work. This is a Δ of one day, and it is not a creep risk. If there is any delay, it is going to be a full one day.

Do not try to combine this information to determine a task's risk factor. We have tried it. It is awkward and does not provide a good contribution number. You should pick the largest contribution from the list of potential overrun causes and use that number, in this case 1.2 days, for the task's contribution to the risk factor.

There is a one-day step-function risk that you would report to the project leader separately if it were bigger than the calculated contribution. In this case, however, it will not impact the calculation of the risk factor and does not need to be noted. If there is a step-function Δ that is bigger than the calculated contribution, you should report this to the project manager for attention when combining contributions to determine the risk factor. If it turns out that the step-function is large—greater than 50 percent—when compared to the risk factor for the task sequence that is calculated, the project manager will lead the team in using the following formula: $\Delta - 50\%$ of Risk Factor = Risk Factor Adjustment.

RISK ANALYSIS WORKSHEET

Risk Contribution 1.20

Task: A

Leader: Tom K

Most of the Time Estimate: 10

RISK ANALYSIS

CAUSE	TYPE	LONGEST	DELTA	% LIKELIHOOD	CONTRIBUTION
1. Person not available	Creep	15	5	20%	1.00
2. Lack of Knowledge	Creep	14	4	30%	1.20
3. Facility unavailable	Step Function	11	1	20%	.20

Figure 9-1

COMPUTATION AND THE LOCATION OF A RISK FACTOR

Each task leader provides his or her risk analysis worksheet(s) to the project manager. The project manager them prepares a table listing each task according to the critical path sequence, what its Δ and likelihood (Y) are, and its creep or step-function character. This table is distributed to each member of the project team. The team then will convene to review this worksheet and pick out the risk factor insertion points. See Table 9-1 for the risk factor contribution worksheet.

It is important that the full body of displayed information be available to the team. The project manager should lead the team through a review. Some team members may wish to discuss the data. If discussion points are raised that lead to line item adjustments, it is good; the task leader, however, always has the final call on what the task contribution for his or her task should be. The team will discuss and decide on risk factor insertion points at the risk factor meeting.

The rule of thumb is to insert a risk factor every 20–30 critical tasks. Whenever a natural sequence completion point (a point where one phase of the effort is completed) within the 20–30 task range emerges, this point should be used. If there is one point where the task start date must be firm, insert a risk factor just ahead of this task to protect this date. For example, if one task is "test assembly in a test cell" and the test cell availability is tightly scheduled, insert the risk factor before this task to be sure that you buffer upstream risks and meet the test scheduled date.

When the risk factor insertion points have been identified, the risk factor's size is determined by adding up all of the contributions in the task sequence leading up to the insertion point. If one or two step-function risks are in the series, and one (or more) step function-risk Δ is nearly as large, or larger, than the sum of the contributions, the risk factor should be adjusted as previously discussed. Step-function Δs significantly smaller than the series risk factor do not need to be given any special consideration.

ANALYSIS OF CONTRIBUTION TABLE

At this time, the break points for inserting risk factors into the critical path task flow have not been decided upon. The team will come together to do this. In Table 9-1, Task 20—GG is a candidate and Task 30—Assembly is a candidate. Assembly seems to be a good choice because it represents a project's milestone. However, Task 22—Test also has some important characteristics. The test facility is heavily loaded, and the test manager has control over any adjustments in the test scheduling. He or she does not like to make adjustments and can create delays for a project if they miss their scheduled test dates. We can assure ourselves of hitting our scheduled test date if we schedule our first risk factor insertion right after Task 21—II, just before the test task.

Table 9-1

	CP Task	Risk Type	Base Estimate Days—M	Longest Estimate Days—W	Delta Days Δ	Likeli-hood–Y	Contri-bution
1	A	C	10	13	3	0.25	0.75
2	B	C	12	13	1	0.10	0.1
3	D	C	8	12	4	0.30	1.2
4	G	C	6	7	1	0.10	0.1
5	J	C	13	16	3	0.30	0.9
6	K	SF	11	12	1	0.20	0.2
7	M	C	3	4	1	0.3	0.3
8	N	C	14	16	2	0.4	0.8
9	P	C	6	7	1	0.1	0.1
10	R	C	4	4	0	0	0
11	S	C	3	5	2	0.3	0.6
12	U	C	7	8	1	0.1	0.1
13	V	SF	2	3	1	0.4	0.4
14	X	C	20	23	3	0.3	0.9
15	Z	C	10	14	4	0.2	0.8
16	AA	C	1	2	1	0.3	0.3
17	BB	C	0.5	1	0.5	0.4	0.2
18	DD	C	11	15	3	0.2	0.6
19	FF	C	6	7	1	0.2	0.2
20	GG	SF	8	12	4	0.2	0.8
21	II	C	6	8	1	0.2	0.4
22	Test	SF	4	8	4	0.2	0.8
23	KK	C	2	3	1	0.1	0.1
24	MM	C	8	10	2	0.2	0.4
25	OO	C	6	8	2	0.3	0.6
26	PP	C	1	2	1	0.4	0.4
27	QQ	C	5	9	4	0.2	0.8
28	BA	C	10	11	1	0.3	0.3
29	BD	C	8	12	4	0.2	0.8
30	Assembly	C	9	11	2	0.2	0.4
31	BK	C	8	11	3	0.2	0.6
32	C1	C	6	10	4	0.2	0.8
33	C3	C	14	15	1	0.2	0.1
34	C7	C	21	23	2	0.2	0.4
35	CJ	C	10	11	1	0.2	0.2

(Continued)

Table 9-1 (*Continued*)

	CP Task	Risk Type	Base Estimate Days—M	Longest Estimate Days—W	Delta Days Δ	Likeli-hood–Y	Contri-bution
36	CK	C	8	11	3	0.2	0.6
37	CL	C	7	8	1	0.2	0.2
38	CX	C	6	8	2	0.2	0.4
39	C2	SF	12	20	8	0.2	1.6
40	D8	C	10	12	2	0.2	0.4
41	D	C	3	4	1	0.2	0.2
42	EA	C	11	12	1	0.2	0.2
43	EK	C	6	9	3	0.1	0.3
44	EL	C	4	6	2	0.2	0.4
45	EM	C	30	36	6	0.2	1.2
46	EZ	C	20	25	5	0.3	1.5
47	GA	C	11	12	1	0.2	0.2
48	GG	C	8	9	1	0.2	0.2
49	GZ	SF	6	8	2	0.3	0.6
50	I-1	C	8	9	1	0.2	0.2
51	I-2	C	8	12	4	0.3	1.2
52	I-K	C	8	9	1	0.3	0.3
53	IL	C	4	6	2	0.2	0.4

This is the review the project manager and the team conduct at this risk analysis meeting. The risk factor that they will insert is the sum of the contributions from Task 1 through Task 21, which is 9.4 days (round this up to 10 days). Within this sequence, there are three step function risks, Task 6—K, Task 13—V, and Task 20—GG. Their Δs are respectively 1,1, and 4. With a risk factor of 10, two one-day step functions do not worry us at all. A step function of 4 with a 20 percent likelihood is not a problem either. If there had been a step-function risk of 8 with a 30 percent likelihood, we would not consider the Risk Factor of 10 to be big enough. Therefore, we take half of the risk factor ($10/2 = 5$), subtract 5 from 8 and add 3 days, making this risk factor 13. However, with the biggest step function being 4 and its likelihood 20 percent, the risk factor of 10 is good.

If there is another "must hit on time" task further along in the sequence we will try to make adjustments to have it preceded by a risk factor. If Assembly (Task 30) is such a task, we have a problem. Eight tasks are not enough to justify full confidence in a risk factor. There simply are not enough tasks to justify the averaging out techniques that we use. The Test Task (#22) is the first task in our second sequence, and it is a step-function task with a Δ of 4 and a 20 percent likelihood. The others are creep risks. Two have Δs of 4; others are relatively small. The calculation contribution summation for the eight tasks adds up to 3.7 days. With only eight tasks, we would not settle for only four days of risk factor even if they were all creep tasks. We feel that we must play it safe but we do not want to unnecessarily pad the time scale. Feeling a little uneasy about using too large a risk factor at this point, we settle on a risk factor of seven days that can be inserted before Assembly (Task 30). Although we may have introduced a project delay of a day or two, we can feel sure that we will arrive at Assembly with all predecessors complete.

Tasks 30 through 53 (Assembly through I L) can make up our last critical path sequence for the project. The sum of the contribution is 12.6 days—we round up to 13 days. We have a step-function Δ of eight days with a 20 percent likelihood for Task 38. Obviously, we need to adjust the risk factor upward. It is reasonable to go with a total risk factor of 15 days. The total of all the Δs in this sequence is 59 days. This number is conservative, but it is not nearly as conservative as if we had simply totaled the longest times for each task. We may not actually use more than the 13 days at the original risk factor, but we can be sure that almost all of it is needed.

Risk factor analysis is not precise. In a world with risks, no one can be precise. Risk factor analysis does keep the buffers reasonable and lets each team member know that although there are buffers, they are needed for real uncertainties and do not allow any room for slacking on task efforts.

ADDITIONAL SOURCES OF PROJECT OVERRUN

Critical path tasks that overrun their most-of-the-time estimates cause project time overruns. Tasks that are not on the critical path can overrun their most-of-the-time estimates without affecting a project's time if the overrun is less than the slack between this noncritical path task and its critical path successor. However, if a noncritical path task overruns by an amount greater than its slack, it can cause a project time overrun (that is, if a task Δ is greater than the slack between it and the following critical path task, it can cause trouble).

So far we have only considered project time overruns caused by the time overruns of critical path tasks. Noncritical path tasks can cause just as much overrun as critical path tasks if their Δ exceeds their slack.

Noncritical path tasks provide a contribution to the risk factor if the difference between their Δ and their slack (Δ − slack), multiplied by their overrun likelihood, is greater than the Δ times the likelihood of the parallel task on the critical path. In this case, the contribution of the noncritical path tasks replaces the contribution of its parallel critical path task in the risk factor contribution table.

Refer back to Figure 7-4 and see Figure 9-2, which is an enlargement of a small portion of Figure 7-4. Plumbing and furnace and ducts are parallel tasks. Plumbing is on the critical path. The furnace and ducts is 0.25 days shorter than plumbing. It has a 0.25 slack. The 2.5 days most-of-the-time task time of plumbing directly contributes to the critical path time. If the worst-case task time for plumbing is three days, Δ is 3 − 2.5, which is 0.5 days. If the overrun likelihood

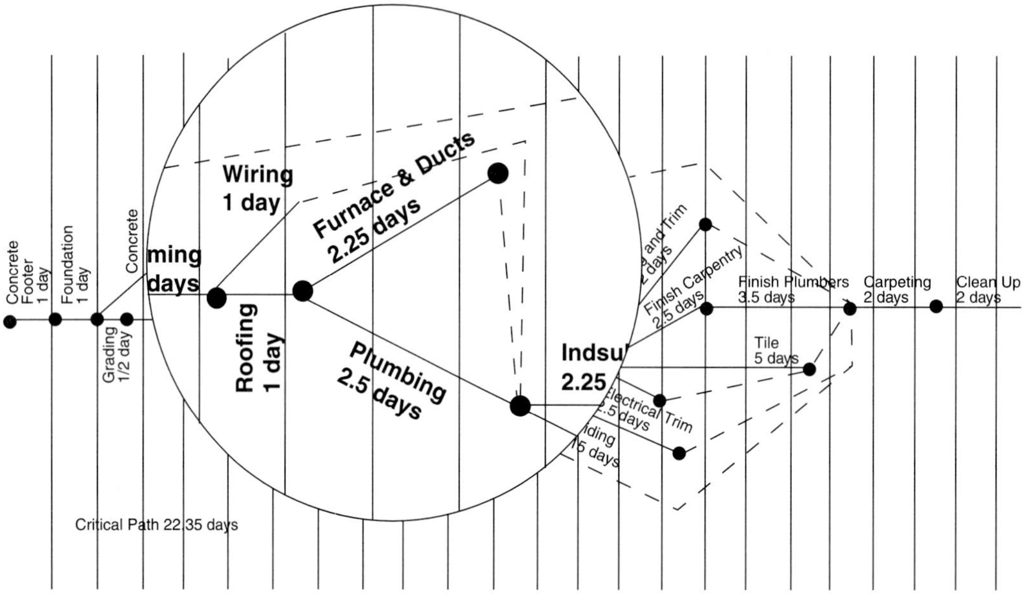

Figure 9-2

for plumbing is 10 percent, plumbing's contribution to the risk factor is 0.5 × 0.1, which is 0.05 days—very small. If the worst case duration for the furnace and ducts is 3.5 days, the Δ for furnace and ducts is 3.5 − 2.25, or 1.25 days. This combines with an overrun likelihood for furnace and ducts of 20 percent. For furnace and ducts, most of the time *plus slack* is 2.25 + 0.25, or 2.5 days. (Most of the time + slack for a noncritical path is always equal to the critical path tasks most-of-the-time duration.) Delta (Δ) − slack is 1.25 − 0.25, or one day. The contribution to the risk factor for furnace and ducts is Δ − slack × likelihood, 1.0 × 0.2, or 0.2 days. Because 0.2 days is much bigger than 0.05 days, the 0.2 days contribution is used on the risk factor contribution table instead of 0.05.

Although these numbers are small, the difference between them is considerable. This same relationship could show up if the tasks were 22.5 days and 25 days, respectively. In this case, the contribution difference would be between half a day and two days. The difference this makes in the risk factor is considerable. Yet, we are looking at only relatively small Δs for both tasks. Some very large, worst-case overruns and worst-case likelihoods can be hidden from analysis if we do risk factor calculations only for critical path tasks.

Because of this possibility, every task leader must conduct a contribution analysis for his or her task and produce a risk analysis worksheet (refer to Figure 9-1). The task leader also must note on the worksheet the slack in days (or weeks) between his or her task and the subsequent critical path task. The critical path arrow diagram that the project manager has prepared and distributed is very useful for task leaders at this time. It clearly shows the slack. The project manager now must ask the task leader of the critical path task and the task leader of the parallel task that has slack to compare their contribution calculations *if the parallel task has a* Δ *that is greater than its slack.* The contribution of the critical path task to the risk factor is $\Delta \times Y$. The contribution of the parallel noncritical path task to the risk factor is $(\Delta - \text{slack}) \times Y$; whichever number is larger is used on the risk factor contribution table.

This still does not take care of all of the overrun threats. Sometimes a critical path task is paralleled by a sequence of tasks that is not on the critical path and ends in slack. A simple example of a two-task parallel stream is shown in Figure 9-3. In this figure, Task A is on the critical path and has a duration of 31 days. It is followed by Task D on the critical path. There is no slack found between A and D. Any task time overrun by Task A will need to be absorbed by the risk factor at the end of the critical path string. Task A has a Δ of three days and a likelihood of overrun of 10 percent. It has made a contribution of $3 \times 0.1 = .3$ day to the risk factor.

Task B is a parallel task—not on the critical path—that is the predecessor of Task C. This creates a string of tasks that must end before Task D can begin. Task D is dependent on completion of both Tasks A and C. There are three days of slack that apply to the B–C stream before Task D starts. Task B has a duration of 24 days. Task B's task leader reports that the task has a Δ of seven days and a likelihood of 30 percent. Task C has a duration of four days, a Δ of one day, and a likelihood of 40 percent.

The worst case impact of Task A on project time could be three days (Δ_A). Tasks B and C have a combined Δ ($\Delta_B + \Delta_C$) of $7+1 = 8$ days). If both tasks overran at their maximum, they would not make an eight-day impact on the project finish date, and they would make only an 8 days $-$ 3 days slack, or five day-later impact on the project finish date. These five days would have to be absorbed by the downstream risk factor. However, the team has not calculated a risk factor contribution that takes this into account. Therefore, the project manager guides the task leaders of Task B and C in calculating a risk factor contribution to substitute for Task A's contribution. Because Task B has the much larger Δ for the string, use Task B's likelihood of overrun (30 percent), to calculate the new contribution. The contribution is $5 \times 0.3 = 1.5$ days.

Because a string of critical path tasks is paralleled by a string of noncritical path tasks that end in slack, the calculations become more complicated, but the principles remain the same.

This analysis is more difficult to describe than it is to perform. It is something that a project manager must understand, however. The real danger is that a task like Task B in the first example is buried in a string of tasks that parallel the critical path and end with what appears to be generous slack. This can lead to ignoring Task B as a risk danger. However, Task B may have a large Δ and a large likelihood, and be capable of greatly overrunning the available slack. Therefore, every task should be evaluated in terms of $\Delta \times Y$ during risk analysis. Any task

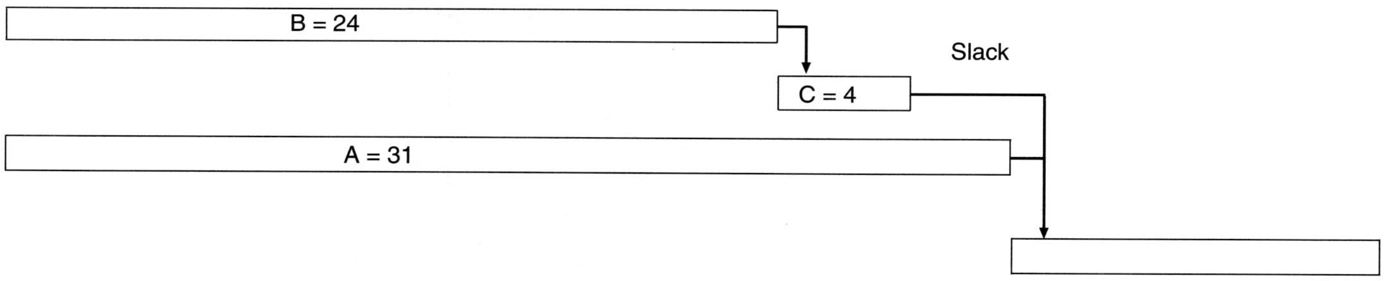

Figure 9-3

leader who sees that his or her task has a potential for a larger risk contribution than the critical path task must talk this problem over with the project manager. Together, they can conduct an examination of the parallel risks and adjust the risk factor as necessary.

One terrible surprise that can impact a project's execution is to discover that an unnoticed task not on the critical path produces a project delay whose possibility has not been accounted for.

The key to completing good risk analysis is to look for a Δ (or a string of Δs) for noncritical path tasks leading up to slack that is much greater than the slack. In risk analysis, the project manager and team always must keep their wits and judgment about them.

It may take two or three closely spaced meetings to cover all risk factor considerations. When the review is finished, the Gantt chart should be revised and distributed to team members, with the risk factors appropriately inserted.

At this point, it is time to print out all the task notes for distribution to the team members.

RISK TASKS AND SOFTWARE TOOLS

Software packages are not designed to make it easy and straightforward to insert and use risk tasks in Gantt charts. If you use Microsoft Project 2002®, you are going to have to tweak it just a little in order to make it work for you. When building the Gantt chart using this software, you must use a linking button to connect the successors to their predecessors. If you do this, you do not have to worry about dates. The software will start the successor the day after the predecessor finishes.

When you are using the software as a project monitoring tool, it will hold an original "Base Line" for you. However, it will extend on the Gantt chart the start dates of tasks that are farther down the line whenever a task runs over. This operation is very helpful when you are monitoring a project's execution. However, You will want the risk task to act as a buffer between the task strings. You do not want the risk factor predecessor to push the risk factor start date out as some task overruns occur. In fact, you want just the opposite. You want the immediate predecessor to show you by its extended end date just how much of the risk factor is used up.

All this means is that when you enter the risk factor on the software Gantt chart, you do not link it to its predecessor. You use a start date instead. You then set the start date to the day after its predecessor is completed. You also link the next task—the first task in the next critical path series—to the risk factor, not the last task in the proceeding series. See Figure 9-4.

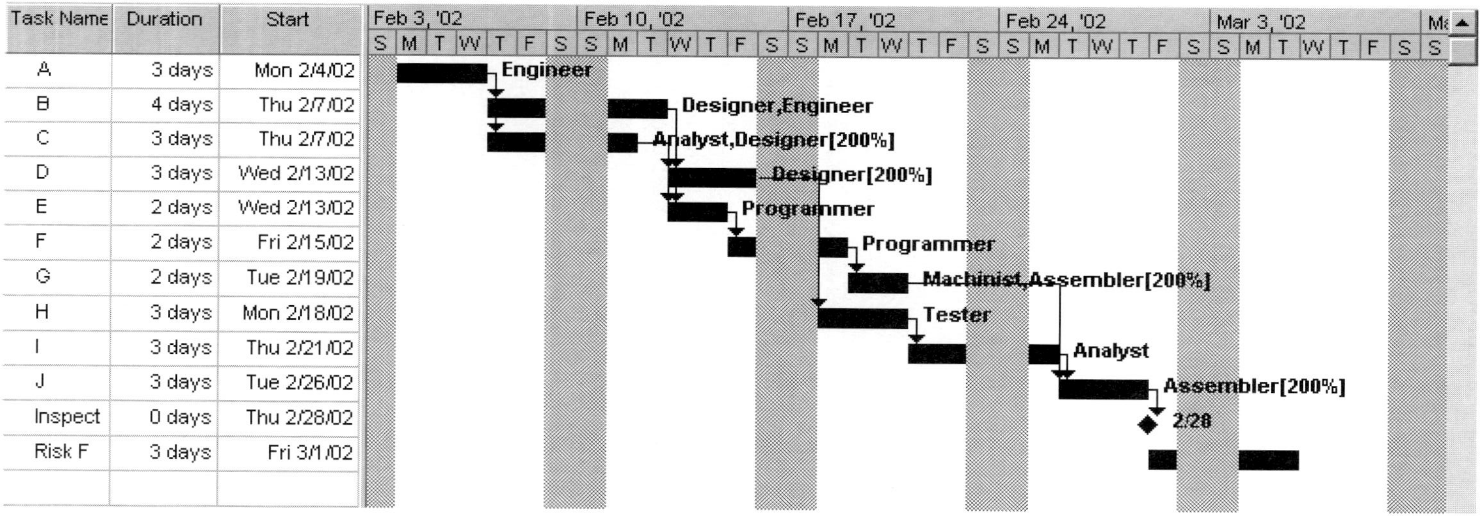
Task Name
Duration
Start
A
3 days
Mon 2/4/02
B
4 days
Thu 2/7/02
C
3 days
Thu 2/7/02
D
3 days
Wed 2/13/02
E
2 days
Wed 2/13/02
F
2 days
Fri 2/15/02
G
2 days
Tue 2/19/02
H
3 days
Mon 2/18/02
I
3 days
Thu 2/21/02
J
3 days
Tue 2/26/02
Inspect
0 days
Thu 2/28/02
Risk F
3 days
Fri 3/1/02
Feb 3, '02
Feb 10, '02
Feb 17, '02
Feb 24, '02
Mar 3, '02
S M T W T F S
Engineer
Designer,Engineer
Analyst,Designer[200%]
Designer[200%]
Programmer
Programmer
Machinist,Assembler[200%]
Tester
Analyst
Assembler[200%]
2/28

Figure 9-4

In linking these tasks, you will wipe out the critical path representations on your Microsoft Project 2002® Gantt chart. Therefore, always print out your critical path series and save it before you enter a risk factor.

SUMMARY

Determining the contribution that a task should make to the risk factor of a stream of tasks requires looking at all the significant possible causes of task overrun. You should always report the risk factor contribution that is largest from this group of causes. In addition, you should also report whether there is a step-function risk in this group. The project manager and the team will combine this information when determining the risk factor to use for the string of tasks.

When the risk factors have been determined for all the successive strings of tasks that make up the critical path and all of them have been inserted into the Gantt chart, the project team has completed the chart, and the finish date of the last task is the date the project is expected to finish.

One must tweak software like Microsoft Project 2002® to enable it to be a satisfactory project-monitoring tool when risk factors are inserted into the Gantt chart.

DISCUSSION QUESTIONS

1. How do you determine the size of a task's contribution when determining a risk factor?
2. What impact does a small-step function Δ from a task typically have on determining the risk factor for its task stream?
3. What impact does a large step-function Δ from a task generally have on determining the risk factor for its task stream?
4. How does a task leader keep track of the possible ways of mitigating or reducing risks that he or she uncovers while doing risk analysis?
5. How much smaller than the total of adding all the critical path Δs together would you expect the risk factor to typically be? Why?

10 BUDGET AND COST

INTRODUCTION

When planning a project using project management software tools, the Gantt chart display system provides a means for determining a project's cost, task by task, and for displaying task and project totals. Thus, as the Gantt chart is developed, time management, resource management, and cost management are achieved. Data also is provided for calculating the costs that are associated with the project's risks.

When project planning is completed, the projected cost as well as the projected duration is clearly identified. This information is available task by task and in the form of subtotals and a total.

TIME, RESOURCE, AND COST MANAGEMENT

Discussions of project management are often broken down into time management, resource management, and cost management. In IPM, these three considerations are all addressed in one package—the project Gantt chart. A task leader in discussion with the task workgroup determines the individual task time. A project's time is displayed as the project manager and the team put these time estimates on the Gantt chart. Additional time management is involved when risk management is done, and the risk factors are added to the project's timeline. Using the risk factors to absorb task overruns must be thought of as part of time management.

Resource management is developed as task leaders report on the team members and other resources that will be needed for each task. This information is recorded on the Gantt chart. If project management software is used the software package captures the task resource requirements and can produce a family of reports identifying each resource that is scheduled to be used, when, how long and how intensely (that is, 100 percent per day used or less) it (they) will be needed, and how much the use of each resource will cost.

The resource utilization reports warn the project manager and the team if any resources are overscheduled (scheduled for more than 100 percent of the available time). Resources may be inadvertently overscheduled as the Gantt chart is being constructed. A check of the resource table immediately flags this error. (Microsoft Project 2002® software has several ways of showing this error. One way is immediately changing the color of the resource's display line on the resource table from black to red.) While building the project Gantt chart, the individual performing the data entry frequently checks the basic resource table. If a resource is overscheduled, the team can make instant adjustments.

When project execution is underway and one task overruns, causing a task member's time to be overscheduled, a resource overschedule warning is immediately flashed, and the task leader and the project manager make adjustments. Resource management is tremendously helped by the systems built into the project management software. Its only requirement is that as the Gantt chart is developed in planning and used in managing a project's execution; resource requirements are entered for every task. Entering resource requirements, task by task, when building the Gantt chart using Microsoft Project 2002® software, automatically builds the basic resource tables and reports. The cost of the project then is determined by the number of resources used. The software's resource screens provide entry points for recording the daily, weekly, or monthly rate of each resource. This is the basic information for the cost of the tasks. Rate times duration yields the cost of each resource used for a task.

Figure 10-1 shows a Gantt chart for a very short project. Each task duration has been determined by the person(s) who will execute the task. The project begins on Monday, February 4. Task A takes three days and is executed by an engineer. This engineer is paid at the rate of $4,000.00 per month. Figure 10-2 shows this rate entered in the project's resource table. (The name of the project is "Budget Builder.") If 20 days is the standard of work days per month, and if the engineer works three days this month, the budgeted cost of this effort should be $3/20 \times 4000 = 600$. When we turn to the cost table on the cost version of the Gantt chart, we find that without any instructions other than those previously noted, the software has calculated and posted $600.00 as the cost budgeted for this

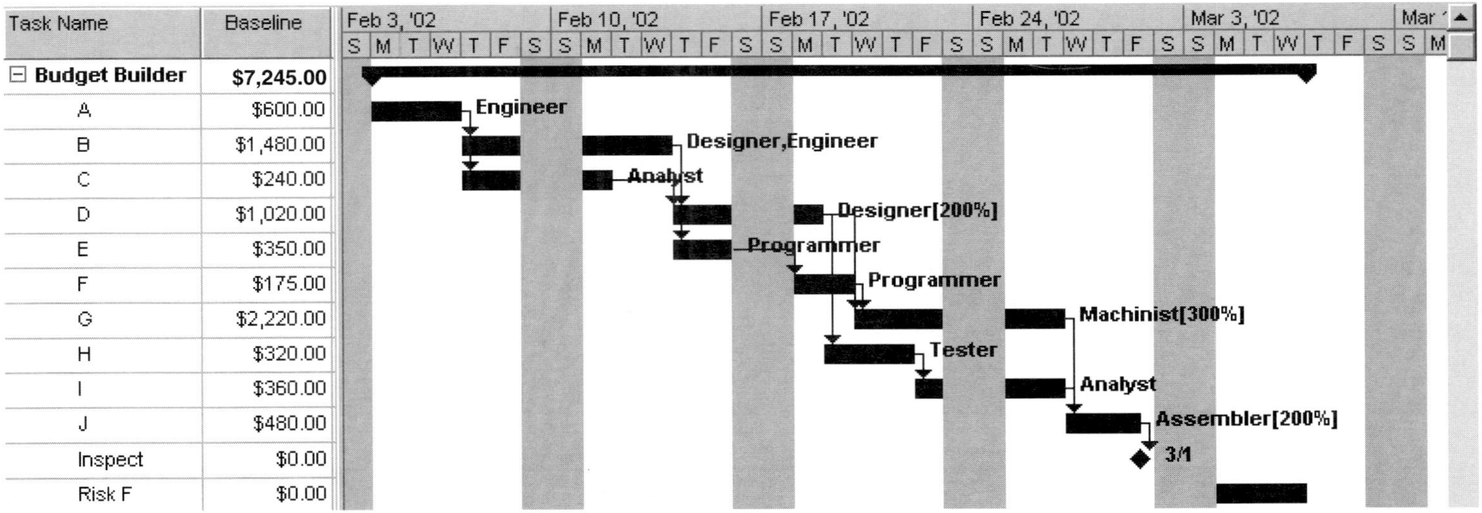
Task Name
Baseline
Budget Builder
$7,245.00
A
$600.00
B
$1,480.00
C
$240.00
D
$1,020.00
E
$350.00
F
$175.00
G
$2,220.00
H
$320.00
I
$360.00
J
$480.00
Inspect
$0.00
Risk F
$0.00
Feb 3, '02
Feb 10, '02
Feb 17, '02
Feb 24, '02
Mar 3, '02
S M T W T F S
Engineer
Designer,Engineer
Analyst
Designer[200%]
Programmer
Programmer
Machinist[300%]
Tester
Analyst
Assembler[200%]
3/1

Figure 10-1

	i	Resource Name	Type	Max. Units	Std. Rate	Ovt. Rate	Cost/Use	Accrue At	Base Calendar
1		Engineer	Work	100%	$4,000.00/mon	$0.00/hr	$0.00	Prorated	Standard
2		Designer	Work	200%	$3,400.00/mon	$0.00/hr	$0.00	Prorated	Standard
3		Analyst	Work	100%	$600.00/wk	$0.00/hr	$0.00	Prorated	Standard
4		Programmer	Work	100%	$3,500.00/mon	$0.00/hr	$0.00	Prorated	Standard
5		Machinist	Work	300%	$18.50/hr	$0.00/hr	$0.00	Prorated	Standard
6		Tester	Work	100%	$20.00/hr	$0.00/hr	$0.00	Prorated	Standard
7		Assembler	Work	200%	$600.00/wk	$0.00/hr	$0.00	Prorated	Standard

Figure 10-2

task. It has prorated the engineer's monthly salary in terms of the three days that he worked on the task and has attributed this prorated salary amount to the task. Each task is processed this way. Task B is a four-day task. A designer, who is paid \$3,400 per month, and the engineer each work full-time on this four-day task. The software calculates and posts \$1,480.00 for this task: $(4/20 \times 3{,}400) + (4/20 \times 4{,}000) = 1{,}480$. The analyst who works two days in Task C is paid by the week: \$600.00 per week. His two days of work on Task C are charged at $2/5 \times 600 = 240.00$. Machinists are paid hourly. We have an eight-hour day set up in the computer as our standard work day. Three machinists work for five days on Task G. Task G is budgeted at \$2,220.00 ($5 \times 8 \times 18.5 \times 3 = 2{,}220$).

Each task is budgeted according to the amount of time a worker (or workers) is scheduled to spend on it and the worker's rate. It does not matter whether the worker is paid monthly, weekly, or hourly, the software has a program that will prorate the worker's salary to the project according to the time spent working a job.

Table 10-1 shows one way that Microsoft Project 2002® calculates and totals up the cost of this project. The same figures can be displayed, task by task, on the cost version of the project's Gantt chart, which is produced in Microsoft Project 2002®.

The cost of the project, just as the time requirement of the project, is understated until the risk analysis is completed and the risk factor costs are included. The risk factor costs depend upon which tasks overrun and absorb the risk factor(s). Because we have no way of knowing in advance which tasks will overrun, the cost overruns that go along with time overruns absorbed by the risk factor have to be estimated. (Never neglect this. If you neglect it the baseline project cost will be understated.) One way of estimating the risk factor cost is to total up the task

Table 10-1 Budget Report as of Sat 2/2/02 Budget Builder

ID	Task Name	Fixed Cost	Fixed Cost Accrual	Total Cost	Baseline	Variance
7	G	\$0.00	Prorated	\$2,220.00	\$0.00	\$2,220.00
2	B	\$0.00	Prorated	\$1,480.00	\$0.00	\$1,480.00
4	D	\$0.00	Prorated	\$1,020.00	\$0.00	\$1,020.00
1	A	\$0.00	Prorated	\$600.00	\$0.00	\$600.00
10	J	\$0.00	Prorated	\$480.00	\$0.00	\$480.00
9	I	\$0.00	Prorated	\$360.00	\$0.00	\$360.00
5	E	\$0.00	Prorated	\$350.00	\$0.00	\$350.00
8	H	\$0.00	Prorated	\$320.00	\$0.00	\$320.00
3	C	\$0.00	Prorated	\$240.00	\$0.00	\$240.00
6	F	\$0.00	Prorated	\$175.00	\$0.00	\$175.00
11	inspect	\$0.00	Prorated	\$0.00	\$0.00	\$0.00
12	Risk F	\$0.00	Prorated	\$0.00	\$0.00	\$0.00
		\$0.00		\$7,245.00	\$0.00	\$7,245.00

costs for all of the tasks that have been executed along the string of tasks used to determine the risk factor. (Be sure to use all of the tasks, not just the critical path tasks, from beginning to end of the sequence. Tasks that are not on the critical path add cost even if they do not extend the project's time.) Dividing this total by the number of days in the sequence gives the average cost per day for the sequence. Now take the number of days for the risk factor and multiply it by the average cost per day of the sequence of tasks. Add this to the baseline—no risk—cost calculation. It will give you a close cost projection for the actual project. In the example shown in Figure 10-1, the string of tasks lasts 19.5 days. The sum of the costs of the tasks in this string is $7,245. The average cost per day is $371.54, and there is a three-day risk factor. The approximate cost of the overrun that we expect is $3 \times 372 = 1{,}116$. In our budget, we add this cost to the cost of the project.

Thus, as the Gantt chart is developed, the cost of the project can be directly determined. This determination comes at the end of project planning. However, the project manager and the team can watch it accruing if they add rates to the resource table as they go along.

BUDGET AND COST

When the project sponsor or customer is considering the project, cost is generally an important item. Because this concern precedes the planning of the project, the budget that the sponsor envisions for the project must be based on other considerations. Many times the sponsor's budget estimate is based primarily on the money that is available for this project. Sometimes this estimate is reduced by the sponsor because he or she is perceived as being financially responsible, as someone who gets a lot done for a little money. One element of the project manager's statement of work should be a feasibility analysis of the proposed budget as compared to the expected outcome cost. As the project specification is being created, the project manager makes cost comparisons between the project's allotted budget and the costs of other similar projects. Project feasibility depends on the relationship between the costs that have been previously charged to similar projects and the budget that the sponsor has allowed for the current project. Whenever similar projects have had significantly greater costs than the proposed project is budgeted for, the project manager presents this information to the sponsor. The recommendation must be: Either cut the outcome expectations or boost the budget.

The sponsor then may make an adjustment or wait until the project plan is completed. Either way, the project manager has alerted the sponsor of the budget-cost discrepancy.

Some projects, particularly projects within and for the benefit of a particular department, may not have a budget, and its cost may not be tracked. They may be folded into the continuing cost of the department's operations.

Technical departments like engineering and IT are sometimes considered project departments, each with a departmental budget. If the department supervisor accepts some project responsibilities, the cost may become part of the overall department expenditure and not separated out. For financial purposes, these departments are not judged according to individual project effort. They are judged overall by how many projects and by the size of those projects that they contribute to annually.

Note: There are fewer projects where cost is not tracked than projects where cost is tracked.

THE PROJECT COST CALCULATION PROCEDURE

The Gantt chart timeline is the primary tool for monitoring and managing a project and its cost. This completed chart clearly defines the project's timeline, but its cost is not obvious without additional processing.

Before software, developing the cost of a project was tedious. A procedure using the Gantt chart for cost projection is attributed to Robert MacNamara, former analyst of the Ford Motor Company. MacNamara's procedure has been incorporated into project management software.

Because the Gantt chart depicts effort and other resource requirements, the budget can be created by applying rates to effort and unit costs to the resource units.

MacNamara's cost method is illustrated in the toy truck example (see Figure 10-3). Inserting a resource cost table under the task list provides a day-by-day and task-by-task cost reference. Purchasers (P), Carvers (C), Machinists (M), Assemblers (A), and Helpers (H) are paid at a rate. With their tasks noted in days, entering the daily rate is essential.

In this example, letters represent the type of workers used in a task, and fractions or whole numbers represent the amount of time a particular type of worker is committed per day for the task. Thus, on the task row "Purchase wood for cab body," the bar covering two days shows the task duration, and the symbol 1/2 P signifies that each day of the task one purchaser will be working half of the time. "Purchase wheels" is a one-day task; 1 P written within the task bar indicates that for one day a purchaser will work full time at this task. The "Carve the trailer body" task is four days long. The 2 C entry indicates that the two carvers will each work full time on this task for all four days.

Task	Days											Task Budget
Purchase wood for cab body	1/2 P											50.00
Purchase wood for trailer body	1/2 P											50.00
Purchase axle wire		1/2 P										25.00
Purchase wheels		1 P										50.00
Carve cab body			1 C									600.00
Carve trailer body			2 C									1200.00
Cut cab axle wire					1 M							200.00
Cut trailer axle wire					1 M							200.00
Assemble cab							1 A					150.00
Assemble trailer							1 A +1 H					230.00
Assemble unit									2 A +1 H			380.00
												Total 3135.00
P-Purchaser @ $50/day	1 / 50	21/2 / 125										
C-Carver @ $150/day			3 / 450	3 / 450	3 / 450	3 / 450						
M-Machinist @ $100/day					2 / 200	2 / 200						
A-Assembelr @ $75/day							2 / 150	2 / 150	2 / 150	2 / 150		
H-Helper @ $40/day							1 / 40	1 / 40	1 / 40	1 / 40		
Labor Cost-$	50	125	450	450	650	650	190	190	190	190	$3135.00	
Labor Requirements-Person Days	1	2 1/2	3	3	5	5	3	3	3	3	31 1/2	
Materials Cost - $		60									$60.00	
Weekly & Total Costs-$	50	185	450	450	650	650	190	190	190	190	$3195.00	

Figure 10-3

Below the body of the Gantt chart is a list of entries that are the forerunners of the resource table screens used in modern project management software. The column lists each type of worker who works on the project and his or her daily rate.

Each type of worker who works on a task on a particular day is identified, and the fraction of time he or she works on a task this day is noted by the cost analyst. Worker time then is added up for each day.

Reading down column one (Day one), two tasks are being executed that day. On each task, a purchaser (P) is working half of the time. Two purchasers working half of the time each is the equivalent to one purchaser working full time. Note that the cell indicating a day on a worker row (Purchaser) is divided into two parts by a slash mark. The full-time equivalent of purchasers working on Day one is one. On the Purchaser row, one (1) is entered in the lower portion of Day one's cell. To determine the cost of the purchaser's effort for this day, the analyst multiplies the figure in the lower half of the cell by the rate shown beside the Purchaser's name, (that is, \$50). Multiplying the number of full-time equivalent purchasers working this day by the purchasers daily rate ($1 \times \$50$) produces the cost number for the upper part of this cell: \$50. Each day column is treated this way for each type of worker who is working that day. Thus, on Day two there is a full-time equivalent of 2 1/2 purchasers working: $\$50 \times 2.5 = 125$. The purchaser labor cost for the second day is \$125.

On Day five, carvers and machinists are both working. There are three carvers working at \$150 per day each. On the Carver row of column five, the number 3 is entered below the slash line. At a rate of \$150 a day, three carvers add \$450 to the project's cost on that day. On the same day, there are two tasks, "Cut cab axle wire" and "Cut trailer axle wire," each with a machinist working full time. Therefore, there are two full-time machinists working that day. The cost analyst enters the number 2 on the lower part of that day's machinist row cell and $2 \times \$100 = 200$ in the upper part of the cell.

The cost per day is arrived at by totaling the dollars listed for that day. Labor, in persons per day, is determined by totaling the number of workers who are listed that day.

Material costs are entered when purchased materials are delivered. Wood for the cab body, wood for the trailer body, axle wire, and the wheels are all delivered on Day two. Each item costs \$15. The cost analyst totals this up and enters it in the Materials Cost row in the cell for the second day: \$60. In this way, all costs for the project can be captured and totaled.

The cost analyst is interested in the cost for each task. To determine it, he or she notes the full-time equivalent of the workers in each category who work on each task. He or she then multiplies the worker days by the worker rate and adds them together to determine the task cost. For example, the "assemble trailer" task requires two days of effort from an Assembler: 2 \$75 = \$150, and two days effort by a helper: 2 × \$40 = \$80. The labor cost for that task is \$150 + \$80 = \$230. (Note: This example and the rates here are taken from an old example, but they were very good rates when McNamara worked at Ford.)

The principles previously described have been written into project management software. Details are embedded in the software but are not displayed as shown in the longhand example. The software, nevertheless, follows and expands upon this formula. If resource cost information is entered on the resource cost screen, the software automatically can calculate and print the cost projections from the Gantt chart information.

As previously noted, before building the Gantt chart, the project manager should enter the anticipated cost of the resources (persons and materials) on the software resource cost screen. It is not crucial, however, that all resources and costs be entered before the Gantt chart is constructed. Microsoft Project 2002® and other packages automatically will list the resources on the resource screen when task resources are entered on the Gantt chart. When resource cost information is entered later, cost projections then can be displayed and printed out.

When resources are identified as people and their names are used, some people may not want their individual rates published. If so, the project manager can get the average rate for this person's category from accounting and simply use that figure.

THE PROJECT PLAN REVIEW

The project costs are determined by the full development of the Gantt chart. The completed Gantt chart is presented to the sponsor and other stakeholders at the project plan review. As soon as this chart has been completed with the project time, resource, and cost requirements fully developed, the project manager can schedule a presentation of this material. The sponsor or customer and key persons who will use the project output, key subject matter experts and key project team leaders, must be scheduled for attendance. All project team members are eligible to attend.

FINANCIALS FOR A MAJOR PROJECT

The "Disk Cleaning Machine A" project Gantt chart was displayed at the end of Chapter 6. It represents the first stage of an actual major custom manufacturer's machine-build project. It focuses on how long the project phase will take and who will execute each task.

If all the team members are identified before the planning starts, the project manager can create the resource table shown in Table 10-2. If only the names or titles are entered, the rest of the page will be blank. However, if project cost is a concern, the project manager will fill in the appropriate standard rates and overtime rates for each team member or task workgroup. The rates entered come from the payroll department. To achieve accurate cost estimates, these rates can be the total cost to the company of each individual's effort—this includes direct pay, social security benefits the company pays, health insurance that the company pays, and so forth. For alternative ways of entering project costs, only the individual's direct pay might be entered. Entries can be pay per month, pay per week, pay per day, or pay per hour. In Table 10-2, overtime rates are entered for hourly employees. Senior technical employees are paid by the month; some special employees are paid by the week. Neither is paid for overtime. Many of the employees are paid by the hour. The manufacturing shop, which represents several employees and some equipment use cost, is charged daily. A task may require several days in the manufacturing shop and 50 percent of available machinist effort during this time. The daily shop rate times 50 percent times the number of days required determines the cost for this task. Time estimates must be uniform. All task time estimates are entered in the same units on the Gantt chart. Days or weeks are the units from which the project managers should choose.

Cost per use is not used in this set of entries. However, the manufacturing shop cost could have been entered in this column if it were desirable. The "Accrue At" column allows for how units of time are charged. Because days is the basic unit used in this Gantt chart, all standard rates are *prorated* according to the proportion of the employee's time, in days, that the employee works on a task. This software feature saves a lot of bookkeeping effort. Note that the base calendar "standard" entry means that all standard holidays are accounted for as nonworking days.

When the resources sheet is preprepared, the software will figure the costs, task by task, as the Gantt chart is being created. If the project manager leads the team to enter the task names before the resource sheet is created, each named task resource will appear on the resource table when entered. Later, the resource rates can be entered, and the software will proceed to calculate the costs. The cost of the project plan can be developed using these procedures with the risk factor cost added as a fixed cost.

When the planning is done, the baseline Gantt chart can be created. Whenever using project-planning software, the project baseline is *saved* and presented at the project plan review meeting. Expected project costs are displayed clearly in Figure 10-4A , 10-4B. and 10-4C.

When the project task action begins, the base Gantt chart is opened for the entry of the actual task effort. The entry of the risk factor cost is deleted because when a task overruns and this data is entered in the operations Gantt chart, the actual overrun costs are calculated, and these costs are the ones the risk factor cost

Table 10-2

Cleaning Machine With Costs							
ID	Resource Name	Initials	Max Units	Std. Rate	Ovt. Rate	Cost/Use	Accrue At
1	P.M.	PM	100%	$7,000.00/mon	$0.00/hr	$0.00	Prorated
2	T	TE	150%	$5,000.00/mon	$0.00/hr	$0.00	Prorated
3	ME 1	ME	100%	$6,000.00/mon	$0.00/hr	$0.00	Prorated
4	EE 1	E	100%	$750.00/wk	$0.00/hr	$0.00	Prorated
5	IT 1	I	100%	$637.00/wk	$0.00/hr	$0.00	Prorated
6	JJ	J	100%	$6,700.00/mon	$0.00/hr	$0.00	Prorated
7	ME2	ME2	100%	$559.00/wk	$0.00/hr	$0.00	Prorated
8	CE	C	100%	$57.00/hr	$77.00/hr	$0.00	Prorated
9	DD1	D1	300%	$37.00/hr	$49.00/hr	$0.00	Prorated
10	Mfg	MF	100%	$6,100.00/mon	$0.00/hr	$0.00	Prorated
11	Mfg Shop	MS	100%	$397.00/day	$0.00/hr	$0.00	Prorated
12	Tst1	T	150%	$567.00/wk	$0.00/hr	$0.00	Prorated
13	Tst hlp	Th	100%	$22.00/hr	$33.00/hr	$0.00	Prorated
14	P1	P1	100%	$54.00/hr	$75.00/hr	$0.00	Prorated
15	DD2	D2	200%	$33.00/hr	$46.00/hr	$0.00	Prorated
16	DD3	D3	200%	$33.00/hr	$46.00/hr	$0.00	Prorated
17	P3	P3	100%	$49.00/hr	$75.00/hr	$0.00	Prorated
18	Tst2	t	100%	$30.00/hr	$45.00/hr	$0.00	Prorated
19	P4	P4	100%	$28.00/hr	$42.00/hr	$0.00	Prorated

	Task Name	Total Cost
1	⊟ **DISK CLEANING MACHINE A**	**$156,755.81**
2	Project Manager	$31,150.00
3	⊟ **Prototype Design**	**$7,014.10**
4	Component specs.	$1,058.22
5	Component interface:	$705.48
6	1st comp skchs	$1,000.00
7	Select prfd skch	$292.50
8	Mech dsn sketch	$900.00
9	Fluid flow sktch	$223.60
10	Elect dsn sktch	$750.00
11	Software spec.	$764.40
12	Revise comp skch	$500.00
13	Design audit	$292.50
14	Finalize dsn sktch	$527.40
15	Milestone	$0.00
16	⊟ **Fluid Flow Dsn**	**$36,634.70**
17	Fluid candidates	$581.00
18	⊟ **Dsn Fld Test Fac**	**$14,662.10**
19	Spec fld pref	$912.00
20	Sketch tst dsn	$1,184.00
21	Pick test pts	$456.00
22	Lay out dsns	$1,480.00

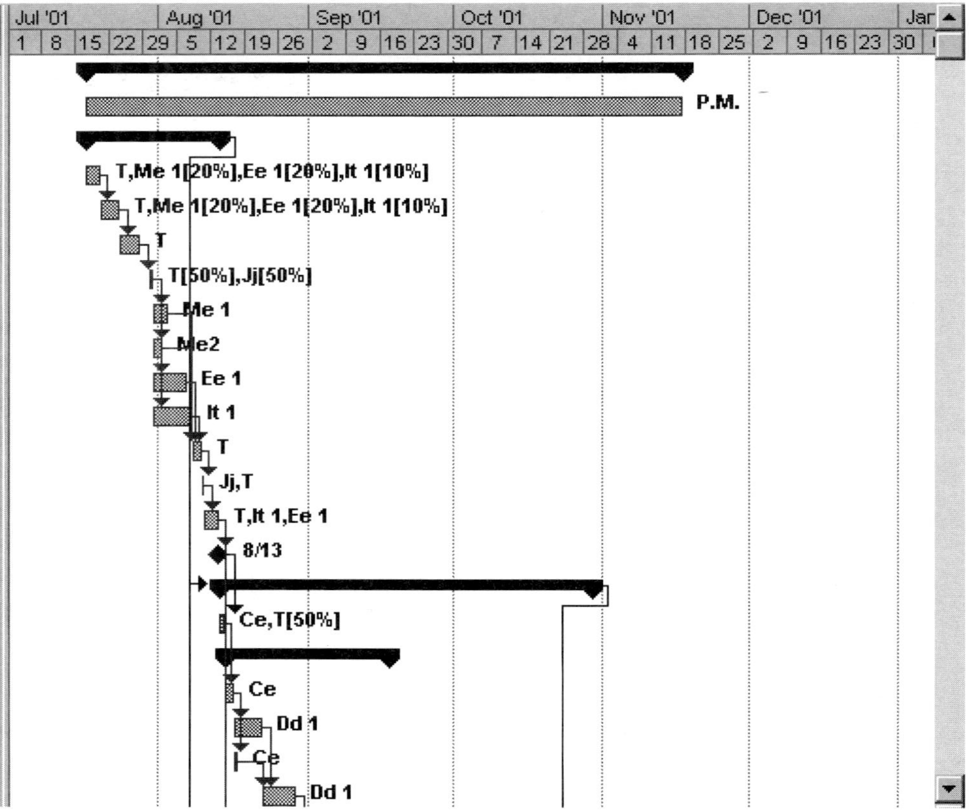

Figure 10-4A

	Task Name	Total Cost
21	Pick test pts	$456.00
22	Lay out dsns	$1,480.00
23	Mfg test parts	$9,932.00
24	Assemble	$698.10
25	Perf test fluids	$1,447.00
26	Select fluids	$581.00
27	Lay out fl path	$1,548.80
28	Pick components	$863.80
29	Order std parts	$4,516.00
30	Design special parts	$3,256.00
31	Mfg spec parts	$9,179.00
32	⊟ **Mechanical Design**	**$57,953.08**
33	Composite layout	$3,384.00
34	Unit dsn frame	$1,320.00
35	Unit dsn handling	$1,848.00
36	Unit dsn housing	$1,184.00
37	Parts design	$6,920.00
38	⊟ **Work Order Make**	**$9,000.60**
39	Parts1-7	$2,643.80
40	Parts A, B, C	$555.80

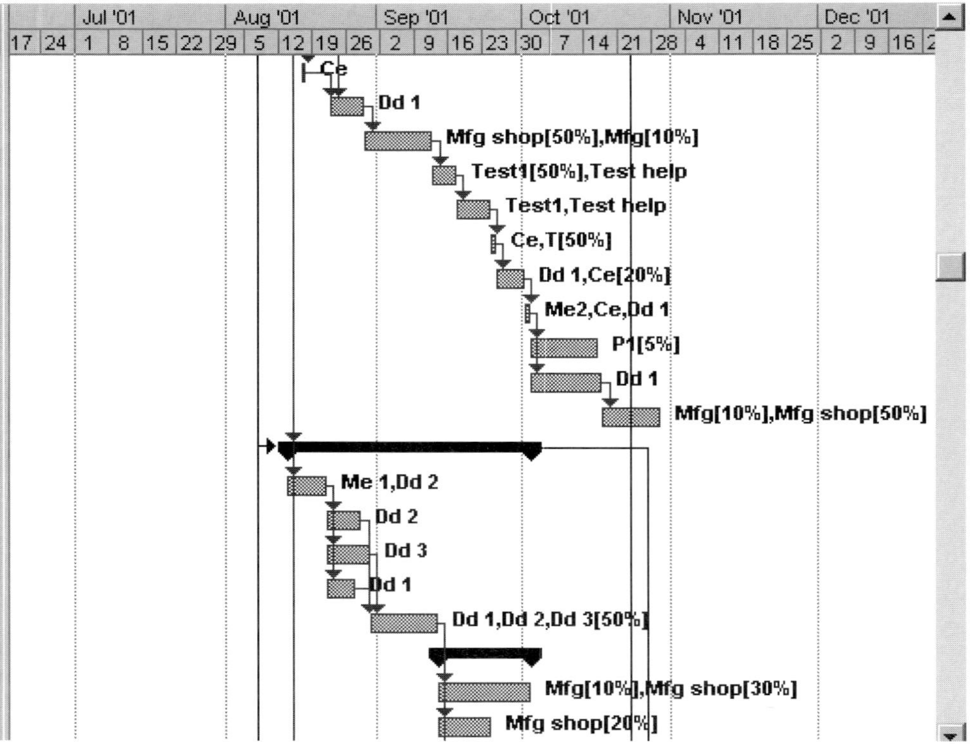

Figure 10-4B

	Task Name	Total Cost
41	Part X	$5,801.00
42	⊟ **Purchase Std Pts**	**$384.48**
43	Group W	$216.00
44	Group Z	$168.48
45	⊟ **Software developmen**	**$5,602.93**
46	Write specs	$892.50
47	Make or buy	$254.80
48	Write	$637.00
49	Purchase	$299.70
50	Design tests	$340.20
51	Purchase test hdw	$2,158.13
52	Install hdw	$113.40
53	Test and debug	$907.20
54	⊟ **Electrical Design**	**$8,981.00**
55	Configure	$1,125.00
56	Purchase std pts	$2,356.00
57	Purchase spcl pts	$5,500.00
58	Milestone #2	$0.00
59	⊟ **Lay Out 3D Design**	**$9,420.00**
60	Lay out	$0.00
61	Team Review	$0.00

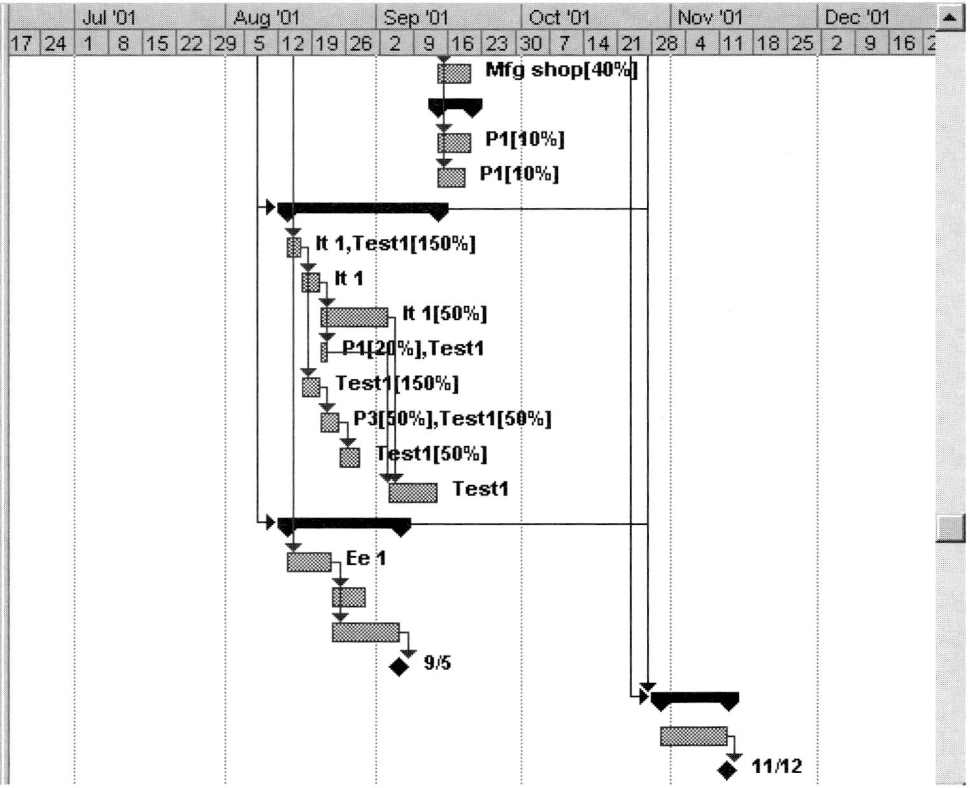

Figure 10-4C

originally was entered to absorb. If a task that a carpenter is working on runs one day over, the software will calculate and charge one more day of the carpenter effort to the project. If the risk factor costs are not deleted from the working Gantt chart, the actual task overruns will be charged twice. As the completed tasks actual dates are entered on the working Gantt chart, the actual costs to date are recorded.

Figures 10-4 are another view of the Gantt chart—the cost view. For each task, the workers assigned to the task are charged to the task by their pay rate times the percentage of time that they work on the task times the task duration. For the first task in Figure 10-4A, "component specs," T works full time, ME1 works 20 percent of the time, EE1 works 20 percent of the time, and IT1 works 10 percent of the time. This chart tells the story of a senior technician (T) who works full time for the duration of the tasks and gets help from a specific Mechanical Engineer (ME1), a specific Electrical Engineer (EE1), and a specific Information Technology specialist (IT1). The mechanical engineer and the electrical engineer will be working 20 percent of their time on the task, and the information technology specialist will be working on the project 10 percent of the time for the life of the task. Each of these workers is paid at a monthly rate. This rate is entered on the resource chart (see Table 10-2) for each person as "Std Rate." When the rate information is entered along with the resource and time information from the Gantt chart, the software can go to work and calculate how much the project should be charged for each person's time. This data then is added together and produces the cost of $1,058.22 for this task.

Note that each of these technical people are paid by the month and that costs are "Accrued at" a prorated basis. In this organization, monthly employees are not paid overtime; therefore, they have no overtime rate.

Note the "Max Units" column in Table 10-2. Each of the engineer employees, indicated as ME1, EE1, and IT1, is an individual. They cannot be used on the project greater than 100 percent. The 100 percent in the Max Units column indicates that there is only one individual. However, there is one senior technician assigned to the project full time, and another senior technician is available half of the time when needed. Therefore, the Max Units column for T is 150 percent.

The costs of each task is figured out in this fashion, and the total labor costs are entered in the total cost column. If there were any material costs associated with this task, this organization would enter them as "Fixed Costs" for a task, as they have for Task 23, "Manufacture test parts," in Figure 10-4A. The machine shop capacity for this task will be used at 50 percent, and the manager of manufacturing will devote 10 percent of his time to monitoring this effort during the time it is going on. These labor costs total $2,290.00. The special materials they will work on cost $7,642.00

Note that even though Task 6 and 7 in Figure 10-4A are on the critical path, there is a two-day delay between Tasks 6 and 7. Task 7 is a very short but crucial task. It is important to make the selection of the preferred sketch a very good choice. JJ is the expert who must do this, but he is not available until August 30.

The material will be ready at the end of the day, August 27. The straight line for Task 6, which looks like slack, is actually an enforced project delay caused by JJ's unavailability.

However, the straight horizontal lines after Tasks 8, 9, and 10 in Figure 10-4A do represent slack. Task 10 has very little slack, and if it has a large Δ, it will be examined as a potential noncritical path task contribution to the risk factor. (The risk factors for this project have not yet been calculated.)

SUMMARY

The sophistication of project management software enables a project manager and a project team to plan the project timing in detail, plan the resource usage in detail, figure up the cost of the project in detail, and present all of this information for a sponsor's review.

When project task action begins, the same software also enables the project manager to monitor actual time usage, resource usage, and accruing expenses in detail.

DISCUSSION QUESTIONS

1. Is the cost estimate produced by IPM planning a rough estimate or a precise estimate?
2. What role does project management software play in the development of cost estimates for an IPM project?
3. How is the cost associated with risks determined?
4. If the planning process indicates a cost that the sponsor cannot afford, where can the project manager look to find the most effective ways to reduce it?

11 PROJECT PLAN REVIEW

INTRODUCTION

When a project plan is completed, it will be reviewed by the sponsor and other project stakeholders. The sponsor may wish to make time adjustments, cost adjustments, or even outcome adjustments. There are always adjustments that can be made. They require a trade-off. Adjustments must be made on a task-by-task basis and with the task leader's approval. The basic Gantt chart provides clues to where these adjustments might be made. Project duration generally can be reduced somewhat but always at an increased cost. Trading longer time durations to reduce cost has limitations. Changing project outcomes means rewriting the specification and replanning the project. These plan adjustments are made for the customer by the project team. After the adjustments are made, a second review may be necessary. When the sponsor signs off on the project plan, execution of the plan begins immediately.

THE PLAN REVIEW

A project plan review is a key event. It consists of showing and explaining to the project sponsor the details of how the project effort will be carried out. The Gantt chart, complete with the risk factors, resource utilization, and project cost, is presented at this time. The completion date defined by the Gantt chart is an item of great importance to the sponsor. The statement of work from the early days of project planning also is reviewed to ensure that everything spelled out in the statement of work has been accomplished.

PROJECT REVIEW ATTENDEEES

The sponsor and the subject matter experts he or she relies upon are the prime audience for the project review. This review will always be scheduled at their convenience. The individuals who will use the project output also should be invited. They are important attendees. Because the review is a discussion of how and why some tasks will be performed, key task leaders from the project team also are needed at this meeting. Resource managers to whom project team members report also should be notified and welcomed. They will better support the availability of these team members for the project if they understand the project plan well. Including individuals from finance and accounting in this meeting also is a very good idea for larger projects.

Most people are invited so that they can gain better knowledge of the project and can knowingly support it. The sponsor is there to inspect the plan, to evaluate time and cost features, and to approve the plan or ask for adjustments. *This is called the sponsor review.* What the sponsor wants, the sponsor gets as long as meeting his or her requirements is feasible.

PRESENTATION OF THE REVIEW

There are many ways to display the project plan. Some customers may be comfortable with an outline; some may respond well to a flowchart display. Either one can be derived from the Gantt chart. An outline can be created directly from the "Task Name" column of the Gantt chart. It is the responsibility of the *project manager* to communicate with his or her sponsor, not the sponsor's responsibility to figure out the project plan from an unfamiliar document. The plan should be shown to the sponsor in a form that best communicates its content. It should be passed out before the meeting in a folder that also includes a basic and a summary Gantt chart, resource utilization charts, cost charts, and the statement of work and the specification that the sponsor signed off on at the beginning of the project. Reviewing the statement of work and the specification at this time ensures a shared starting point for discussing the project plan.

With our current technology, there are several possible ways to present the project's statement of work and specification to the project sponsor. If the statement of work and the specification are to be presented to a small group (3–5 people), it may be easier to distribute copies for review prior to the meeting. During the meeting, the statement of work and the specification will be reviewed by the group, item by item, to ensure agreement by all in attendance.

For larger groups (6 or more people), the previous method can be used but it can be frustrating. It is much easier to display the information via a projector that is connected to a laptop computer. This display enables the team to focus on the information displayed on the screen, with the project manager leading the presentation. If the document is stored in a word processor format, open the document and display it half a page at a time, on the screen.

The project manager will lead the presentation, initially focusing on the project's results and subsequently walking through the detail of how the results will be achieved.

Summary Gantt charts show project duration and major task durations, in addition to project cost and major task costs as illustrated by Figure 11-1 and Figure 11-2. The detailed basic Gantt chart from which the summations are taken are shown as Figures 11-3A, 11-3B, 11-3C, 11-3D, 11-4A, 11-4B, and 11-4C. These displays are stored in the computer being used and will be displayed using a projector hooked up to the computer as needed. Expanded time scales can be introduced for discussion purposes.

ADJUSTMENTS

When the project plan timeline and costs have been presented to the sponsor, the sponsor frequently requests adjustments. The timeline may run too long, the budget too high, or both may require downward adjustments. The detailed Gantt chart with its accompanying cost chart is the tool for making such adjustments.

Note: *One adjustment method will not work;* it cuts time and costs out of key tasks without lowering the expectations of the project outcomes. Doing so will always create the counter-productive result that sponsor expectations will not be met. Adjustments to meet customer needs can be made, but they must always respect the integrity of the Gantt chart.

If the project sponsor requests that both time and costs must be reduced, the project outcomes must be cut back, and the specification must be appropriately rewritten! A careful look at the Gantt chart often discloses those outcomes most expensive to achieve. It leads to the conclusion that some outcomes and associated tasks can be scaled back to reduce both the project's time and cost.

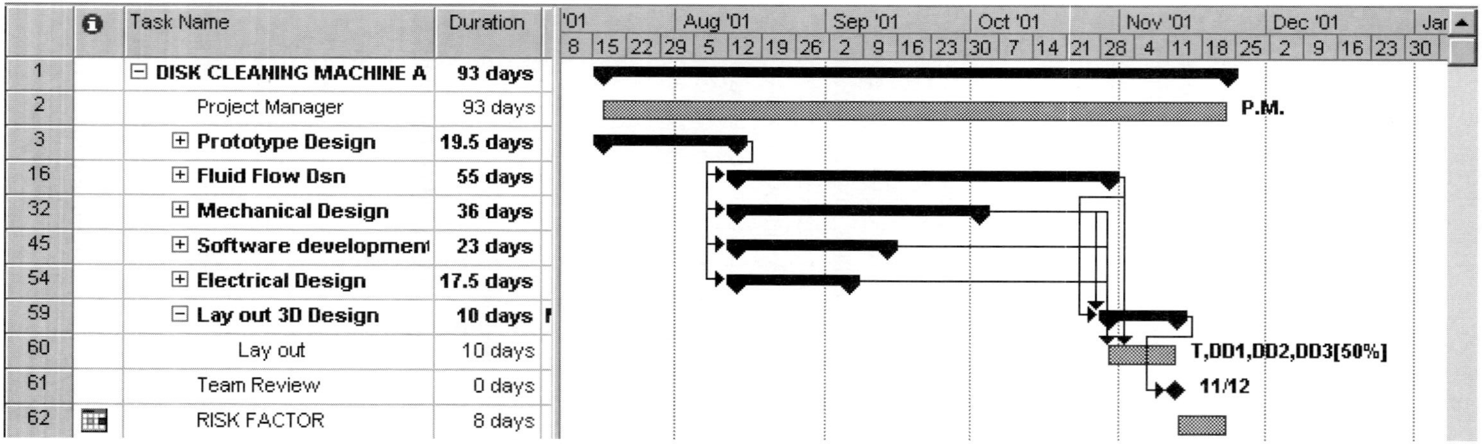
Task Name
Duration
'01
Aug '01
Sep '01
Oct '01
Nov '01
Dec '01
Jar
8 15 22 29 5 12 19 26 2 9 16 23 30 7 14 21 28 4 11 18 25 2 9 16 23 30
1 DISK CLEANING MACHINE A 93 days
2 Project Manager 93 days
3 Prototype Design 19.5 days
16 Fluid Flow Dsn 55 days
32 Mechanical Design 36 days
45 Software developmen 23 days
54 Electrical Design 17.5 days
59 Lay out 3D Design 10 days
60 Lay out 10 days
61 Team Review 0 days
62 RISK FACTOR 8 days
P.M.
T,DD1,DD2,DD3[50%]
11/12

Figure 11-1

	Task Name	Total Cost
1	⊟ **DISK CLEANING MACHINE /**	**$172,155.81**
2	Project Manager	$32,550.00
3	⊞ **Prototype Design**	**$7,014.10**
16	⊞ **Fluid Flow Dsn**	**$36,634.70**
32	⊞ **Mechanical Design**	**$57,953.08**
45	⊞ **Software developme**	**$5,602.93**
54	⊞ **Electrical design**	**$8,981.00**
59	⊞ **lay out 3D design**	**$9,420.00**
61	Team Review	$0.00
62	RISK FACTOR	$14,000.00

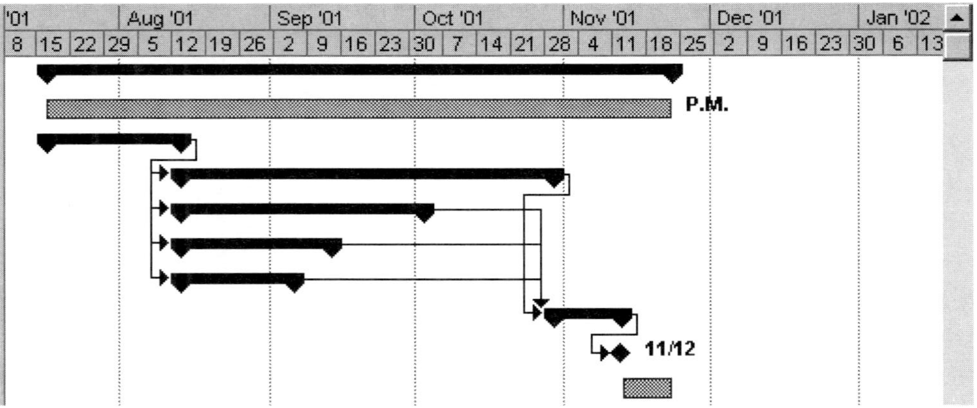

Figure 11-2

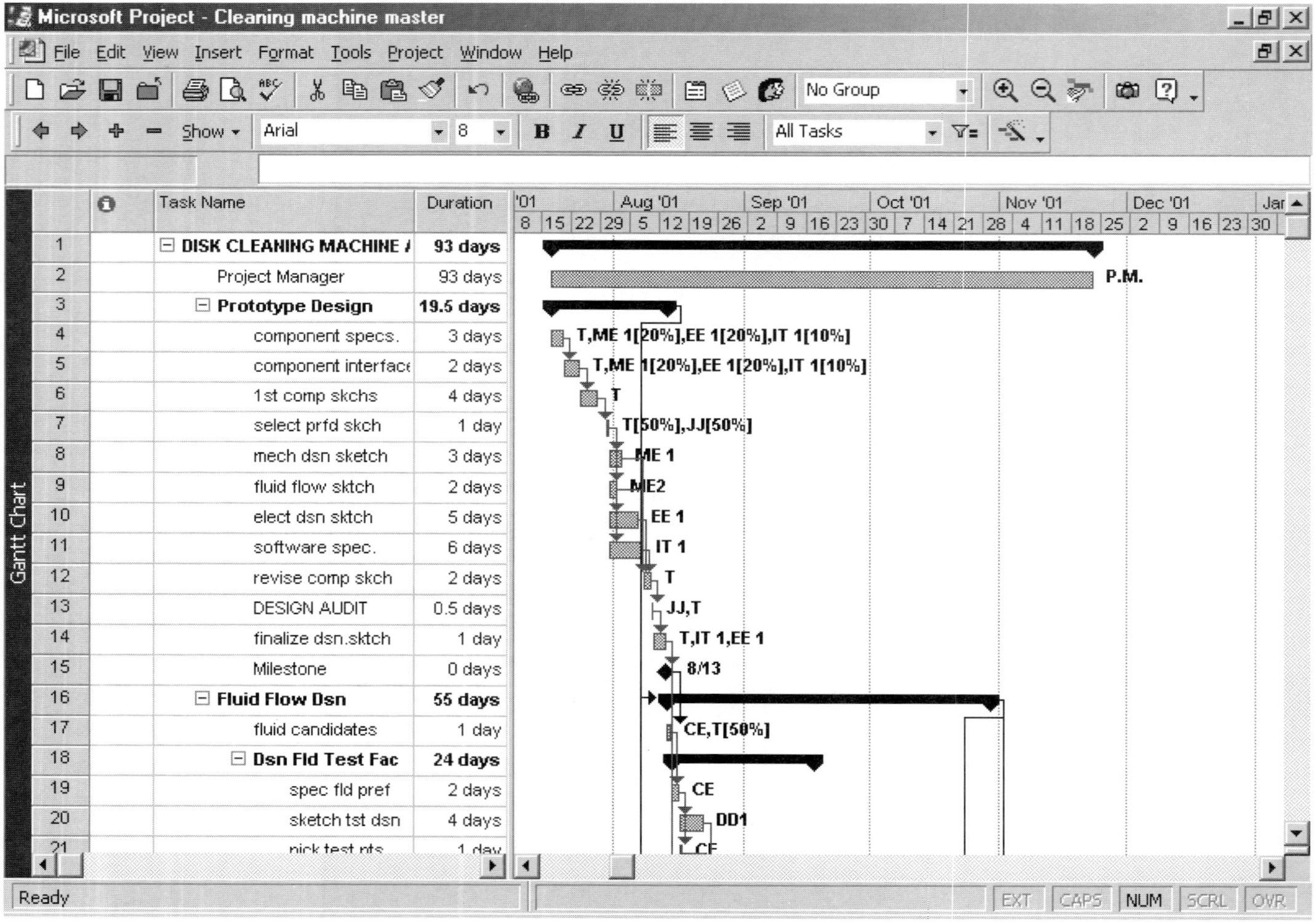
Microsoft Project - Cleaning machine master
File Edit View Insert Format Tools Project Window Help
No Group
Show
Arial
8
All Tasks
Gantt Chart
Task Name
Duration
'01
Aug '01
Sep '01
Oct '01
Nov '01
Dec '01
8 15 22 29 5 12 19 26 2 9 16 23 30 7 14 21 28 4 11 18 25 2 9 16 23 30
1 DISK CLEANING MACHINE 93 days
2 Project Manager 93 days
3 Prototype Design 19.5 days
4 component specs. 3 days
5 component interface 2 days
6 1st comp skchs 4 days
7 select prfd skch 1 day
8 mech dsn sketch 3 days
9 fluid flow sktch 2 days
10 elect dsn sktch 5 days
11 software spec. 6 days
12 revise comp skch 2 days
13 DESIGN AUDIT 0.5 days
14 finalize dsn.sktch 1 day
15 Milestone 0 days
16 Fluid Flow Dsn 55 days
17 fluid candidates 1 day
18 Dsn Fld Test Fac 24 days
19 spec fld pref 2 days
20 sketch tst dsn 4 days
P.M.
T,ME 1[20%],EE 1[20%],IT 1[10%]
T,ME 1[20%],EE 1[20%],IT 1[10%]
T
T[50%],JJ[50%]
ME 1
ME2
EE 1
IT 1
T
JJ,T
T,IT 1,EE 1
8/13
CE,T[50%]
CE
DD1
Ready
EXT CAPS NUM SCRL OVR

Figure 11-3A

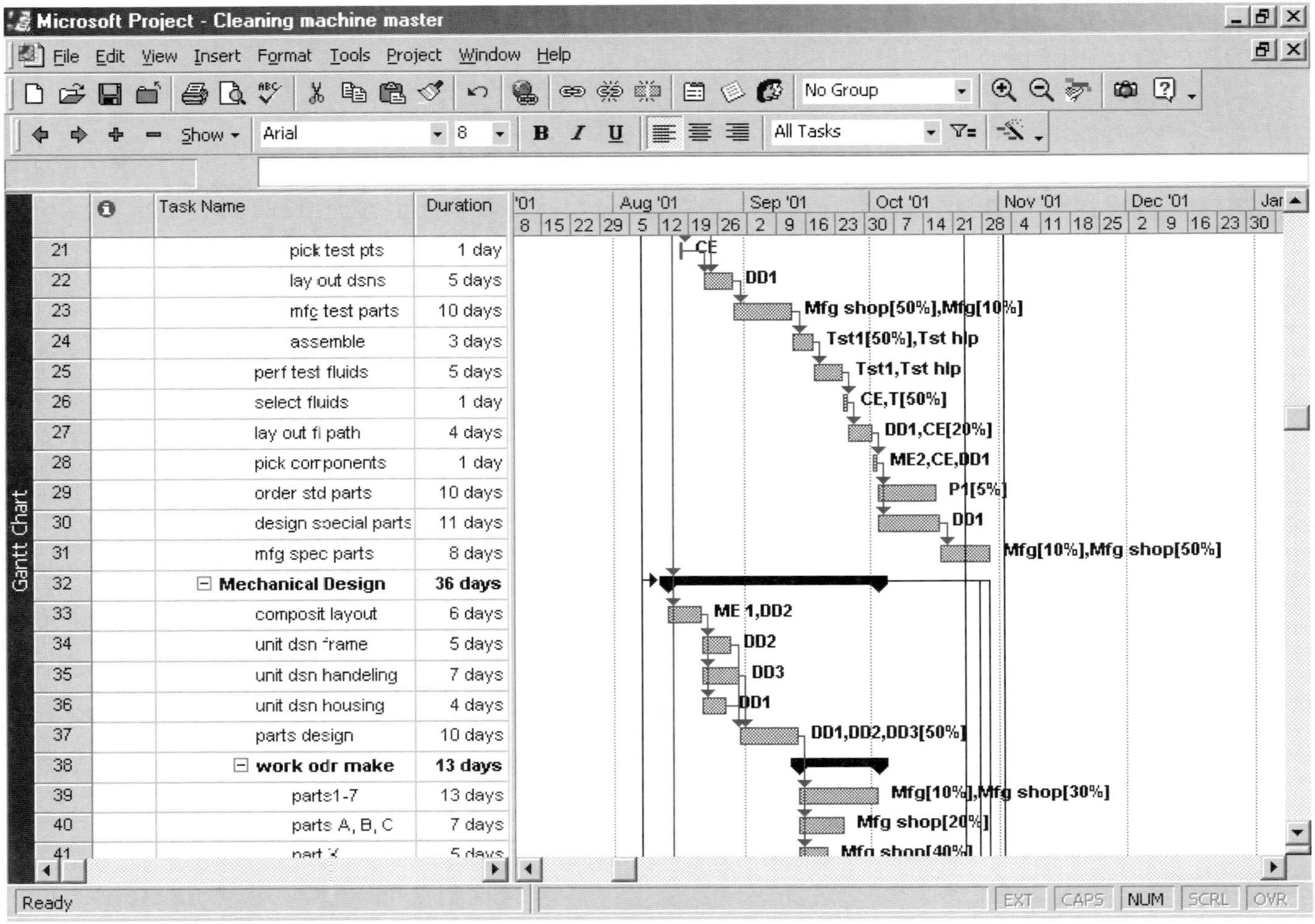
Microsoft Project - Cleaning machine master
File Edit View Insert Format Tools Project Window Help
No Group
Show
Arial
8
All Tasks
Gantt Chart
Task Name
Duration
'01
Aug '01
Sep '01
Oct '01
Nov '01
Dec '01
Jan
8 15 22 29 5 12 19 26 2 9 16 23 30 7 14 21 28 4 11 18 25 2 9 16 23 30
21 pick test pts 1 day
22 lay out dsns 5 days
23 mfg test parts 10 days
24 assemble 3 days
25 perf test fluids 5 days
26 select fluids 1 day
27 lay out fl path 4 days
28 pick components 1 day
29 order std parts 10 days
30 design special parts 11 days
31 mfg spec parts 8 days
32 Mechanical Design 36 days
33 composit layout 6 days
34 unit dsn frame 5 days
35 unit dsn handeling 7 days
36 unit dsn housing 4 days
37 parts design 10 days
38 work odr make 13 days
39 parts1-7 13 days
40 parts A, B, C 7 days
CE
DD1
Mfg shop[50%],Mfg[10%]
Tst1[50%],Tst hlp
Tst1,Tst hlp
CE,T[50%]
DD1,CE[20%]
ME2,CE,DD1
P1[5%]
DD1
Mfg[10%],Mfg shop[50%]
ME 1,DD2
DD2
DD3
DD1
DD1,DD2,DD3[50%]
Mfg[10%],Mfg shop[30%]
Mfg shop[20%]
Ready
EXT CAPS NUM SCRL OVR

Figure 11-3B

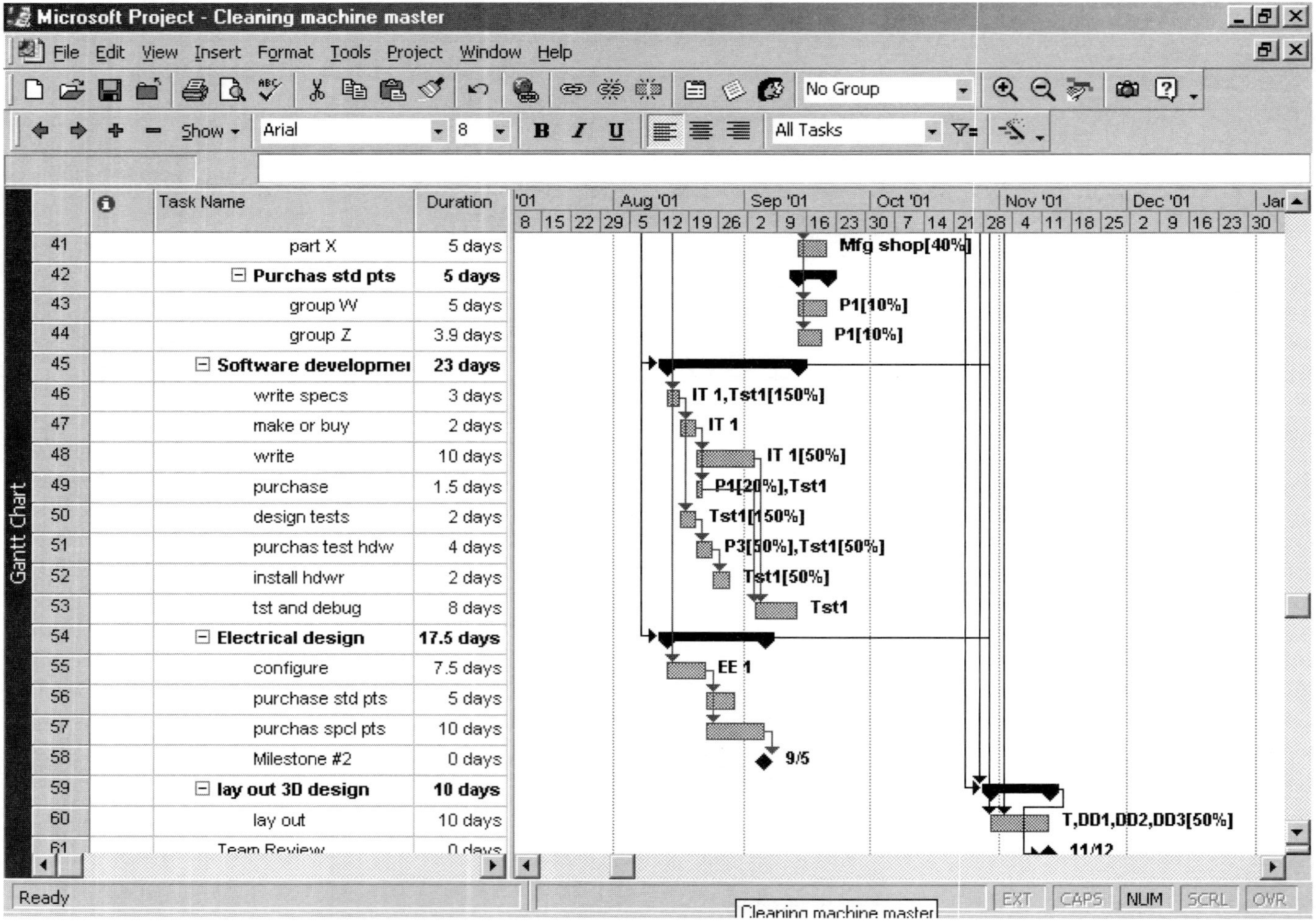
Microsoft Project - Cleaning machine master
File Edit View Insert Format Tools Project Window Help
No Group
Show
Arial
8
All Tasks
Task Name
Duration
41 part X 5 days
42 Purchas std pts 5 days
43 group W 5 days
44 group Z 3.9 days
45 Software developmei 23 days
46 write specs 3 days
47 make or buy 2 days
48 write 10 days
49 purchase 1.5 days
50 design tests 2 days
51 purchas test hdw 4 days
52 install hdwr 2 days
53 tst and debug 8 days
54 Electrical design 17.5 days
55 configure 7.5 days
56 purchase std pts 5 days
57 purchas spcl pts 10 days
58 Milestone #2 0 days
59 lay out 3D design 10 days
60 lay out 10 days
'01
Aug '01
Sep '01
Oct '01
Nov '01
Dec '01
Mfg shop[40%]
P1[10%]
P1[10%]
IT 1,Tst1[150%]
IT 1
IT 1[50%]
P1[20%],Tst1
Tst1[150%]
P3[50%],Tst1[50%]
Tst1[50%]
Tst1
EE 1
9/5
T,DD1,DD2,DD3[50%]
Gantt Chart
Ready
EXT
CAPS
NUM
SCRL
OVR

Figure 11-3C

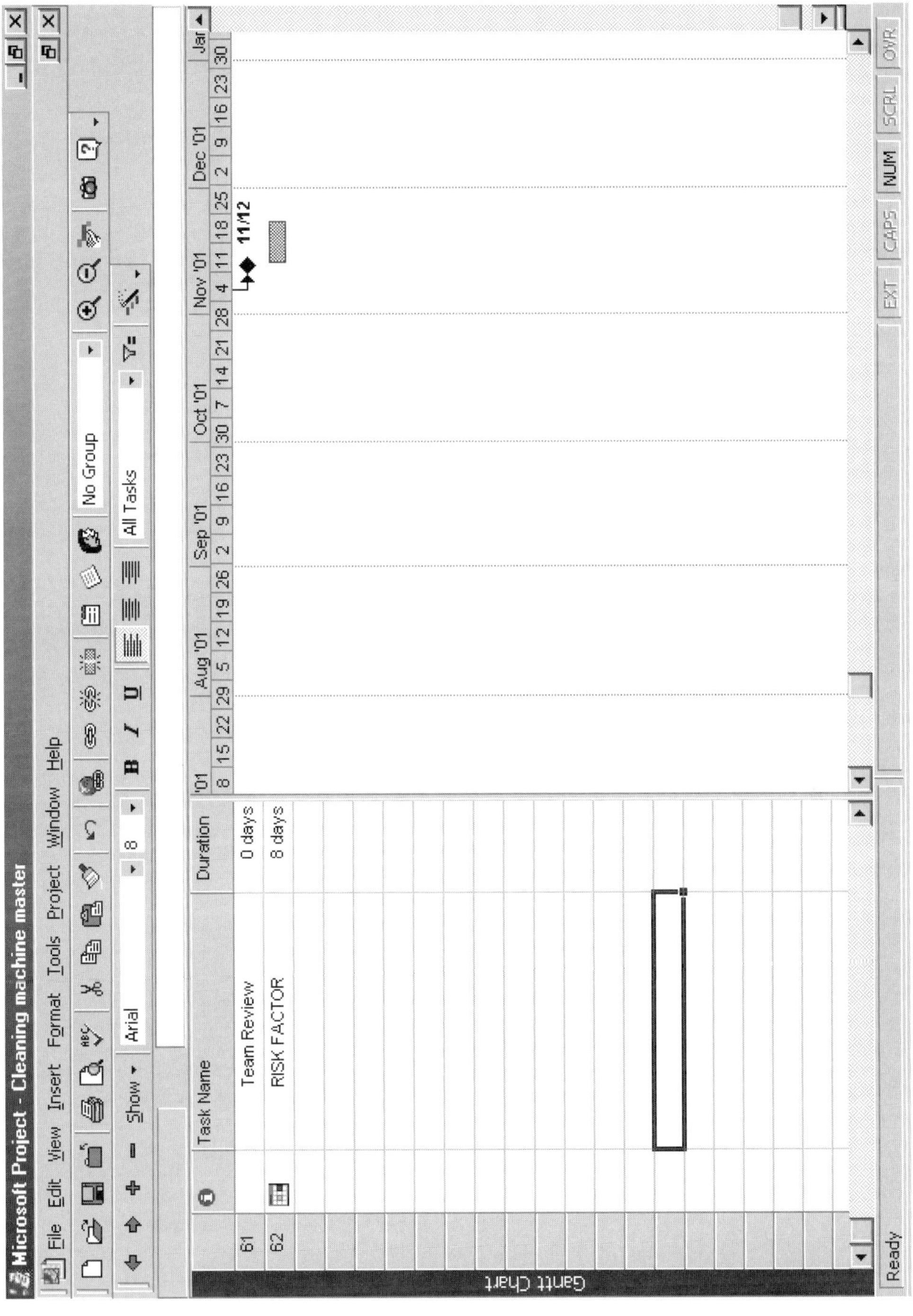
Microsoft Project - Cleaning machine master
File Edit View Insert Format Tools Project Window Help
No Group
Show
Arial
8
All Tasks
Gantt Chart
Task Name
Duration
61 Team Review 0 days
62 RISK FACTOR 8 days
'01
Aug '01
Sep '01
Oct '01
Nov '01
Dec '01
Jan
8 15 22 29 5 12 19 26 2 9 16 23 30 7 14 21 28 4 11 18 25 2 9 16 23 30
11/12
Ready
EXT CAPS NUM SCRL OVR

Figure 11-3D

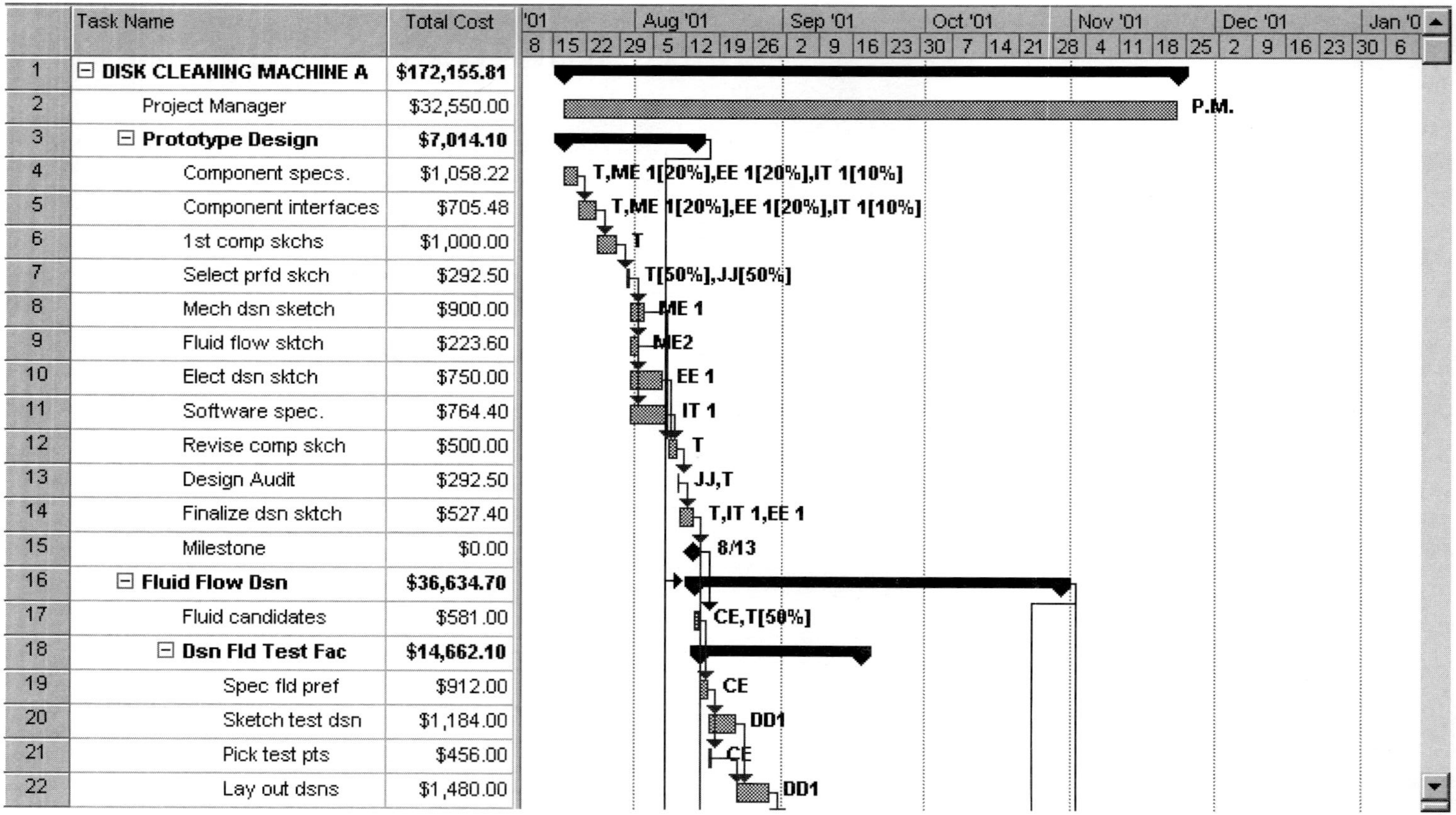
Task Name
Total Cost
'01
Aug '01
Sep '01
Oct '01
Nov '01
Dec '01
Jan '0
8 15 22 29 5 12 19 26 2 9 16 23 30 7 14 21 28 4 11 18 25 2 9 16 23 30 6
1 DISK CLEANING MACHINE A $172,155.81
2 Project Manager $32,550.00
3 Prototype Design $7,014.10
4 Component specs. $1,058.22
5 Component interfaces $705.48
6 1st comp skchs $1,000.00
7 Select prfd skch $292.50
8 Mech dsn sketch $900.00
9 Fluid flow sktch $223.60
10 Elect dsn sktch $750.00
11 Software spec. $764.40
12 Revise comp skch $500.00
13 Design Audit $292.50
14 Finalize dsn sktch $527.40
15 Milestone $0.00
16 Fluid Flow Dsn $36,634.70
17 Fluid candidates $581.00
18 Dsn Fld Test Fac $14,662.10
19 Spec fld pref $912.00
20 Sketch test dsn $1,184.00
21 Pick test pts $456.00
22 Lay out dsns $1,480.00
P.M.
T,ME 1[20%],EE 1[20%],IT 1[10%]
T,ME 1[20%],EE 1[20%],IT 1[10%]
T
T[50%],JJ[50%]
ME 1
ME2
EE 1
IT 1
T
JJ,T
T,IT 1,EE 1
8/13
CE,T[50%]
CE
DD1
CE
DD1

Figure 11-4A

	Task Name	Total Cost
23	Mfg test parts	$9,932.00
24	Assemble	$698.10
25	Perf test fluids	$1,447.00
26	Select fluids	$581.00
27	Lay out fl path	$1,548.80
28	Pick components	$863.80
29	Order std parts	$4,516.00
30	Design special parts	$3,256.00
31	Mfg spec parts	$9,179.00
32	⊟ **Mechanical Design**	**$57,953.08**
33	Composite lay out	$3,384.00
34	Unit dsn frame	$1,320.00
35	Unit dsn handling	$1,848.00
36	Unit dsn housing	$1,184.00
37	Parts design	$6,920.00
38	⊟ **Work Order Make**	**$9,000.60**
39	Parts1-7	$2,643.80
40	Parts A, B, C	$555.80
41	Part X	$5,801.00
42	⊟ **Purchase Std Pts**	**$384.48**
43	Group W	$216.00
44	Group Z	$168.48

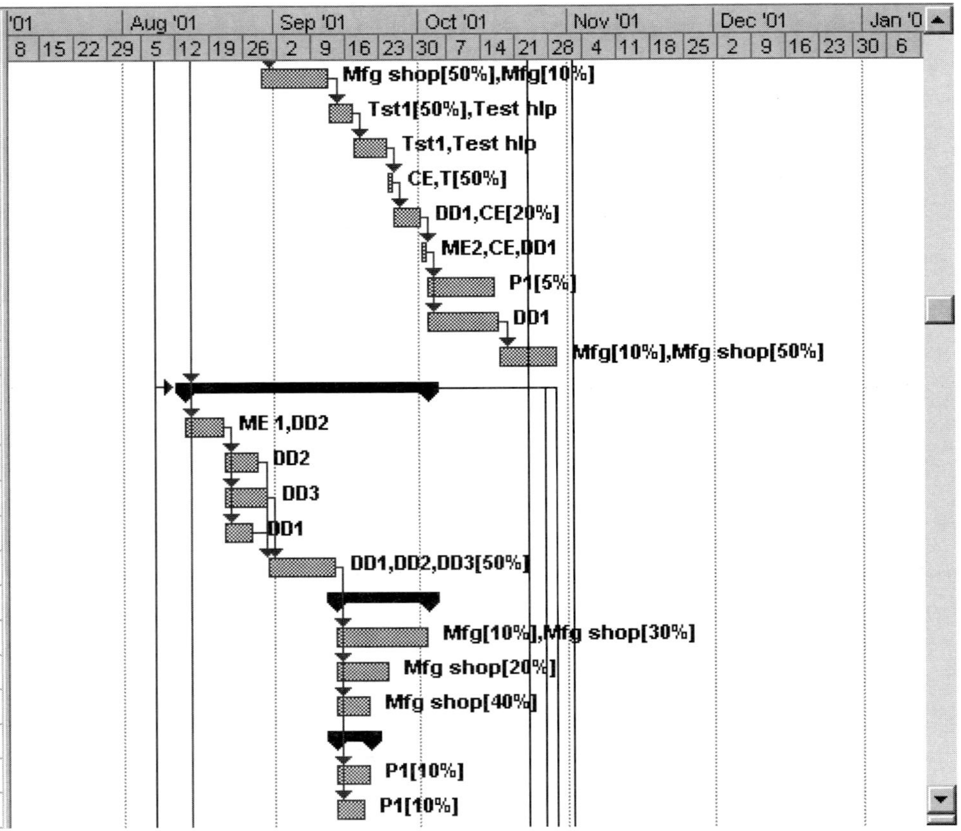

Figure 11-4B

	Task Name	Total Cost
45	⊟ **Software developme**	**$5,602.93**
46	Write specs	$892.50
47	Make or buy	$254.80
48	Write	$637.00
49	Purchase	$299.70
50	Design tests	$340.20
51	Purchase test hdw	$2,158.13
52	Install hdw	$113.40
53	Test and debug	$907.20
54	⊟ **Electrical Design**	**$8,981.00**
55	Configure	$1,125.00
56	Purchase std pts	$2,356.00
57	Purchase spcl pts	$5,500.00
58	Milestone #2	$0.00
59	⊟ **Lay out 3D Design**	**$9,420.00**
60	Lay out	$9,420.00
61	Team Review	$0.00
62	RISK FACTOR	$14,000.00

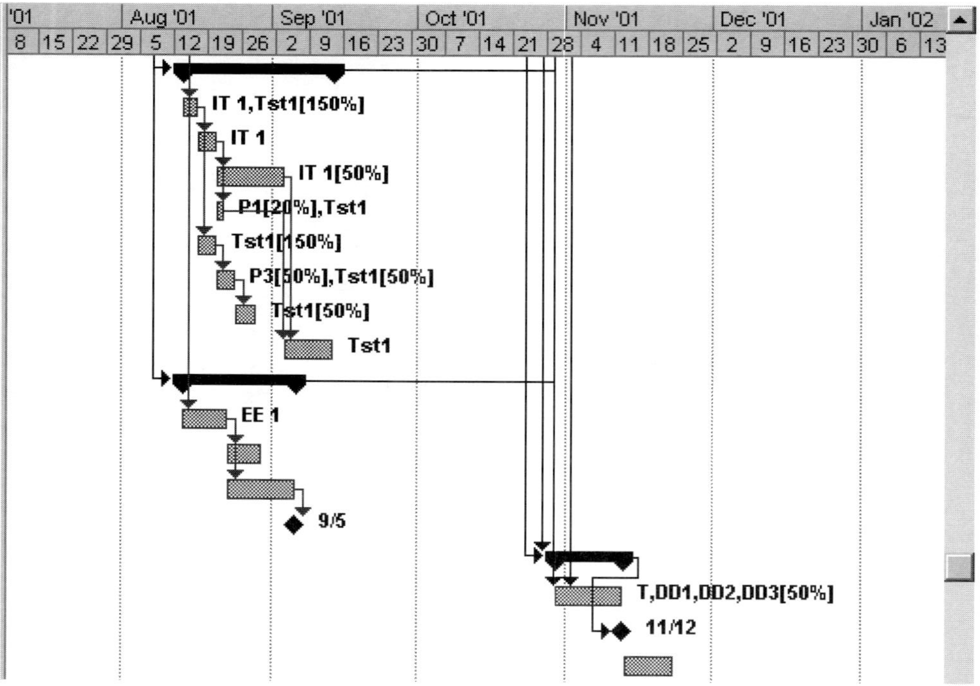

Figure 11-4C

Using the toy truck example, shown in Figure 11-5, little is gained by using less expensive material. Materials only make up a small amount of the total cost. The largest costs are associated with carving the truck parts. To change the specification from "carve truck units to a smooth, rounded modern body design" to "carve truck units to a squared-off symbolic body design" may reduce the carver's cost and time. The sponsor can change the specification accordingly, and the team easily can replan/redraw the Gantt chart. Only the carver task durations will change on the Gantt chart.

If time is pressing, different adjustments can be made without sacrificing outcome quality. Using the toy truck example, one may be able to do the following:

- Schedule carvers and assemblers to work overtime and/or over the weekend to achieve an earlier finish date.
- Contract out the truck's assembly to an organization that could complete the task in a shorter time period.
- Bring in two temporary assembly helpers to shorten the assembly times.
- Pay a premium to shorten delivery time for materials, particularly the wood used to carve the truck and the trailer.

These options can be detected by carefully reviewing the Gantt chart and by discussing the situation with key team members. Such adjustments will lead to a shortened timeline but at the expense of increased cost. Suppliers often charge more to provide a shorter delivery time. Scheduling the carvers and assemblers to work overtime increases the resource costs. When "time is money," this increase can be justified.

When the cost is too high and quality cannot be sacrificed, look for ways to reduce costs by extending the project's timeline. Using the toy truck example, one might be able to use only one carver and a helper to carve the trailer body (which would take longer), trade one assembler for another helper and assemble the final product, all at the cost of one additional day's time. Such adjustments only can be made if task leaders agree to the replanning and its outcomes. *The ability to reduce cost by extending time is generally very limited.*

In most projects, there are many ways to reduce time, but they are inevitably expensive. Adding people, working overtime, and farming out tasks to specialists are frequently used tools. Paying premiums to shorten material delivery time sometimes can be done. As with any changes in the project, these changes also call for some replanning.

The Gantt chart plans must be part of the review discussion. The summary Gantt charts, which are condensed to show the major work packages and their relationships to each other, are the key project plan disclosure items (refer back to Figure 11-1 and Figure 11-2). A large project such as the Disk Cleaning Machine discussed earlier has a detailed Gantt chart that is shown in Figures

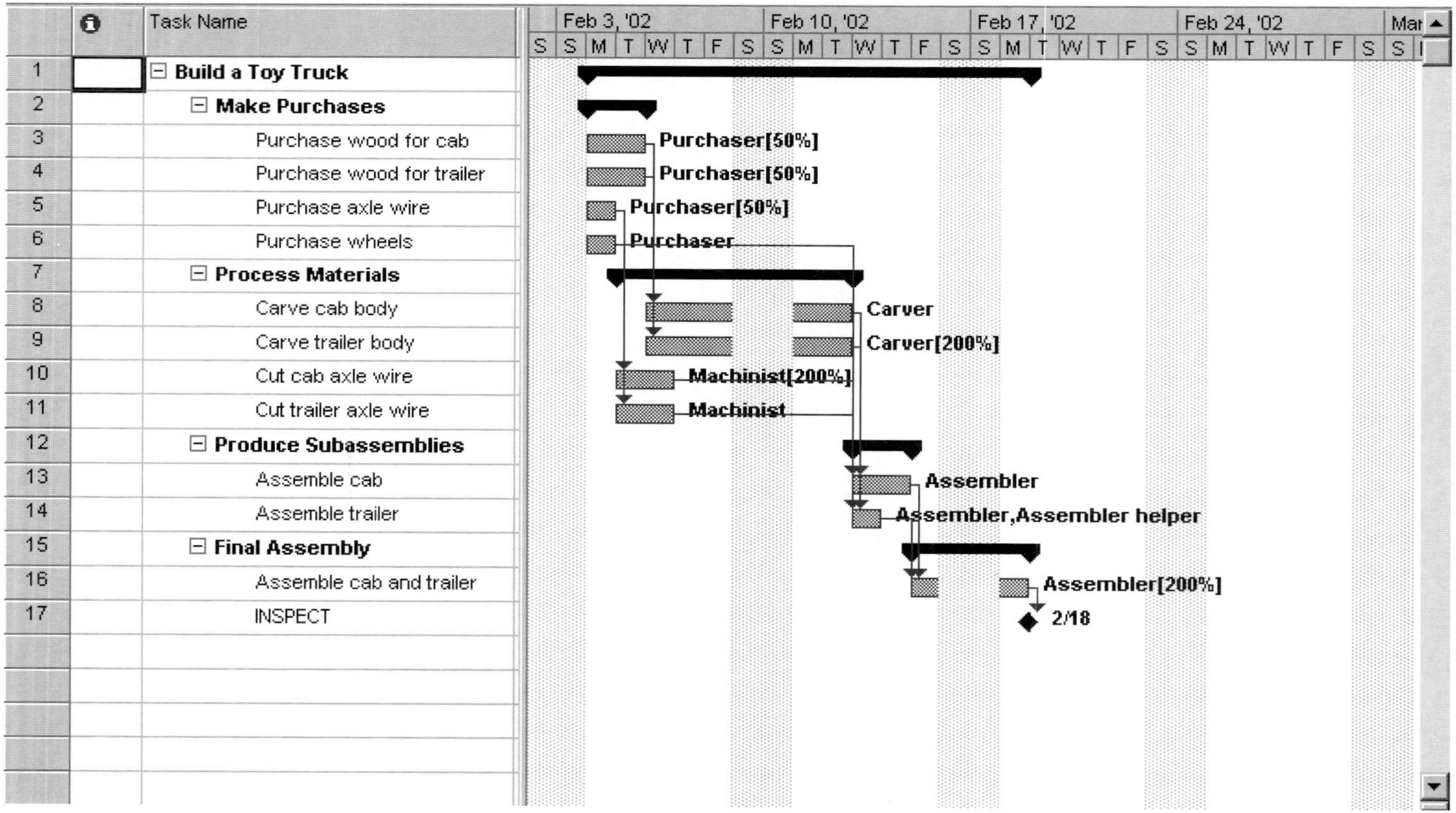
Task Name
Feb 3, '02
Feb 10, '02
Feb 17, '02
Feb 24, '02
Mar
1 Build a Toy Truck
2 Make Purchases
3 Purchase wood for cab
4 Purchase wood for trailer
5 Purchase axle wire
6 Purchase wheels
7 Process Materials
8 Carve cab body
9 Carve trailer body
10 Cut cab axle wire
11 Cut trailer axle wire
12 Produce Subassemblies
13 Assemble cab
14 Assemble trailer
15 Final Assembly
16 Assemble cab and trailer
17 INSPECT
Purchaser[50%]
Purchaser[50%]
Purchaser[50%]
Purchaser
Carver
Carver[200%]
Machinist[200%]
Machinist
Assembler
Assembler,Assembler helper
Assembler[200%]
2/18

Figure 11-5

11-3A, 11-3B, 11-3C, 11-3D, 11-4A, 11-4B, and 11-4C. In discussing the details of a plan's adjustment, the use of these charts is necessary. However, many sponsors and customers will get lost in the details of Gantt charts like these. It is enough for them to see the project in terms of major tasks. Initially, you should show the sponsor the Gantt chart in the form of a summary of tasks. This summary shows the time requirements for each of the major tasks. It also shows the dependencies among those major tasks. Figure 11-2 shows the cost of each major task.

If the customer is concerned about cost, he or she probably notices that the Mechanical Design is the biggest major task cost in Figure 11-2. When the customer suggests trying to reduce this cost, the project manager and the key project team leaders from mechanical design should display the details on that part of the Gantt chart. The project manager and the team leaders then must explain that each task is dictated by the final design sketch. The mechanical design sketch (Item ID-8 in Figure 11-3A) is driven by the project's specification. According to the chart, the mechanical design sketch was produced by ME 1. This person can explain to the customer how the sketch was guided by the project's specification. Explaining this in some detail, ME 1 can help the customer understand how the project's specification drives the mechanical design. The customer and ME 1 then can explore the possibilities for modestly reducing the specification's expectations in order to simplify the project's mechanical design and to save some mechanical design costs. They cannot expect to save time this way because the mechanical design is a 36-day task and is parallel to fluid flow design, which is a 55-day task. The mechanical design has 19 days of slack.

If the customer wants to save time, he or she and the team must look at the fluid flow design. They will soon see, by looking at the details, that they can save some time on fluid flow. The most promising tasks are "order standard parts," "design special parts," and "manufacture special parts." The time for the design and manufacture of special parts may be reduced by workers working overtime and on nonworking days. This overtime, however, costs additional money. Perhaps, with careful planning and resource utilization, some 15 days can be cut out of the project with a considerable increase in cost. The cost can be slightly reduced by simplifying the specification as it impacts mechanical design.

It is possible to continue by going through the project task-by-task in order to reduce project time, but given the type of tasks involved (design sketches and fluid flow sketches), doing so will threaten the quality of the product in many cases.

More imaginative things can be done with some projects. Some principles are illustrated in the projects that can build a modern home in three days. On several occasions, demonstration projects have been executed to build a modern, $200,000 high-quality home in two or three days. Videos are available showing the work progress from a bare lot to a ready-to-live-in house. As one would expect, the house being built looks like it is being swarmed over by human ants. *Note:*

Before the building starts, a great deal more planning must be done for this house than is done for a traditional home. But, even with the time that must be put into this additional planning, this home project will be done much faster than in the traditional time allottment of two to three months. These three-day homes are not prefabricated homes. They are each original, unique architectural designs and were framed, plumbed, wired, roofed, and finished by traditional craftsmen using their traditional techniques.

The word "traditional" did not extend to the materials. Giving the concrete footers and basement walls time to set up could use up two days by itself. However, fast setting concrete is available. This concrete costs more and comes from a special supplier. It sets up in a very short period of time and gets the building of the house off to a fast start. One principle involved is that if you want to shorten the time of a project, go looking for materials that are faster and easier to use and that do not degrade the quality of the project.

When the foundation and basement walls are set for the accelerated build-a-house project, framing begins. Traditionally, one crew of three or four carpenters and helpers frame a house. They follow architectural plans; sometimes, adding creative touches to make up for the architectural plan's lack of detail. To accelerate this process, the architects can break the general framing task down into a number of separate tasks, and a separate crew of carpenters can be called to execute each task. *Architectural details must be more carefully specified*, and a special carpenter foreman working with each crew is necessary to be sure that the crew get the fits right. With this task breakdown, careful instructions for each crew, and with skilled supervision, framing for the house can be completed in a few hours.

The basic message here is: If you must speed up the project, look for tasks that can be divided into subunits with skilled people working on each subunit in parallel and with a highly skilled supervisor coordinating their work. For this approach, all workers must have very high skill and motivational levels. The process of breaking down tasks and linking them will need to be much more carefully planned and documented than in the original plan. It is desirable to have all of the workers or a key person from each subunit sit in on the detailed planning effort.

Plumbing, wiring, heating, and air conditioning can all be treated in the same way. Look for components that require the least amount of effort for installation. The architectural plans show the details, and a purchaser must prelocate these supplies and personally ensure their presence at the work site when needed.

In addition, there are tools that speed up the work for builders. For example, carpenters and roofers will be supplied with nail guns. Planning will focus on set ups that support the use of sophisticated hand tools.

At the heart of this effort to speed up the building of a house is much more detailed planning and greater resource identification effort. The three-day house plan certainly requires at least three weeks more planning time than the traditional three-month house. At some point while using the more detailed planning approach, the added time consumed in planning may exceed the time saved in the building of the house. This longer planning time must be considered when special techniques are being considered to shorten the time required to complete the project.

Instant landscaping for the instant house also is feasible. Landscapers do this sort of thing all the time. There are limitations, however: For example, the big, mature oak tree that the new homeowner wants in a back corner of the lot is going to take at least 40 years to mature, and nothing can be done about that. This message about the limitations of speeding up a project is even clearer: "You cannot produce a baby in one month by putting nine women to work on it."

A project that has been planned for a traditional task-oriented 8–5 world generally can be shortened somewhat. It only can be done with more intensive and time-consuming planning. It must focus on the Gantt chart, task by task, and it generally will cost a lot more than the original plan. Some things cannot be shortened. At some stage, every project will come to the point where there is no way to cut the project's time any further. Because cutting time is heavily dependent on more intensive planning, cutting time out should done at the beginning of a project. Cutting out time during a project's execution using the methods cited here can be tremendously disruptive and counterproductive. Nevertheless, circumstances do emerge where this is necessary. *Always proceed with great care!*

EXAMPLE

At one company, a project to produce a new valve is underway. The Gantt chart for this project has been created and supported. The date for the first finished product to come off the production line also has been firmly set.

The department's chief executive receives word from corporate headquarters that a competitor expects to have the same product on the market six months ahead of ours. We are ordered to cut six months from our two-year schedule.

As project manager, you and your team proceed to examine the Gantt chart to determine the amount of time that can be taken out of the schedule by using overtime and outsourcing. As a group, you form a conclusion on what can be done and on the additional costs that will be attributed to the acceleration.

In addition, you also examine the project's tasks and determine whether any can be compressed by using more detailed planning and parallel teams, and whether the deliveries of materials can be shortened with premium payments.

You and your team also concentrate on the critical path tasks and consider only noncritical path tasks when a shortened critical path task has made one of the noncritical tasks critical. You and the team also must consider any other task where Δ is greater than the slack.

After all this is completed with the appropriate risk analysis, your project team knows what can and cannot be done. In fact, six months may have been cut out of the original project timeline, but at great expense. Upper management now will have to decide whether this plan is cost effective.

LAUNCH THE PROJECT

After adjustments have been made and the sponsor and the project manager have signed off on the completed plan, it is time to launch the project. Planning should have been done so that project tasks without predecessors will start the next day!

SUMMARY

After the project Gantt chart and all the associated planning documents have been completed, it is absolutely necessary that the project manager and the key project team members review the plan with the project's sponsor. This review includes a look at the original statement of work to be sure that all of the outcomes noted there have been addressed.

The review tells the sponsor how long the project will take, what resources will be needed, and how much the project will cost. If the sponsor feels that the project is going to take too long, there are ways that the project's completion time can be shortened. However, this always costs more than the cost of the original plan. There are stringent limits to how much cost reduction can be achieved by lengthening the project time. If both the time and cost must be reduced, the requirements of the specification also must be reduced. The project Gantt chart shows the way to make these time and cost reductions. Note: There is a point where further reductions cannot be made.

DISCUSSION QUESTIONS

1. Why should every project plan be reviewed by the sponsor before the project is launched?
2. Who attends the project reviews? Why?
3. What information and materials are presented for the sponsor's review?
4. How can projects be shortened?
5. Can all tasks be shortened if the sponsor is willing to bear the cost?
6. What comes after the review?

12 PROJECT EXECUTION

INTRODUCTION

When the sponsor has approved the project plan, the project manager must make sure that the team gets to work. The tasks that have no predecessors must start immediately. It is not automatic. The project manager must make sure that the leaders of the first tasks are all ready to go and do, in fact, start. As the tasks are approaching completion, the project manager must make sure that the successor task teams are ready to go, and do start working. Tasks leaders who are not scheduled to start their tasks until the project is well underway may lose track of their start date unless the project manager keeps them well connected to the project.

The project manager keeps him- or herself well connected to the project by visiting with task teams who 1) have just finished their task, 2) are currently active, 3) are successor teams to the currently active teams. This visiting, discussing activities, and providing assistance with problem solving is called *walk-about management*, which is part of the project manager's full-time project management job.

Holding milestone meetings and continuously updating the working Gantt charts, supported by frequent status reports, also are a project manager's responsibilities. He or she must keep all the task team members, the sponsor, and other project stakeholders continuously connected to the project.

NOTES ON THE PROJECT LAUNCH

The basic principle of IPM is plan the work and then work the plan. When IPM principles have been followed, the project is well planned in detail by the time the sponsor signs off on the complete statement of work and the baseline Gantt chart. All of the task leaders for the project have been involved in the planning and now understand the plan. All have or have ready access to the complete and detailed basic Gantt chart and the statement of work. Now there is nothing to it. The team proceeds to follow the plan and to complete the project to specifications, on time and within budget.

Strangely enough, this is very often not the way it happens. After having carefully planned the project, many task leaders and task workgroups forget that they have a plan. A few workers on the project are committed full time to the project from beginning to end. Most have other things to do—other things that generally are not as well planned and scheduled as their project commitment. These workers may truly intend to do their tasks as scheduled. But, if it is not going to start for some weeks or months, they may lose track of their commitment to a start date. When the start date does arrive, they are in the middle of another effort and do not want to drop what they are doing to begin the project's task. Therefore, they will do the project task as soon as they finish what they are presently doing. (This is something for risk analysis to consider.) This posture, on the part of one or several task leaders, can blow the project plan apart.

There are many variations on why task leaders are not ready or willing to start their tasks at their committed time during planning. Some, who contribute enthusiastically to creating the plan, just never believed it was real; it is just a document that they can refer to as they work through the project. "But you never really expected it would actually happen the way we planned it, did you?" is their way of thinking.

The project manager must be aware that this attitudes exist among at least some of the project team. He or she also must realize that his or her job is not just to facilitate the creation of a good project plan; it is to make sure that the team works the plan and that each team leader is prepared to start his or her team's task as soon as the predecessor task(s) is finished. It is to make sure that the team approaches the task with due diligence. It is to make sure that each team leader keeps risk contingency plans in mind and is prepared to use them whenever warnings emerge during the task effort.

The project manager's job is to get the job done! THERE IS NO SUCH THING AS A GOOD EXCUSE! This means that he or she must have a thoughtout scheme for how to manage the project day by day and how the tools that he or she has available to manage this project will be used to make the plan work. This all begins at the project launch, which should take place at a meeting the day after the sponsor signs off on the project. All project team members must attend this project launch meeting.

THE PROJECT LAUNCH MEETING

At the project launch meeting, the project manager will cover the following points with the team. During project execution, the project manager intends to:

- Ensure that each task without a predecessor starts immediately.
- Ensure that each subsequent task starts on schedule, by keeping in touch with the successor's task leaders.
- Practice walk-about management and keep task leaders communicating with each other.
- Keep the operations Gantt chart up-to-date with printouts posted and replaced at regular intervals.
- Support task leaders in securing any necessary resources.
- Support task leaders in using reserves, when necessary.
- Maintain discipline and order within the project.
- Give special attention to the preparation of the user documentation.
- Gather information for and prepare the project report. He or she should keep a project diary.
- Schedule milestone meetings; publicize, schedule, and prepare agendas for the meetings.
- Give special attention to the successful achievement of the project outcomes!
- Convene and lead the post project review.
- Plan and implement a project closure celebration.

PROJECT MANAGEMENT

After the plan has received customer approval, it is time to launch the project's activity. At this point, the project manager's role changes somewhat from facilitator to manager. This does not mean, however, that the project manager adopts a top-down authoritarian style, but rather takes on a modern management role with "walk-about" management. Walk-about management is done when a manager gets out of the office and visits with the people who are executing the project's tasks.

The *Wall Street Journal* once attributed walk-about management to Bob Packard of Hewlett-Packard Corp. Packard was an outstanding manager, but walk-about management goes further back. In fact, it was widely practiced at General Electric in the 1940s.

Modern management was further defined when Tom Peters, the widely read commentator on management practices, interviewed John McConnel, CEO of Worthington Steel Corp. Peters asked McConnel how a large steel company could operate—and operate very well—using only a two-page operating manual (which only stated the company's basic principles.) McConnel replied, "We talk to each other."[1]

During the project's execution, the project manager practices walk-about management by regularly talking to team leaders and encouraging them to *talk to each other*. Walk-about management is visiting with team leaders where they are working every day or as close to every day as possible. The project manager must always visit a task leader shortly after his or her task has started.

The project launch begins as each task lacking a predecessor gets started on time. Without attention, this may not happen. When a project's completion is weeks, months, or years away, on-time startup may not seem urgent. However, start delays translate into completion delays. Consequently, the project manager makes a point of conferring with the task leaders before the launch date, making sure that they have all necessary resources, and are prepared to begin their task at 8 A.M. on the startup date. If any help is needed to meet this date, the project manager helps! THEY TALK TO EACH OTHER.

Walk-about management is practiced if task leaders are around the corner or around the world. For example, a project manager leading an information systems project for an international company spent much time in Canada, England, Japan, and stops in-between. This high-tech operator used e-mail and conference calls extensively, but he also traveled to far-flung venues and visited task leaders, face-to-face. THEY TALKED TO EACH OTHER.

When face-to-face meetings are not possible due to budget constraints, logistics, or corporate policy, the project manager must arrange video conferences or teleconferences with the team leaders who are working on current tasks. Frequent communication between the project manager and these team leaders must go well beyond checking on the team leaders when their tasks begin and end. The project manager must follow up on each of these conversations with an e-mail summary. E-mail exchanges between the project manager and the task leaders who are currently working on tasks is valuable. The project managers should ask, "What have you done this week? Any problems? What will you do next?"

Walk-about management helps to gather up information. The project manager saves the baseline Gantt chart as a baseline reference. (Microsoft Project

[1]From a personal conversation with John McConnel.

2002® has a procedure for saving the baseline and later comparing it to the operating Gantt chart as work proceeds.) As tasks start, the project manager indicates a task's startup on the operations Gantt chart.

THE OPERATIONS GANTT CHART

The mechanics of monitoring a project using the operations Gantt chart is illustrated in the following simplified example. You should assume that there are enough tasks on the critical path to justify calculating a risk factor. Note: the demonstration provided also works for larger projects.

Figure 12-1 represents a condensed basic Gantt chart for a product development project. For each task, the task's duration is entered. The people who will be working on the task are designated following the task bar; two designers will work on Task C and D; two machinists will work on Task G; and two assemblers will work on Task J. The relationship of the predecessor and successor is represented by one-line arrows that end with an arrowhead at the successor task. A risk factor, which has been calculated for the string of tasks, also is represented. Its duration is three days; it is entered at a fixed date; and it is not connected to any prior tasks by dependency arrows. The risk factor starts the day after the last task in the string (J) finishes. A zero duration inspection point is entered as Task J finishes. This point is connected to Task J by a dependency arrow. This baseline task is printed out, and it is saved as a baseline within software storage.

After the baseline has been saved, the basic Gantt chart is brought up on the Gantt chart display screen. As the tasks are finished, their actual durations are entered on this screen by the project manager. The software draws a thick black line within the task bar to represent task completion (see Figure 12-2). If the project manager enters percent completion for a task that is less than 100 percent, the black line only fills up that percent of the full length of the task bar.

As shown in the Figure 12-2, Tasks A and B finish on time. The critical path is A-B-D-H-I-J. Task C finishes half a day late, which will add cost to the project but not add time. Task C is not on the critical path. There is one day of slack between Tasks C and D. Task C has room to run over its estimate. Task D runs one day over. Task H depends on Task D; Task I depends on Task H; and Task J depends on Task I. When Task D overruns, Tasks H, I, and J will have to start one day late. (This should not be a big surprise.) Task workers for Tasks H and I and the team leader for Task J are on the project team. They know that their tasks are on the critical path and by the time the project gets to Task H, it is very likely that the A-B-D sequence of tasks may overrun. Nevertheless the project manager reminds all three to expect a late start as soon as he notes that Task D will overrun. Tasks E and F finish on time. Task G overruns by one day, which does not add to the project overrun because the task string E-F-G has three days of slack. Note how the project manager records this and prints out a partially completed Gantt chart (See Figure 12-2).

Task Name	Duration	Start
A	3 days	Mon 2/4/02
B	4 days	Thu 2/7/02
C	3 days	Thu 2/7/02
D	3 days	Wed 2/13/02
E	2 days	Wed 2/13/02
F	2 days	Fri 2/15/02
G	2 days	Tue 2/19/02
H	3 days	Mon 2/18/02
I	3 days	Thu 2/21/02
J	3 days	Tue 2/26/02
Inspect	0 days	Thu 2/28/02
Risk F	3 days	Fri 3/1/02

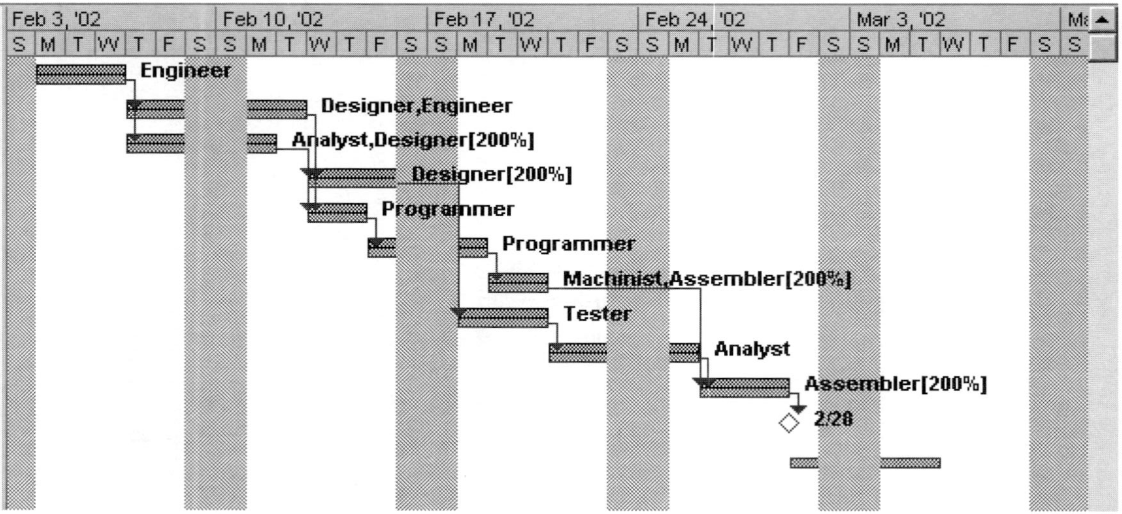

Figure 12-1

Task Name	Duration	Start
A	3 days	Mon 2/4/02
B	4 days	Thu 2/7/02
C	3.5 days	Thu 2/7/02
D	4 days	Wed 2/13/02
E	2 days	Wed 2/13/02
F	2 days	Fri 2/15/02
G	3 days	Tue 2/19/02
H	3 days	Tue 2/19/02
I	3 days	Fri 2/22/02
J	3 days	Wed 2/27/02
Inspect	0 days	Fri 3/1/02
Risk F	3 days	Fri 3/1/02

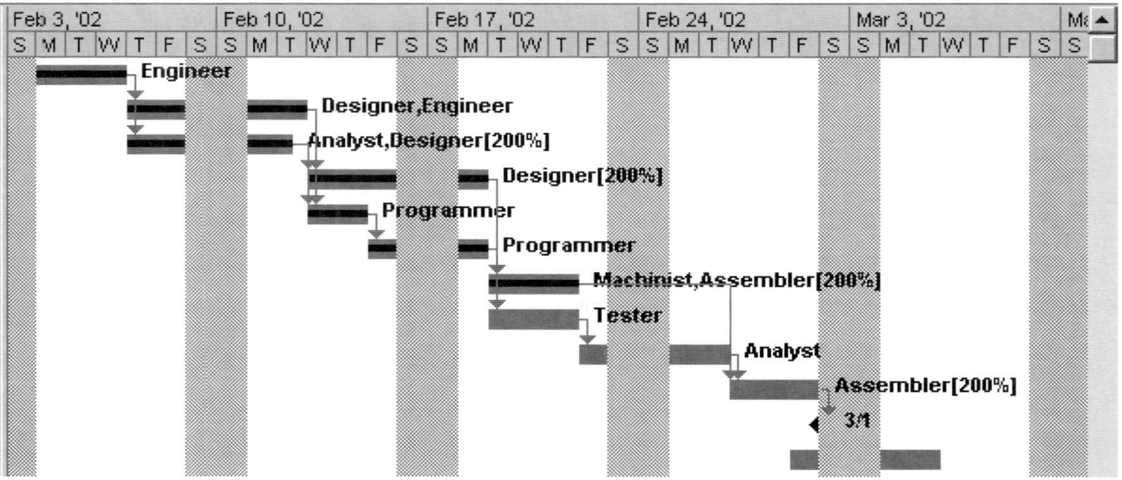

Figure 12-2

When Task H overruns one day (Figure 12-3), the project manager sees that two thirds of the risk factor is used up. With Microsoft Project 2002® the project manager has saved a base line and can print a tracking Gantt chart with lightly shaded bars and completed tasks with dark shaded bars.

Note the baseline Gantt chart shows its no risk duration point with a white diamond and the actual duration point (Inspection) with a black diamond. The black diamond travels above the risk bar, which does not move. It shows all the interested parties that when Task H is completed, the project has used up two days of the risk factor. This may seem easy to see here. But when there is a string of 20+ critical path tasks and numerous other non-critical path tasks, it is very good to be able to view the solid diamond with reference to the risk factor to see how much of the time buffer the project has used up.

The project manager cautions task leaders for Task I and J to look at their notes and use extra resources if they suspect that they might overrun. Task I finishes on time. Task J runs over a half-day (See Figure 12-4).

All but one-half day of the risk factor has been used up. The next string of tasks can start as planed on March 6, 2002.The risk factor worked very well. This is just what a project manager generally can expect.

This means of tracking a project's progress works for small projects and for very large projects. For very large, basic projects, having the critical path broken down into units of approximately 20 tasks and risk factors inserted at the breaks gives the project manager and the team better control of the project's time performance than having the risk factor at the end.

Using Microsoft Project 2002®, we indicate a task's startup by assigning five or 10 percent completion using software utilities. We do not enter further percent completion until the task is 100 percent complete. Percentage completion can be interpreted in different ways, which can result in a misleading display. We keep track of the progress of a task with notes written into our project diaries during a walkabout and teleconferencing. We regularly ask team leaders, "How many days of work are left?" and we use this information to show a task's percent completion. If the task is running over: it shows up on the operations Gantt chart when the days left are entered. It is the result when the task's completion date is pushed out by adding the days left to current date. Both of us are diligent about knowing how the task is progressing during a task's execution. Waiting until a task is completed to track and record the overrun limits is not what a project manager should do to help a task that is in trouble.

The operations Gantt chart is the planned project Gantt chart that is set up so that the task's actual duration can be entered as the work progresses. If a task runs over, the project manager enters the actual finish date for this task to the chart. The software then automatically moves all subsequent, dependent tasks further out in time. The task leaders of the successor tasks then are informed when the chart shows that their task will actually start later than scheduled.

Task Name	Duration	Start
A	3 days	Mon 2/4/02
B	4 days	Thu 2/7/02
C	3.5 days	Thu 2/7/02
D	4 days	Wed 2/13/02
E	2 days	Wed 2/13/02
F	2 days	Fri 2/15/02
G	3 days	Tue 2/19/02
H	4 days	Tue 2/19/02
I	3 days	Mon 2/25/02
J	3 days	Thu 2/28/02
Inspect	0 days	Mon 3/4/02
Risk F	3 days	Fri 3/1/02

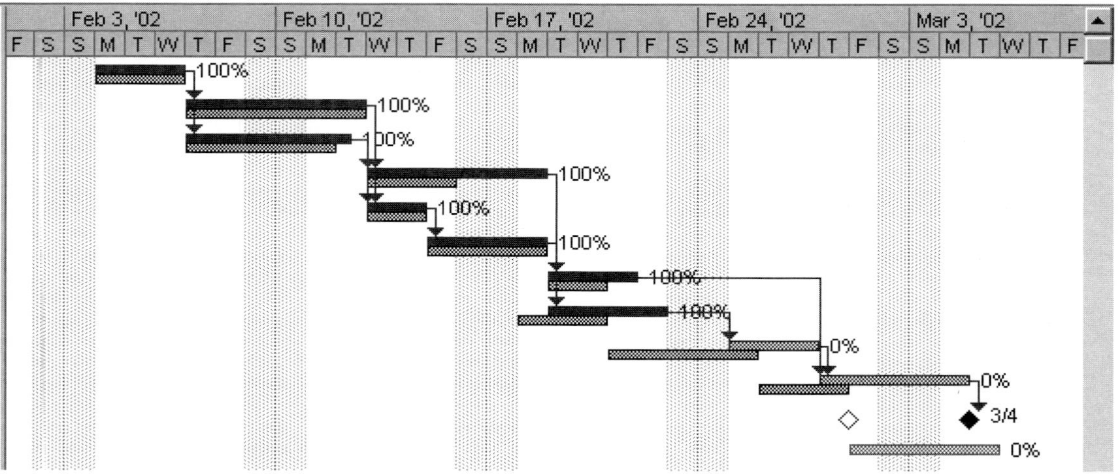

Figure 12-3

Task Name	Duration	Start
A	3 days	Mon 2/4/02
B	4 days	Thu 2/7/02
C	3.5 days	Thu 2/7/02
D	4 days	Wed 2/13/02
E	2 days	Wed 2/13/02
F	2 days	Fri 2/15/02
G	3 days	Tue 2/19/02
H	4 days	Tue 2/19/02
I	3 days	Mon 2/25/02
J	3.5 days	Thu 2/28/02
Inspect	0 days	Tue 3/5/02
Risk F	3 days	Fri 3/1/02

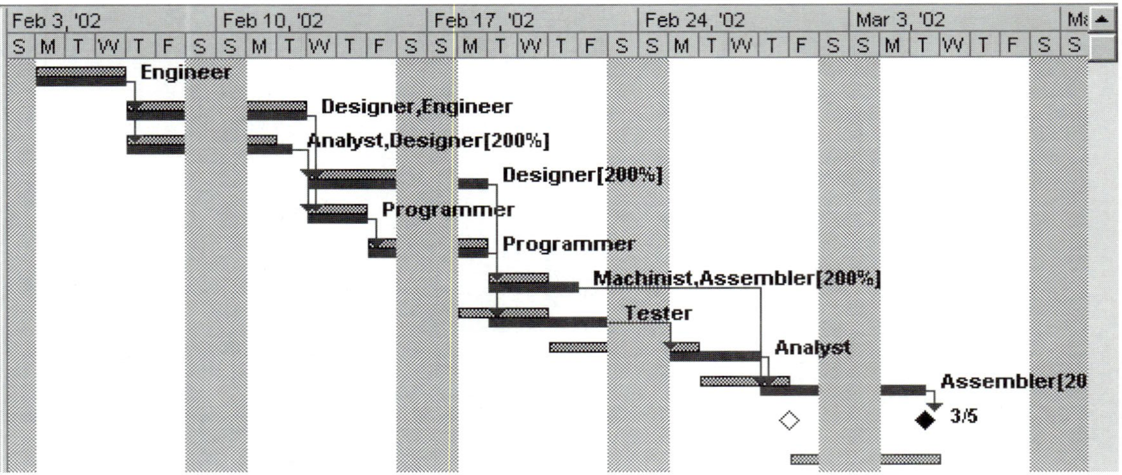

Figure 12-4

The Gantt chart has been set up so that the risk factor task does not move. Displayed above the risk factor task is a diamond symbol (if Microsoft Project 2002® is used) that moves out in time as some tasks overrun. This diamond points down to the risk factor bar and represents—at any specific time—how much of the risk factor has been used up.

Because the downstream task leaders helped to develop the risk factor, they should not be surprised when their actual start dates are moved out somewhat farther than indicated on the basic Gantt chart. This also is easy to forget. The project manager, performing walk-about management; must remind the task leaders that their task's start-up could be delayed by as many days as indicated by the risk factor but never by more than the full amount of the risk factor. It is up to the project manager to keep the operations Gantt chart current. He or she must enter each task completion date the day that it happens. When one string of tasks ending in a risk factor is completed, the next task's start date is the day after the end date of the preceding risk factor. *No one else is ever permitted to enter a completion date on the working Gantt chart.* (Always put the chart in a password-protected file and specify a read-only access for everyone except the project manager.)

The project manager must find a good place to display the operations Gantt chart. A long hallway or a large conference room wall works best for large projects. An office wall works best for small projects. The chart must be changed every time a task is completed. The project's team leaders should have access to the operations Gantt chart on their PCs.

WALK-ABOUT MANAGEMENT AND COMMUNICATIONS

The key concept in walk-about management is communication. An informed team is a well-functioning team. There are no surprises in this type of management.

An e-mail announcement sent out by the project manager to each task leader every time a task is completed helps ensure that the task workgroup leaders are alerted to what is happening in the project.

The project manager must use every means of communication at his or her disposal—walk-about managing, posting the current charts, e-mail, telephone calls, and interoffice memos—to make sure that the team members, *the sponsor*, and other stakeholders of the project are fully aware of its progress.

When a task workgroup's achievement is noteworthy, the project manager should congratulate the workgroup and make sure that the congratulations are distributed. E-mail is an effective way to announce congratulations to all of the project's team members, resource managers, and other stakeholders.

The project manager pays great attention to what is happening within the project. He or she visits with the teams that have just finished their tasks and discovers and shares any helpful information that they have gained with downstream task workgroup members who use the task's output. He or she also visits with the workgroups that are currently engaged in the project's tasks. The project manager thus learns about developments that may help downstream task leaders (whose tasks will start soon), and provides them information that will help them start and perform their tasks.

By practicing walk-about management, the project manager is often able to help a workgroup uncover issues and problems and to deal with them as they occur. Often, when a workgroup member is working on an issue, a short conversation with the project manager can help this person think around the obstacle. In fact one of the authors is often heard to say, "explain it to me as if I were a five year old".

DISCIPLINE AND ORDER

The world of projects is a world in which most workers will devote due diligence to the effort in which they are engaged. With the opportunity to participate in planning, attention from the project manager, recognition, rewards, and opportunities to demonstrate skill and competence, most IPM task team members will make a serious effort to successfully complete their project commitments after they start. Starting on time, as previously noted, is something a project manager must give attention to, and walk-about management is one tool used to ensure that this happens.

As the project manager keeps in touch with current tasks, he or she asks task leaders for help in understanding where they are in their task effort, what they need, and what information he or she can pass along to successor task leaders that will be helpful in the task's transitions. This gives the project manager opportunities to evaluate the level of diligence that is being devoted to the task. It gives him or her the opportunity to praise and support the team members, and to identify any unsatisfactory task performances. Although the latter does not happen often, it does occasionally happen, and every project manager must be prepared to deal with it. Dealing with an unsatisfactory performance is something many project managers prefer to avoid. However, they must deal with it because it impacts overall project performance. Overall performance is the project manager's responsibility. Remember: "There is no such thing as a good excuse."

Line supervisors also must deal with unsatisfactory performance. In fact, there is a long history and a great amount of literature on how to do it correctly. An authoritarian approach has its limitations, and the project manager has limited authority. The project manager must approach an unsatisfactory performance firmly but with sophistication.

The first thing the project manager must do when he or she suspects an unsatisfactory performance is to determine why it is happening. For example, the project team may be bogged down with a problem that they do not know how to fix and are unwilling to admit they have a dilemma. The project manager can begin by asking questions about what they are doing and what they might be doing. A project manager's questions often help a task workgroup's members solve their own problems. In addition, the project manager also may help them get outside assistance that they are reluctant to seek. This project manager is solving performance problems as a resource person and as a mentor.

When the project manger discovers that the unsatisfactory performance is basically caused by lack of effort on the part of a task leader or the task team, he or she faces a classic disciplinary problem. Lessons derived from the training of supervisors will guide this response.

The project manager must clearly and precisely identify what is not happening that should be happening. Opinions and impressions do not stand up here—data of some relevance must be uncovered. If work progress during the time the task has been underway can be compared to other similar efforts and it is clear that the task is unreasonably and slowly progressing, then this data must be discussed. If work progress is much slower than the task leader committed to during discussions while preparing the Gantt chart, then this data must be discussed. If problems that will affect the outcome have emerged and have not been addressed, then this must be discussed. Never approach a project team member with the statement, "I think there is a problem with how the task is progressing" unless and until you are well prepared to explain why you think there is a problem.

Whenever the project manager raises a question about task performance with a task leader, it must be presented with this attitude: *We* have a problem, let's try to figure out what *we* can do about it.

The problem is always addressed as soon as possible, with the task leader *in private* and *on the task leader's own turf*. The project manager always goes to the task leader. The project manager never asks the task leader to come to him.

At this point, the project manager and the task leader discuss whether or not there really is a problem. If the task leader accepts the perception that there is a problem, the discussion proceeds to "What can *we* do about it?" When this discussion ends with action items, it is desirable that the action items are captured in a written work plan on which both the task leader and the project manager are willing to sign off.

If the task leader does not accept the perception that there is a problem, even though it is clear that the task will not be performed well or as scheduled, more firm discipline is required. The project manager writes out his or her perception of the problem with consideration of the current and projected project impact, gives the task leader a copy, and invites him or her to a discussion with the resource manager or supervisor to whom the task leader permanently reports. With or without the task team leader, the project manager promptly schedules a meeting with the resource manager using the prepared documentation. The project manager then asks the resource manager for backup with disciplinary action to get the task back on track, or if necessary, the removal of the task leader and the assignment of a satisfactory replacement. If this does not work, the project manager takes the problem to the project sponsor, seeking his or her help. This help is necessary. There must be discipline and order in the project's workplace and among the project's team members.

There are variations possible for this approach that all seek the same result—due diligence devoted to the project task. The project manager must always be prepared to act when discipline is called for. Always discipline workers using a careful, responsible process; give team members every chance to make corrections at steps along the way but do not ignore the problem and hope it will go away. In addition, be sure to document your actions. You are a manager with managerial responsibilities!

It is very important to follow the procedure described here before taking the problem to the project sponsor. It should be clear to everyone on the team that all reasonable steps will be taken before seeking outside intervention; they must believe that this approach is not a threat to any of them. At the same time, the team must realize that the project is important and that the project manager will not ignore unpleasant problems.

MILESTONES AND PROJECT REVIEWS

Milestone project review meetings are points where the team and other stakeholders briefly reconvene. A milestone meeting is scheduled at a point where the project plan has progressed and some of the tasks have been completed (see Figure 12-5). The attendees review the project's success and risk factor utilization. In addition, they use the opportunity to keep downstream task leaders in touch with the project. They do not, however, critique individual performances, nor do they micro manage. Milestone and review meetings should *never bring about any surprises or replanning*. Milestones celebrate success. The project manager and the individual team members handle the other factors offline, before the milestone meetings.

Two milestone points seem to identify themselves on the "Build a House" critical path chart shown in Figure 12-5 (originally presented in Chapter 8). The roughing-in phase is finished at the end of Day 8. The morning of Day 9 is a natural milestone and point for a brief project review meeting. The main finishing work is completed at the end of Day 19. The morning of Day 20 also makes a very good milestone point. It calls for a project review just before the final touches of the house are applied.

Milestone points are often appropriately placed after a risk factor. One would not insert a risk factor until Day 20 on the "Build a House" path because not enough tasks are on the critical path to justify an earlier risk factor calculation. (Only six tasks are on the critical path at the Day nine milestone.) Six tasks do not provide enough risk distribution to justify calculating a risk factor here. By Day

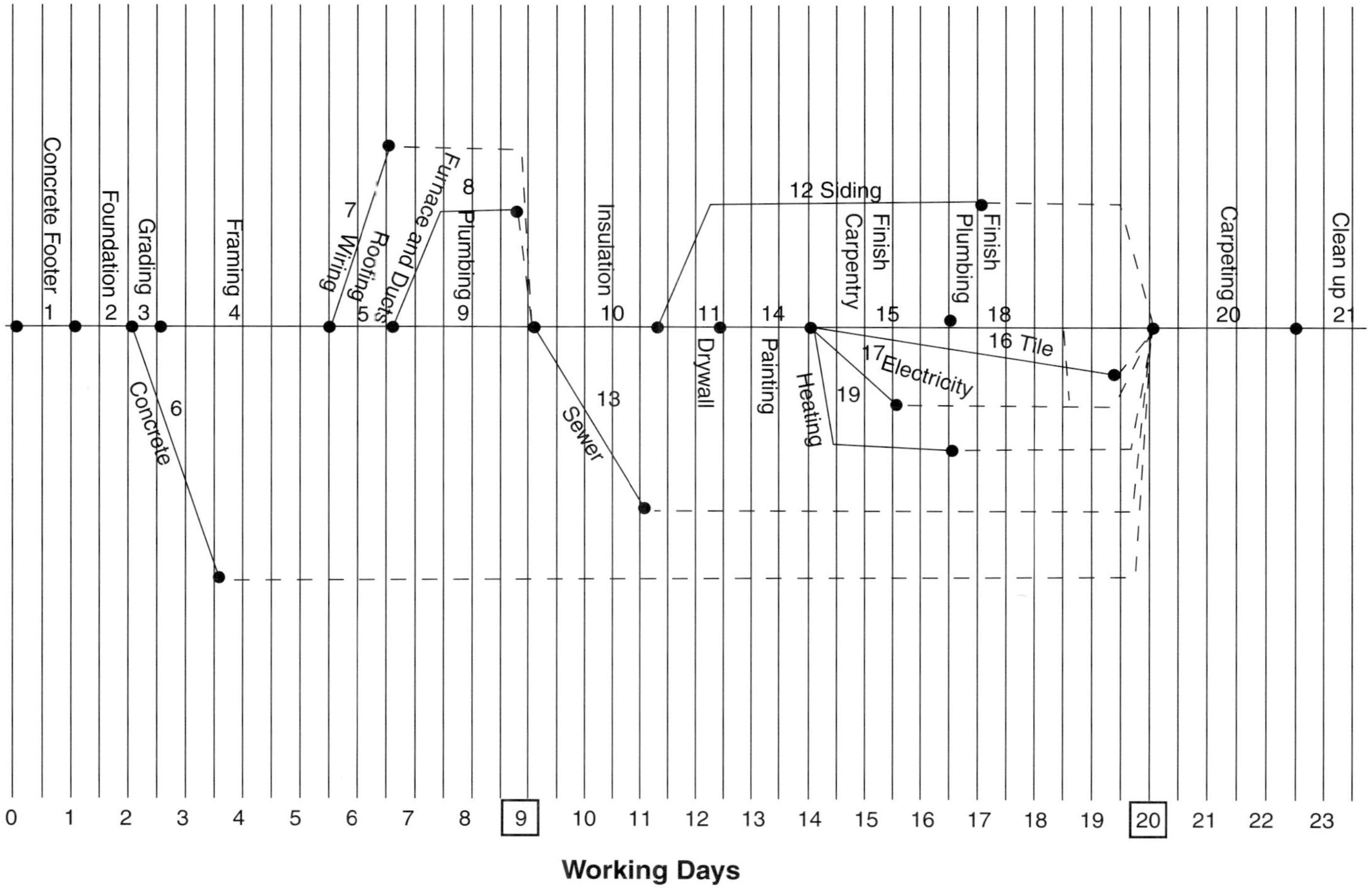

Concrete Footer 1
Foundation 2
Grading 3
Framing 4
6
Concrete
7
Wiring
Roofing 5
8
Furnace and Ducts
Plumbing 9
Insulation 10
13
Sewer
11
Drywall
14
Painting
12 Siding
Finish Carpentry 15
Finish Plumbing 18
16 Tile
17 Electricity
19
Heating
Carpeting 20
Clean up 21
0
1
2
3
4
5
6
7
8
9
10
11
12
13
14
15
16
17
18
19
20
21
22
23
Working Days

Figure 12-5

20, 11 tasks on the critical path are completed, which gives just enough spread to support a risk analysis and risk factor calculation. If this did not represent the end of the project, the milestone would stand, but the risk analysis would be delayed until at least 20 critical path tasks had been completed.

THE REASONS BEHIND MILESTONE MEETINGS

Milestone meetings are important. These meetings are discussion meetings about what is happening and what is projected, and they follow an agenda that is prepared and distributed by the project manager. The minutes of the meeting are kept by a designee of the project manager and are distributed to all of the team members and the project stakeholders. The milestone meeting is one tool for keeping the project's team members connected to the project. As previously noted, the team members, whose tasks do not begin for months into the future, can easily lose track of where they fit in the project. Milestone meetings and the minutes of these meetings are distributed to help keep them connected. (You should distribute the minutes by e-mail along with a personal e-mail note to each team leader.)

Persons whose tasks are far in the future may not attend the current milestone meetings, but everyone whose task is recently completed, whose task is currently ongoing, or whose task will start within the next two months, should get a personal invitation from the project manager to attend. Task leaders will be scheduled to report the following:

- What we have done and how that may affect "you" downstream
- What we are doing, how it may affect parallel tasks, and how this may affect task teams downstream
- What the team members downstream need from the team members who are currently working on tasks

Some task leaders have special needs that are met at milestone meetings. The people who have responsibilities for writing user's guides, installation manuals, service manuals, hot line resource dictionaries, quality assurance, testing, and other product or service support documents find it much easier to do their jobs if they can regularly attain information as it develops.

The completion of every project should include the compilation of a project report that the project manager excerpts from his or her project diary. The milestone meetings and the minutes of these meetings provide an excellent supplementary source for this report.

The sponsor, resource managers, financial managers, suppliers, and the product or service line managers need to be kept abreast of a project's progress. All of them should be invited to the milestone meetings and receive the milestone minutes.

The project manager should have a tight agenda, limit the discussions to project team participation, and take care of the concerns of non-project team attendees "off line." The meeting should be as short as is functionally satisfactory and should never be more than two hours.

It can be difficult to get all of the project team members and stakeholders together for a review of the project's progress. If this happens, the project manager may have to substitute an effective status report at the time of a scheduled milestone meeting. The project status report should cover three primary areas of the project: Time, cost, and scope.

The time report covers the tasks completed during the past period, tasks that are underway, tasks to be started during the next work period, and tasks that were expected to be completed but have not been completed. For tasks expected to be completed but not yet completed, the report should cover how the team will be resolving the issues and when completion is projected. Note that these currently incomplete tasks are using up an identifiable portion of the risk factor.

When reporting on cost, the report should review current expenditures to date, over budget and under budget areas, and how these facts relate to the budgeted reserve associated with the risk factor. The cost operating Gantt chart is the source of this information.

When reporting on project scope, the report should cover any changes that have been proposed for the specification and their disposition. If the changes have been accepted and replanning has been done, you should include the revised Gantt chart in the report and explain the rationale behind accepting these changes.

Conversely, there are important things that the milestone meeting and status reports do not do. They do not manage the project. The project manager manages the project with walk-about management and individual consultations with task leaders or small groups of task leaders, which occur as the circumstances require. Any problems, including discipline problems, are handled by the project manager during the project manager's walk-about managerial efforts.

The project manager keeps tight control over the milestone meeting and squelches anyone's attempt to change or micromanage the project. A special warning is in order here. Too often, project meetings are wide open, where many people try to tell others what to do and how to do it. Individuals can come to a meeting with a chip on their shoulder and want to criticize others. Individuals also may bring suggestions for project changes. *None of this can be allowed!* Although well-organized IPM projects do not have much trouble with this, the project manager always must be alert.

The project manager often can manage meetings and guide team and sponsor expectations through the use of up-to-date project documentation as disclosed on the operations Gantt chart. This project documentation is made up of the statement of work, which includes the project scope discussion and the specification, the updated working Gantt chart and related charts and tables, all change request and reports of their resolution, risk documentation, and budget/cost information. The project manager must always keep in mind that this documentation is only as good as the updates. If the operations Gantt chart is not kept up to date and is not fully representative of all of the approved changes, it is of little value to the project team.

For projects that are not set up with IPM plans and IPM discipline, milestone meetings often turn into angry discussions. Thus, the project falls apart.

The action item that result from a good milestone meeting is that the project will proceed as planned, with some intensified communication between some team members who particularly need to talk to each other.

MOVEMENT TOWARD COMPLETION

By using an updated operations Gantt chart as an ever-present reference, walk-about management, milestone meetings, and an open door policy, a project manager can move a project toward the time when the team can clearly, unequivocally, and measurably demonstrate that they have met the projects objectives.

SUMMARY

The project manager gets the project started on time and keeps it on time. He or she stays in close contact with the project by walking about and talking to the project's task leaders. He or she does not sit in an office waiting for information to arrive. The project manager stimulates task problem-solving by asking probing questions during walk-about and by offering to help secure outside assistance. The project manager keeps team members and stakeholders connected to the project through milestone meetings and updated status reports. He or she ensures that the project team members talk to each other.

If discipline is called for, the project manager does not shy away from this managerial responsibility. In disciplinary action, he or she carefully observes the modern rules of due process.

DISCUSSION QUESTIONS

1. What are the perceptions of task leaders that can cause a project to start late and for successor tasks not to start as scheduled?
2. What is walk-about management?

3. How is the project manager's mentor/support role played out during a project's execution?
4. What is the function of a milestone meeting; of a status report?
5. What does a status report cover?
6. What are the steps of due process when administering discipline?

13 PROJECT CHANGE

INTRODUCTION

Few projects proceed from beginning to end without some change in the specified outcome(s) or in the methods used to achieve these outcomes. The introduction of change into a project must be managed carefully, or the project will fall apart. A change committee, consisting of a customer representative, key task leaders, and a financial representative, that is chaired by the project manager must be established at the project's inception. This committee must develop a set of change procedures that will be rigorously followed.

MANAGEMENT OF CUSTOMER INDECISIONS

A project manager must begin working on a project with the expectation that the customer will request change at least once, perhaps several times, regarding the project outcome(s). The project manager must be prepared for the possibility that a task leader or an external subject matter expert will discover and present a new or better way to perform tasks after the completion of the task list. If the proposed change occurs during the project planning period, it can be accommodated by backing up the planning process and replanning with the change(s) in mind. Before this is done, however, the project manager must create a new, revised specification statement and clear it with the customer, appropriate subject matter experts, and key team members. The project must always be working toward one clear goal, and all prior specifications must be destroyed.

Change requests that arise during the project's planning process are not hard to deal with if they are few and infrequent. Changes do interrupt the planning process and cost time and money, but aside from that and the frustrations the team experiences, they can be handled effectively. When a customer is uncertain about exactly what he or she wants and frequently changes his or her mind this must be dealt with as a special case.

Customers often want a project to begin before they have decided on a precise outcome. They may not expect to be able to precisely define what they want for some time. However, IPM is based on the premise that a precise outcome statement—specification—must be decided upon before planning can begin. Both experience and logic support this proposition. Nevertheless, when thinking is at the scope level, it is often reasonable for the customer to be uncertain of the precise outcomes. Can an integrated project be started under these conditions? The answer is yes. A preliminary specification can be created. A project manager begins the project by leading the creation of this specification.

As the project manager helps migrate the project from scope to specification, he or she aims for a precise specification that will capture the *current* best estimates of what the outcome should be. This specification will be used in the initial planning and execution of the project. At the same time, the project manager puts in place a project specification change procedure to deal efficiently with the outcome changes the customer may desire later on.

Experience has proven that this approach is more efficient than simply starting in a general direction, then adjusting, redirecting, and reorganizing as an outcome concept emerges. It must be understood that in IPM, replanning will be a major event and will not take place piecemeal. It will not occur often during the life of the project. Small and frequent modifications of the specification must be prevented because such practices kill projects.

The rationale for insisting on the creation of a specification before starting project planning derives from the processes that must take place when the change in a project is executed. Before a project can be changed, there must be something to change. The effort to get the customer to agree on what the "current" best estimate of what the outcome should be is defined within the statement of work. Sometimes, customers do not decide on exactly what they want until they see what is involved in providing them with what they think they want. Sometimes, the general dimensions of an outcome are identified, but the exact characteristics of the outcome must wait on "research in progress." The customer and the project manager agree that a precise outcome definition within the general framework of the expected outcome will enable the project manager to begin the project planning.

It also will provide for the startup of project execution. The initial plan is expected to be relevant when the revised outcome statement is decided upon.

Creation of the initial project plan gives the project team something useful to do now, and it creates a good plan for the team to examine and change when a specification revision is presented. This fits in with the fundamental process of project change. When a change is proposed, the original project plan—the Gantt chart and the resource table—is the necessary reference for the considerations of what can be done and what this will cost.

THE CHANGE COMMITTEE: STRUCTURE AND PROCEDURES

Change is inevitable. It is unrealistic to expect to execute a project exactly as planned—although sometimes it does happen. Allowing change to haphazardly creep into a project at the task level is fatal. When planning is completed, it is devastating to be expected to fudge tasks and add elements to accommodate new objectives without also changing the project Gantt chart. Therefore, it is absolutely necessary at the kickoff meeting to appoint a change committee to implement change procedures covering all possibile changes. The project manager should chair this change committee. He or she should keep the records, receive the change requests, and promptly convene the committee to deal with these requests. The project manager may be able to personally deal with the requests for small changes. Yet, even in the case of small changes, he or she must document the changes in a report that is given to the person requesting the change, the change committee, and the project team.

To be efficient, the change committee must be kept small. It also must be able to call on various subject matter experts to help evaluate any proposed changes. Committee membership should include at least one empowered customer representative, an accounting representative (to provide cost analysis), and key project task leaders.

Change procedures are simple and straightforward. Written approval from the change committee is mandatory before a change can be implemented. Every change, including the customer's change must be submitted in writing on the following change request form and the change committee will respond with its report:

Project Change Request

1. List the benefits from the change, or why the change is necessary. The reason for requesting this change is______________________.
2. What does the change consist of?
3. What time and resource requirements are associated with the change?
4. How will the change affect the cost of the project?

Change Committee Report

1. Disposition:
   Change approved
   or
   Change rejected
   or
   Change approved in part
2. How is the project affected?
3. The rationale for the committee decision is____________________.

A person requesting the change must provide the following information:

- The reason for the change and how it will benefit the project
- What the change consists of and how it will affect the project's outcomes, process, and timing
- Estimates, with explanations of any new timing and resource requirements believed to be needed
- An Estimate on how the change will affect the cost of the project

Having to think through and document these items will eliminate many frivolous change requests. It is especially important that the customer understands and agrees to use this process, because it is clearly in his or her best interest.

The procedures that the change committee follows must be clear to all members of the project team and to all of the stakeholders. Change requests are to be submitted to the project manager, who will always give them prompt attention. He or she will examine the change request and place it in one of three categories: Trivial, Feasible, or Not Feasible.

Trivial changes are changes that the project manager can easily deal with. They clearly do not negatively affect project process, cost, or outcome. They do need to be addressed, and their disposition must be reported. One example of a trivial change might be a customer's request to have the project reports bound in flex bindings with blue instead of red covers. Although this change is very simple, it must be documented and passed on to the task leader who is responsible for publishing the project report, or it will not happen. No cost changes or time changes seem necessary.

A very conscientious task leader may discover that with a small additional effort, he or she can produce an outcome that significantly improves the accuracy of a measuring instrument being developed for the project. A question for the project manager to deal with is, "Does this improved accuracy contribute to the objective(s) of the project?" Technical people often are fascinated with achieving exquisite outcomes. They enjoy doing things very well. But, if the project does not profit from the improved accuracy, the extra effort should not be supported. The project manager, through direct inquiries, can determine whether "improved accuracy" contributes to the value of the project's outcome. If the project outcome can become more valuable to the outcome users as a result of this change in the task effort and the cost is negligible, the project manager may consider this change for approval.

There are other considerations, however. With reference to this and most proposed changes, the project manager looks at the Gantt chart and the resource table. Is there slack available for this task, and is the task team's time open for the additional effort? If people are available, task timing on the project permits it, the costs are negligible, and the project output gains value for the customer, the project manager approves the change. Checking with people, and checking the charts, tables, and the cost for something like the proposed change often does not take much more of the project manager's time than it takes to read about it. Although documenting the process and the decision may take a little longer, it must be done. Documentation of negative decisions is as important as documentation of positive decisions. Sometimes, the same proposal comes up repeatedly. Having good documentation means that you only have to consider the proposal once.

Changes that are not feasible generally cost too much, take too long, or both. The project generally has a time and cost upper limit, which is defined by the sponsor explicitly or implicitly. The sponsor may request a change that is outside this realm without realizing it. The project Gantt chart and the resources table are the measuring tools that the project manager uses. He or she examines the proposed change and compares it to the work packages and tasks on the Gantt chart that are related to it. If it costs $100,000 to do one easily identifiable part of the work, and the change being considered will require a very similar addition of effort, the project manager can reasonably estimate that the change will add another $100,000 to the project's cost. Without the Gantt chart as a reference, the project manager probably would have to do a good deal of analysis to arrive at this conclusion. However, because these changes are always somewhat related to what has already been planned, there is a good chance that their costs can be estimated by referring to work that has already been planned. The project manager can determine an approximate cost that is not obvious to the customer, and can report this cost with an explanation of how it has been determined. The customer makes the final decision about cost feasibility. Knowing the customer's constraints, the project manager will report the cost of the change as something that does not appear feasible.

A similar consideration, analyzed with reference to the Gantt chart, may be related to a resource's availability. The change being requested for may call for the use of resources that are not available and never will be.

Dealing with trivial changes and changes that are not feasible generally does not require a meeting of the change committee. Dealing with such changes, however, does call for a report to the change committee, the change requestor, and the interested stakeholders.

The remaining category of change request—feasible changes—deals with adding time and effort that appears to be within the cost and time tolerance limits. A detailed examination of what additional tasks or task extensions are necessary must be done to determine what affect the change would have on the project and whether or not it can be considered to be cost effective. To deal with this type of change, the project manager will convene the change committee and invite the appropriate subject experts to draft a rough plan for including the change in the project. Because changes always relate to what has been planned and what has been done, the Gantt chart and the resource table are important sources of data for extending the project. (If the change proposal is not related to what is planned for the project, the proposal calls for a new project.)

When the rough plan for the inclusion of the change request has been worked out by the change committee, the approximate cost, and the time and resource requirements for the change are identified. These costs and resource demands can be measured against the benefits achieved by a successful change to provide a basis for the change committee's decision. The final call on this change is generally up to the customer, but the change committee has provided good data for the customer to use in making a decision.

If the customer decides that the change effort is worth the cost in terms of the benefits that accompany it, the project manager reconvenes the project team or the affected units of the project team and, replans the project in detail. The new specification—the specification that includes the outcomes the change is to achieve—is published along with the *new* Gantt chart and resource table. All older materials then must be taken out of circulation.

If the change is approved, the project team will reconvene to replan the project. With a major change, the basic project planning steps—creation of a task list, Gantt chart redesign, and risk analysis—must be carried out. Work resumes when the new project plan is completed.

Project change does not involve tearing up the Gantt chart and starting over. The existing chart provides a major reference for replanning the project. The new Gantt chart will significantly resemble the old chart. Although replanning will not require as much time as did the original project planning, it still is absolutely necessary. The old chart must be permanently set aside, and the new one must be used exclusively. Remember, the new chart reflects the project's changes!

If the change is fundamental, the old Gantt chart must be torn up, and planning must be redone, which means starting a new project. In this case, it is important to close out the old project before starting anew.

As the project progresses, suggestions for small changes often are made. However, continually dealing with small changes is never functional. The project leader must make judgment calls as to their consideration. Generally, these changes are processed after being batched and considered together. The process of making changes and replanning must not occur often. In a one-year project, generally only one or, at the most, two, major project changes should be processed. If multiple changes are allowed throughout the life of the project, it can cause a specification creep. In many organizations, this is called "scope creep." Monitoring and managing the changes to the specification is the key to delivering of the project on time and within budget.

If the change is not approved, the project manager should ensure that the reasons for its denial are documented with the change request. This documentation is imperative for all projects, but more so for major and macro projects due to changing team dynamics. As project sponsors or team members are added or removed from the project, many of the same changes may be requested. By keeping a change log of all of the requested changes, the project manager is able to quickly bring any new team members up to speed.

PROJECT CHANGE CONTROL

When changes must be made that will change the plan, the project manager must control and track them. The following are the guidelines for controlling changes

Guidelines for Controlling Change

1. Changes can be requested by anyone associated with the project, but submitting the Project Change Request Form to the project manager and the project change committee will start the change process.
2. Project change requests must be evaluated to determine the effect of a request.
3. The project manager and the team must estimate the effort, dependencies, and resources required to institute the project change.
4. The project manager must communicate the impact of proposed changes in terms of cost, scheduling, and performance to the customer.
5. If a change is approved, the signatures of the client and the project manager authorize the project team to make the requested change.
6. The project plan must be revised after the change has been approved for implementation.
7. The project manager must inform the project team of all approved, unapproved, and deferred changes.
8. The Project Change Request Form must be logged, regardless of its approval or denial.

EXAMPLES OF CHANGE REQUESTS AND CHANGE PROCESSING

The following are examples of project change requests and their processing:

1. The Project: Build a house on a designated lot according to its architectural plans.

The Change: Add a bedroom over the garage—the house construction is already in process.

The Action: The change committee takes a look at the new architectural drawings and notes that no additional skills are needed for the project team to make the addition. If the project has not passed the framing stage, no work has been done that will need to be removed or changed. The change committee directs the project manager to call together the necessary members of the project team to revise the project plan in order to accommodate the change. This change does not require any masonry or plumbing work. However, it will require extending the work of most of the other teams, but it will not require them to perform tasks different from those already scheduled.

The project manager convenes the project team, minus the masonry and plumbing task leaders. Beginning at the task level, the project manager leads the team in expanding the project to accommodate the change. Because only familiar efforts are involved in adding the change, it can be expected that replanning will be a short process and that the project can proceed with the extended time and cost requirements in an orderly fashion. The most serious problem may be scheduling the availability of the skilled craftsmen to take on additional effort. The availability of the skilled craftsmen may cause a significant delay in completing the project. If so, the customer must be informed. The customer has the choice of accepting the delay or directing the project manager to finish the project as originally planned. A new project to add the room can be considered later if the change is not made at this time.

This last consideration is a familiar one in facing project changes. Is it better to add a change, achieve a desired improved outcome, and fold the work into the project now or finish the original project and add on the improvement at a greater cost later? The basic mantra of project management is, "Finish the project, do the enhancements later." The rationale is that finishing the project brings satisfactory closure and provides a useful product. Adding enrichments to the project may "never end," and the product may be flawed in the process.

2. The Project: Develop a software package for a "modern" PC used by a small business that will process income and expenses and produce a monthly profit and loss statement and a balance sheet.

The Change: Add a payroll processing system to the package.

The Action: The change committee takes a look at the new requirement statement and asks for explanations from the customer's representative and the accounting subject matter expert. These specialists explain how a payroll system is processed, using paper and a pencil. The team notes that an accounting team and an IT systems analyst will need to work together to precisely define the project outcomes and to lay out the basic system for achieving these outcomes. There is a desirable interface with the originally planned accounting package, and the same people who can use one can use the other. However, the payroll system is fundamentally a new project. The change committee recommends to the customer that the development of a payroll system to go along with the original accounting package be treated as a separate basic project. The two basic projects can proceed as two units of a major project, and a major project manager can be appointed to lead the two basic project managers in developing the interfaces.

3. The Project: Develop a sheet metal cleaning machine that will remove all dust and oil from 4′ by 10′ sheet metal sheets up to 1/4′ thick before they are processed in the presses.

The Change: Add the capability of removing rust and corrosion in the cleaning process.

The Action: The change committee convenes with the subject matter experts on rust and corrosion. They learn that the basic cleaning process and the mechanical design may remain the same, but that the degreaser liquid used will have to be supplemented with another solvent, and perhaps, an added brushing process. The project manager will have to reconvene the project team and add a solvent subject matter expert. This new team will create a fundamental product redesign—one that can use some of the already developed parts. This is a new project that uses some of the parts the old project has created. The team will be able to move faster in the redesign and development planning because they have covered much of this information before.

It will be possible to arrive at a rough cost estimate for the new product because the original plan will support an extrapolation of the time and cost estimates. It is essentially, however, a new project whose time and cost cannot be confidently determined until the new project plan is completed. The customer will receive this information and will make the decision regarding whether or not to implement the change. Until the customer makes this decision, in most cases, the project team will continue with the original project plan.

SUMMARY

A project manager works with the project customer to ensure that project execution always will be directed toward a precise objective while maintaining flexibility so that the customer can change the objective somewhat while project work is in progress. Such a change requires that a project change committee be formed to handle it. In addition, a well-defined and disciplined change procedure must be implemented, which can be used to modify the project objective(s) and—when change is decided upon—modify the project plan.

DISCUSSION QUESTIONS

1. If a project task leader, during a project's execution, comes up with a bright idea that will significantly improve the effectiveness of the project's product, how should he or she proceed?
2. Who has final authority over what, when, and how the changes are introduced into the project?
3. Why is it very important to document change requests?
4. Why is it important to document decisions of the change committee?

14 ACHIEVING CLOSURE

INTRODUCTION

As a project nears completion, the project manager continues to support the team by visiting their workstations to check on their progress and to track their tasks. Working with the change committee to clear up any confusion that may have resulted when changes were approved is especially important at this point.

The final steps that the project manager is responsible for are: 1) ensuring that the project's achievement is demonstrated, 2) getting the sponsor to sign off on a project after having successfully met the objectives, 3) preparing a project report, and 4) working out the details of the project completion celebration.

PROJECT CLOSURE

Managing a significant project is absolutely a full-time job. The project manager is kept extremely busy near a project's end, monitoring its progress and preparing for shutdown. When walking about and visiting the workstations, he or she must re-emphasize the need for good communication among task leaders; encourage the give and take that supports the internal customer principle; be attentive to the project timetable; actively help task leaders get their tasks started and completed on time; monitor the Gantt chart; and as some original estimates overrun, alert downstream task leaders to the scheduling changes. If a task finishes early, which occasionally happens, more time is bought for the risk factor. With an early finish, the project manager must help downstream task leaders readjust their start time; when a task overruns, he or she helps marshal the resources identified in the task notes file to cover the overrun.

Should a change in the project become necessary, the project must be replanned, with the project manager scheduling the replanning meetings, drafting agendas, and leading the meetings. When a revised plan has been approved, and the sponsor and the project manager have both signed off on it, all of the old plan's Gantt charts must be destroyed, and every downstream task leader—for tasks starting after the change was inserted—must be given a copy of the new Gantt chart.

The project manager must be alert to not allow changes that were initiated within tasks sneak into the project. Engineers and other technical people have a tendency to "over-engineer" their work to make their product exquisite. Generally, "good" is all that is needed; exquisite takes longer. During the walk-about, the project manager should watch out for "exquisite" and keep the task leaders focused on "good."

PROJECT ACHIEVMENT DEMONSTRATIONS

As the project nears the finish line, the project manager must keep the team focused on the project achievement demonstration that proves the specifications have been met. Often, team members tend to move toward a kind of "we did it; we know we did it; let someone else test it and prove it works" thinking. However, the demonstration is built into the project plan, and the project manager must ensure that the workers and other resources assigned to it are ready, and that the demonstration begins as scheduled.

The sponsor, or a chosen representative of the sponsor, must be present at the specification's demonstration to formally accept the project's completion and to sign off on the project. The project manager must ensure that the demonstration is efficiently and effectively presented and that the official is there and actually signs off on the formal acceptance of the project's completion. Remember, "If it isn't in writing, it hasn't been said."

THE PROJECT REPORT AND OTHER DOCUMENTATION

Any organization that is serious about completing projects to specifications, on time and within budget, makes a project report mandatory. Written by the project manager, this report explains how the project was done and why specific procedures were used. The information in the report is helpful to anyone using the project's product, and it serves as resource material for a project manager embarking on a similar project in the future.

The project manager's diary, notes from the milestone meetings, the original statement of work, the operation Gantt chart, and the task notes held in Gantt chart software become the principle sources for the information in the project report. One copy of this report goes to the project sponsor, and another is filed in the organization's archives.

The most important piece of documentation for future project planning is the project operation Gantt chart and its associated software products. Two versions should be preserved: The baseline Gantt chart that displays details of the original project plan; and the operation Gantt chart that displays the actual time and effort, task by task, used in executing the project. Anyone undertaking a similar project, or a project with similar work packages and tasks, can learn a great deal by looking at these charts.

With the advancement of project software, many software products are available to help manage project planning and execution. Many of these applications make use of a data warehouse or project repository. These applications have the ability to import and export project files and store the information from within their data files. The use of a data warehouse and project repository enables access to all project information and can aide a project manager and the project team in the creation of future projects.

The project manager must see to it that these documents are archived, along with important project elements, such as parts and assembly drawings, data dictionaries, data tables, and the results of technical analysis. An unfortunate tendency exists for project managers and team members to walk away from a completed project without capturing its basic project information and without reflecting upon what they have learned and how this can help others within their organization.

With the end in sight, the project manager should be alert to the possibility that a task team may have become so intrigued with what they are doing that they do not want to stop. It must be made clear to these people and to the accounting department that once the project has delivered on all objectives the project work has ceased, and no additional work may be charged to the project.

Two final responsibilities remain for the project manager: To distribute the project report (or a summary of it) to every team member and to convene the team to discuss "what we learned from the project." This discussion should be documented and amended to the report. All too often, what was learned in a project is lost. The review will help the team members recognize and retain the project's information, which then becomes a resource for future project planners. After the review has ended, it is time to celebrate!

PROJECT CLOSURE CELEBRATION

The workforce achieves project closure through a celebration. For a small project, this can be a pizza and pop luncheon in the conference room. A few appropriate coffee mugs might be presented to individuals who have made particularly significant contributions. These people also should be given copies of the commendation letters that the project manager forwarded to their function managers for their personnel files.

Larger projects mean larger celebrations. One large research systems analysis organization operates projects that typically take one year or more. Many hundreds of thousands of dollars go toward the project's personnel salaries. Their closure ritual is distinctive: On the hour that the project report is delivered to the customer, several support personnel and some project team members roll back the partitions dividing the auditorium, bring in an audio system, unlock the liquor cabinet, send out for hors d'oeuvres, pass the word throughout the organization, and telephone spouses, vendors, customers, directors, and other appropriate persons, to announce an open house. The partying can last 24 hours! It ends with a speech from the CEO and with the project manager handing out appropriate symbols of recognition.

These people end projects in grand style! Not surprisingly, their firm has a reputation for being very efficient and effective, with great creativity and a high morale.

EXAMPLES OF PROJECT CLOSURE

To finally close out a project, it is necessary to demonstrate that project goals have been achieved. This often requires a substantial, well-organized effort, which is planned early on, as is shown in the following examples.

Closing a Course Catalog Project: The project specification to produce a course catalog for a university management center states: Develop and produce 5,000 copies of a catalog describing each course, seminar, and workshop offered; it is to be organized by subject matter and provide the instructors' names and qualifications, the date, time, and place of the offering, and a statement of the benefits to be derived from attending the offering. The material must be organized so that a training manager or a prospective student can read it and easily find the needed course or seminar. This catalog must be suitable for mailing, according to the criteria of the U.S. Postal Service.

This specification sets forth the project's goals. Every detail outlined in the specification is a goal that must be accomplished. After it has been demonstrated that each detail has been taken care of, the catalog can go to press, and the project can be declared finished.

The center director served as the project sponsor of the catalog project, and the marketing manager was its project manager. To ensure that each specification detail would be completed properly and that none were left out, the sponsor and the project manager agreed that several people should review the finished galley proof. Each management center's subject area manager would read the catalog before its final printing, checking for overall accuracy and correct instructor qualifications. The scheduling clerk would check the date, time, and place for each offering. An independent training director was to sample the listings to ensure that the benefits were well stated and that it would be easy for a potential customer to find the needed seminar or course. An outside editor would be paid to review the galley proofs for correctness of form, punctuation, and spelling. Corrections would be made as required.

When all the reviews and the corrections were made and a clear galley proof was delivered, the project manager was ready to authorize the printer to print 5,000 copies and secure U.S. Postal Service approval for the catalog mailing. The center mail clerk eventually counted the boxes of catalog to ensure that 5,000 had been printed. This well-organized effort brought the project to a satisfactory closure. Anything less would have resulted in confusion for students and chaos for the management center.

Closing a Project for an Accounting System Designated for Small Commercial Firms: The project specification states: Develop a software package that will provide an accounting system capable of holding up to 500 accounts. The program shall provide for 1) entry of sales information of accounts receivable for up to 200 customers, with entries accurate to the penny, and up to $100,000; 2) an accounts payable entry system for 100 vendors, with the same dollar constraints; 3) the ability to automatically bill customers monthly, specifying a finance charge option of one percent a month for accounts 30 days overdue; 4) the ability to automatically write checks for vendors whose payments come due, with a manual override for checks to be issued selectively; 5) a monthly profit and loss statement and balance sheet. The program will be written in C++ language to run with a UNIX operating system on a machine with 9 GB of disk storage.

A demonstration of every item in the specification is necessary before this project can be considered closed. Early on in product development, the project manager and the sponsor carefully considered how to do this. The project team would develop ways to test the components and a package using the names of a hypothetical chart of accounts and balances at the beginning of an accounting period and a list of transaction entries for a hypothetical one-month accounting period. They would enter the account data into a computer in the firm where the software package was to be tested, and they would introduce transactions through journal entries. They would create the situation of an overdue account, issue some special checks to vendors, close the books at the end of the accounting period, and print out a profit and loss statement and balance sheet.

However, this was not enough for closure. One product of the project was a user guide for the customer, explaining how to set up and use the software. Because the product was developed for a broad range of customers who were to buy the software package, several potential customers would have to test it. This type of test, which is done by a customer's staff at the customer's site, is called a *Beta test*. The hypothetical material used in the initial testing was incomplete. The customer's staff, following the user guide to install the software and install their data on the software, would do so over a certain period of time. This must be a time period already processed using paper and a pencil. The customer would repeat processing the test month, using the computer to show that results were identical with the paper and pencil procedure.

While the product was going through its Beta test, the project manager was writing up a report that included the information needed by a "hot line" operator or the customer service specialist, to deal with the bugs that inevitably would emerge.

The project was ready for closure when the Beta tests were successfully completed, and the project report was completed, discussed, and delivered. Then, the project was complete, and it was time to celebrate!

The software package is not a unique example. Many projects require the same type of treatment to be brought to closure. A project not brought to closure remains uncertain in that it is always being fixed, adjusted, or improved. Sometimes, it even drifts away from the satisfactory results that were once achieved. There is a bit of wisdom in project management that says, "Finish the project; leave the improvements to the next edition."

The project manager should work with the sponsor and the customer early in the project to formulate a plan to demonstrate project completion, and they should stick to it!

Closing a Project to Build a House: Some closure is simple. When a good contractor finishes building a house, he arranges a walk-through for the customer to look over the house. He then makes notes on the necessary touchups, completes the touchups, and literally *closes* the sale. But, as with other projects, some owners move in early, and their houses never get finished.

SUMMARY

There is a necessary intensity in a project manager's walkabout practice as project completion approaches. The project manager and the customer must have agreed at the beginning of the project how successful project completion will be demonstrated. As closure approaches, the project manager focuses the project team on successfully performing this demonstration. Closure also requires that a project report be prepared by the project manager and distributed to the customer and project team leaders and filed in the company's project archives.

After everything is finished, the project manager gathers the team together to review "what we have learned" and wraps it all up with a project completion celebration.

DISCUSSION QUESTIONS

1. How do you know when you are finished with a project?
2. What do you do when you are finished?
3. Why does a project manager prepare a project report?
4. Who benefits from this project report?

15 ON BEING AN IPM TEAM MEMBER

INTRODUCTION

The roles played by IPM team members differ greatly from those played by teams using other project management methods. The big differences center around planning and communication.

Most frequently with other methods, the project manager does all the planning. Sometimes a project manager will seek task recommendations and time estimates from specialists who may end up doing the project work, but their input is advisory. The project manager will act on this input to develop the final project task list, the sequence list, and the task times estimates, and will assign team members tasks within the expected sequence, indicating how long each task should take. When a task worker or group completes a task(s), their association with the project often ends. Frequently, workers do not even discover they are involved in a project until just before their input is needed. They are simply assigned a task, and they do it.

IPM team members have far greater project involvement. They are recruited for the project and learn about the project's objectives and IPM methodology before planning begins. Each team member must accept the responsibility to ask questions and share in discussions during team meetings until they all understand the project's objectives and how they are to cooperatively plan the project and achieve its objectives. They must be prepared to help schedule meetings, participate in collaborative leadership at these meetings, reach outside their own experience to gather task suggestions, and develop task time and risk estimate data. They also must communicate effectively at the meetings and during the project's execution and contribute to the project's report.

If the team members accept these responsibilities and enthusiastically take ownership of a project, it has a very good chance for success. If not, the project will depend heavily on the project manager. It will take longer to execute and have less chance for success.

DETAILS OF TEAM MEMBER PARTICIPATION

During recruitment, the project manager thoroughly explains the role of a team member to each recruit. To ensure good communication, recruits should ask questions to clarify terms and concepts and make a frank and accurate assessment of how other commitments may impact their participation within the project. If necessary, the recruit, accompanied by the project manager, must be willing to discuss availability for the project with the recruit's supervisor.

While working on project it is important for a team member to show interest in the project and be committed to it, but *only he or she can make this happen.* Interest and commitment begin by understanding a project's goals and the priority that the project has been given within an organization. The team first learns this information at the kickoff meeting. All the details of what the project is to accomplish and why it is being undertaken are spelled out in this meeting. Because they are encouraged to query the project manager to clarify anything puzzling, no team member should leave the kickoff meeting not understanding a project's goals and priorities.

Understanding IPM project planning is equally important. Project planning is at the heart of IPM, and it likely will be new to most team members. The project manager will work hard to explain the process. Team members should ask questions until they fully understand the process.

Each team member must participate in a collaborative decision-making process. This process begins by taking part in the effort to create the norms to be used during the project meetings. Team members then must accept the norms and support them.

Team members are asked to play team leadership roles. The project manager will explain the collaborative leadership process and the roles to be played at the kickoff meeting. A team member must be prepared to spontaneously remind the rest of team that they are violating their own norms, when this seems appropriate. A team member must feel free to ask the team to invite input from a knowledgeable but silent member, and to alternatively remind them to hear and respect each person's input. A team member must be alert should a leadership opportunity arise during the team meetings, and must not hesitate to voice a norm reminder, request feedback or broad participation, or emphasize the importance of moving toward consensus. At the same time, other team members must be encouraged to play collaborative leadership roles. In short, it is important that team members participate as partners with the project manager in managing and planning the project—but be careful not to dominate the procedure.

This is a big order. It calls for a level of involvement, judgment, and maturity not always expected of individuals in the workplace. Yet, many people respond positively when given a chance and a good reason to do so.

The activities required of team members go beyond collaborative leadership participation. It is crucial to successful project planning for the team to develop an all-inclusive task list. To contribute effectively to this effort, each team member should request help in identifying tasks from others persons who have experience in similar projects.

Seeking outside input does not end with the development of the task list. The project manager will communicate the importance of good task time estimates. To develop these estimates, the team member must again, "ask other experienced people for help," and if this becomes a problem, the team member must request assistance from the project manager. The required estimates include the "most of the time" task duration, the worst-case time requirement, and the likelihood of not finishing on time, which is given in a percentage.

The estimates then are brought to team meetings and presented to the team. Each team member must be willing to share constructively his or her opinion of the others' estimates and recognize that after discussion, the team member responsible for a task has the final say. When presenting estimates, a team member must listen thoughtfully to suggestions before making the final decision.

A team member must review risk sources and calculate a risk factor for each task, identify step-function risks if they might occur, and participate with the team in identifying risk insertion points for the risk factors and in determining the size of the risk factor at each insertion point.

When the planning is finished and project execution begins, each team member is responsible for keeping in touch with the project's progress and for timing his or her participation. Although much help will be forthcoming from the project manager, it is the team member's responsibility to pay close attention to the project.

Team members can aid a project's execution by communicating their needs to each other and by sharing information about their task's progression. They must be willing to play the two-way role of internal customer and to promptly communicate with the project manager if any problems arise.

None of this is easy. Many individuals have expressed doubt over the willingness of American workers to take on so much responsibility. There is much skepticism, with the skeptics resorting to authoritarian project management. However, in the modern American workplace, teams have repeatedly proven to be effective and productive. *Industry Week* magazine is a premier, down to earth, manufacturing management publication. In *Industry Week*'s yearly review of America's most productive manufacturing organizations, teams and teaming are consistently the prime elements in the success of "America's best companies."

Teams work well for project management. If a supportive environment exists in the organization undertaking the project and the team members give teaming a chance, all will be well rewarded.

SUMMARY

Project success depends heavily on team members' willingness to share in the collaborative leadership of the project, to responsibly gather task data, and to proactively contribute to a project's internal communication.

DISCUSSION QUESTIONS

1. What is the difference between the roles that members of a traditional project workgroup are expected to play and the roles that IPM project team members are asked to play?
2. How does a team member's unwillingness to play IPM team member roles impact a project's outcome?
3. Is being an IPM team member easy?
4. If you were appointed to an IPM project team, would you
   - Know how to carry out the role of an effective IPM team member?
   - Be willing to take on IPM team member responsibilities?
5. What are the consequences when a competent IPM project manager inherits a workgroup whose members are unwilling to play IPM team member roles? What can be done about this?
6. Does the history of American industry show the workers' willingness to learn and play team roles?

16 BASIC PROJECTS, MAJOR PROJECTS, AND MACRO PROJECTS

INTRODUCTION

Integrated Project Management (IPM) has evolved over many years. It owes its form and processes to the concepts and practices developed by project managers, and to managerial developments in other areas.

The collaborative project team emerged out of many team-focused managerial experiences, but it particularly owes its procedures to the concept of the self-managing work team. Self-managing work teams became significant in the late 1980s and have found a place in american industry. Consensus decision-making skills and collaborative leadership are self-managing work team practices.

Conflict resolution practices emerged out of modern industrial psychology and mediation practices. Good communication practices come from basic modern management. The affinity diagram is derived from modern quality initiatives. Elements of risk analysis were drawn from Taguchi's method of designing experiments to identify inputs that most affect the output of a process.

Discipline and order methods are taken directly from contemporary lessons for line supervisors. Discussions of Hewlett-Packard management styles led to the focus on walk-about management. It was John McConnel of Worthington Steel who reminded all of us to *talk to each other.*

The product of all of these concepts and practices has led to the creation of Integrated Project Management (IPM), and it works very well. IPM works for basic projects, but there are many projects that are too large and too complicated to be managed as basic projects. Basic projects can be the foundation for all projects; however, additional management structure is necessary for managing larger, more complicated projects.

Two levels of project management structure provide the framework for all projects above the basic project level. For us, it has been useful to classify projects as basic projects, major projects, and macro projects. However, the terms "basic project," "major project," and "macro project" are not widely used in project management literature.

BASIC PROJECTS AND THEIR LIMITATIONS

There are important reasons why the IPM practices used to manage basic projects are exceptionally efficient. These IPM practices are as follows:

1. Collaborating, competent project team members *share* in the project planning.
2. Planning time is kept short, and attention to planning is intensified by having project *team members working at planning efforts in parallel,* instead of sequentially.
3. Good communication and coordination is achieved by *short, efficient planning meetings* and by *walk-about management.*
4. *Risk analysis can be carefully done at the task level*, and risk time buffers are determined and applied at the project team level.

The IPM project management practices noted above that produce IPM results have the following limitations:

1. Collaborative management, team communication, and cooperation break down with more than 30 project team members. (Conventional wisdom, particularly regarding self-managing work teams, suggests that 12 members is a good upper limit for a collaborating team; however, the project management team has a structured, well-defined series of planning meetings with a facilitator and a well-developed plan to follow for execution that makes a somewhat larger group doable.)

2. Projects that involve several different technologies or methodologies can produce a situation in which one project manager does not have the breadth of knowledge and experience to effectively facilitate the planning and organizing in each subject area.

3. Walk-about management and communication facilitation capabilities for one individual can become overloaded when too many parallel tasks are being executed at the sametime.

A good solution is to break down the project into several parallel or sequential basic projects and add a level of management to coordinate the work of the several basic project managers. The project that takes on these characteristics is called a major project. A major project can function well with up to eight basic projects within it. When the needs of a project suggest a more complex pattern of management relationships than this, we refer to it as a macro project.

Categorizing projects as basic, major, and macro is useful when dealing with the full range of projects. Because these three types of projects vary in size and complexity, the project manager must approach the job of managing a project in each category differently.

THE BASIC PROJECT

After a project manager and a sponsor agree on a project's specification, the project manager can proceed to develop a work breakdown structure. Identifying the major tasks that can be broken down into work packages is the beginning of the project planning procedure. The project manager recruits the specialists indicated by the work packages for the project team, and with their assistance, he or she develops the project task list, assigning each task to a member of the project team to execute or to lead colleagues to execute. (A task is a work unit that needs no further breakdown to guide the task worker or task workgroup in executing the effort.)

When the work breakdown structure suggests that no more than 30 task leaders will be needed, the project fits the model for a basic project. The project team will be small enough so that the IPM principles of collaborative leadership can be comfortably and efficiently used.

Many small- and medium-sized project efforts have this characteristic; however, the designation of "small" or "medium" does not necessarily mean that a project will be short or simple. Altogether, the project could encompass several hundred tasks, some of which may be very challenging, possibly requiring several planned iterations to "get it right." Task workgroups may each be responsible for several or even dozens of tasks. Some tasks may take weeks or months to accomplish. Nevertheless, if one team of task leaders numbering 30 or less can cover all task responsibilities, the project is deemed to be a basic project and can be executed according to IPM methodology, with one person working full time in the project management role.

At some point, the project manager may recruit team leaders to assist with management as well as to participate in collaborative leadership. However, a single project manager can handle the responsibility of monitoring and guiding the execution of a basic project; a single project team can collaborate to do the work (see Figure 16-1).

THE VERY SMALL BASIC PROJECT

As with larger projects, the work breakdown structure must be created for a very small basic project: It can be embarrassing to omit this step and later discover that a work package was forgotten. In this type of project, the project manager should identify and recruit a project team (even if it consists of only three or four people) and gather them around a conference table and discuss the project planning with them. They should make out a plan and then work it. A single person, such as a graphic artist, circuit designer, or insurance actuary, may very competently perform a task but should not be left to work in isolation; simple IPM principles to keep in touch work well. It is important to have a project Gantt chart, to visit all team members during the project, to keep good communication flowing among them, and to keep their work coordinated, and by all means, the project manager should strive to finish on time. Small basic projects will often run on and on and never finish because the project manager did not bother to clearly define and coordinate the project.

A very small basic project often has a technical specialist acting as the project manager. In this project, this is a person who can and will perform some of the tasks. He or she will identify the other specialists needed for the project and will lead them in the project planning process. It is important that this project manager set aside some time to perform project management functions and realize that these functions must have top priority.

In some instances, a project manager may be responsible for several very small basic projects at the same time. The scheduling and timing of each project must be handled carefully so that no project gets short shrifted. Even though these projects may be managed informally, IPM fundamentals must be observed: The project manager should visit and communicate with team members and keep all the Gantt charts up to date. Overseeing multiple projects requires that the project manager be good at time management. Software packages, like Microsoft Project Management 2002®, can help, because they offer tools for planning and tracking small basic projects that are managed in parallel.

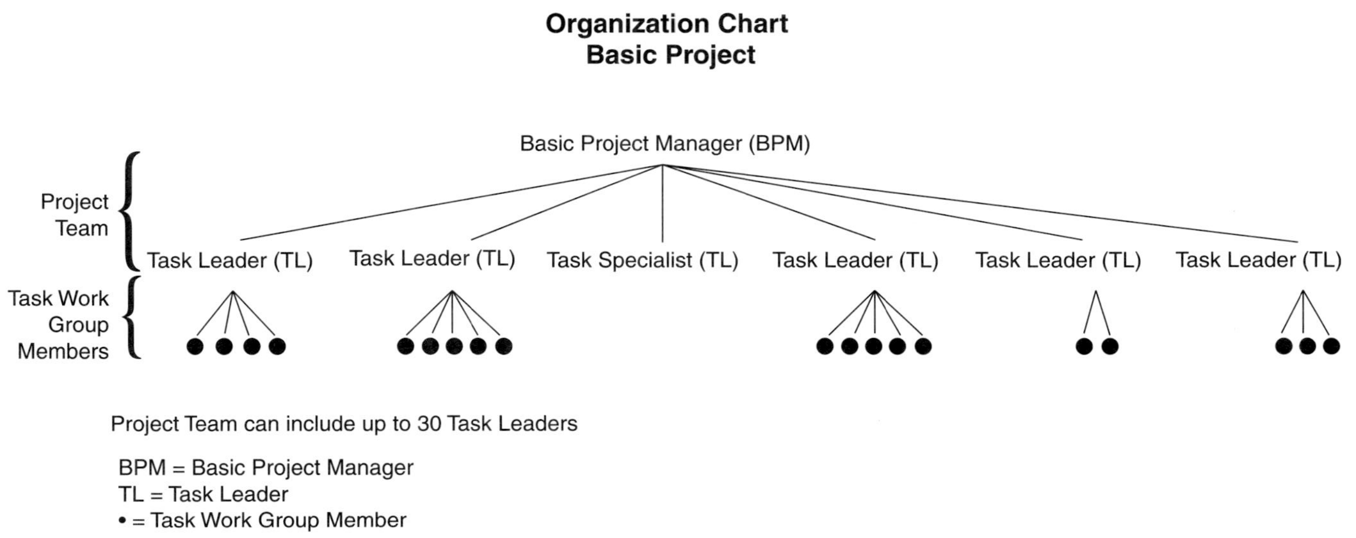
Organization Chart
Basic Project
Basic Project Manager (BPM)
Project Team
Task Work Group Members
Task Leader (TL)
Task Leader (TL)
Task Specialist (TL)
Task Leader (TL)
Task Leader (TL)
Task Leader (TL)
Project Team can include up to 30 Task Leaders
BPM = Basic Project Manager
TL = Task Leader
• = Task Work Group Member

Figure 16-1

THE MAJOR PROJECT

When the work breakdown structure is being disaggregated into major tasks and work packages and it becomes clear that the project team will require more than 30 task leaders, the project is classified as a major project.

A major project is too big for the IPM collaborative planning and leadership used for a basic project. However, this does not mean that IPM should be abandoned. Rather, the major project manager should proceed to identify the major tasks or work packages that can each be treated as basic projects within the larger project. *Project managers, not task leaders, must be chosen to manage each of these basic projects within the larger project.* Each basic project manager will work with the major project manager to create the specification statement, which defines the basic project's objectives. The major project manager will act as the sponsor for each basic project. Each basic project manager will proceed to recruit a team, plan the basic project, and then execute the project's plan.

The family of basic projects that the major project manager is responsible for is what classifies this as a major project. The roles played by the major project manager are different from those of a basic project manager.

As the major project manager proceeds to develop the work breakdown structure, he or she will identify the work packages within the project that can be treated as separate projects. He or she should attain help from potential basic project managers, subject matter experts, and other persons with experience on similar projects.

Often the breakdown of a project is relatively easy. Major projects often break down into a sequence of basic projects. Each basic project delivers an output that serves as the starting point for the next basic project. Some basic projects may run parallel to each other, with the same overlap and slack characteristics that tasks have within a basic project. When each basic project is semi-autonomous, the major project manager's role is that of coordinator. *The major project manager does not walk about and micromanage basic project tasks*! He or she does, however, stay in close contact with each basic project manager and makes sure that the same communication, which is important in a basic project, occurs among the basic project managers. The major project manager acts as a coordinator and is a key source of support if difficulties do arise.

The major project manager collects the project plans of the basic projects as they are developing and consolidates them into a major project Gantt chart. Microsoft Project 2002® has a capacity for large, major projects, but as they grow to include many basic projects, software that has greater capacity, such as Primavera®, is useful.

One feature among parallel basic projects that often emerges is an interdependence where a task output within one project is not only necessary for its own project but also is necessary for a task within a parallel basic project.

In Chapter 7, a basic project with two critical paths is described. This project not only happens to have two critical paths, but it also is easily divided into two basic projects (see Figure 16-2).

If the sales work package (Tasks A-D-F-G-H) had 30 tasks or more with 20 separate task leaders, it would have been handled as a basic project that was parallel to a marketing and materials preparation parallel basic project (I-O-V-W-X-CC). Even with the tasks as shown, if each task had required a different task leader, breaking down the project into two basic projects would be reasonable; the two basic projects would proceed in parallel. There are two points where the tasks from the basic "marketing/materials" preparation project provide the necessary inputs for the "sales task" basic project tasks. Task F of the "sales task" project requires an input from Task I of the "marketing/materials preparation" project; and Task G of the "sales task" project needs an input from Task BB of the "marketing/materials preparation" project.

The major project manager of this "national marketing and sales" project must ensure that the basic project managers and the team leaders who are most concerned (team leaders I, F, BB, and G) maintain good communication with each other so that the interdependencies would work out smoothly.

The "disk cleaning machine" project of Chapter 6 with its Gantt chart also can easily grow into a major project (see Figures 16-3A, 16-3B and 16-3C).

As shown in Figure 16-3A, "prototype Design" could be a basic project. Its project output would be "finalized design sketch," which is the necessary predecessor for the other basic projects that follow it. If the subsequent work packages—fluid flow design, mechanical design, software development, and electrical design—had many more tasks within them, each would be a basic project. All of these packages lead up to "layout 3D design" (shown in Figure 16-3B) which might be treated as another small basic project that is followed by a string of basic projects of assembly, test, final manufacture and delivery to customer, and installation to complete the major project.

This group would be a major project made up of a sequence of basic projects and, a family of parallel basic projects that are included in the sequence. The basic project managers should use IPM principles to plan and execute their projects. The major project manager will act as the sponsor and interproject coordinator for the basic projects. He or she does not micromanage basic projects, but does attend basic project milestone meetings and schedules major project milestone meetings for all of the basic project managers to ensure good intraproject communication and coordination.

The actual project refered to here was a very large basic project that could have been handled easily as a major project. It works as a major project because it easily uses two levels of project management. See Figure 16-4.

Critical Path

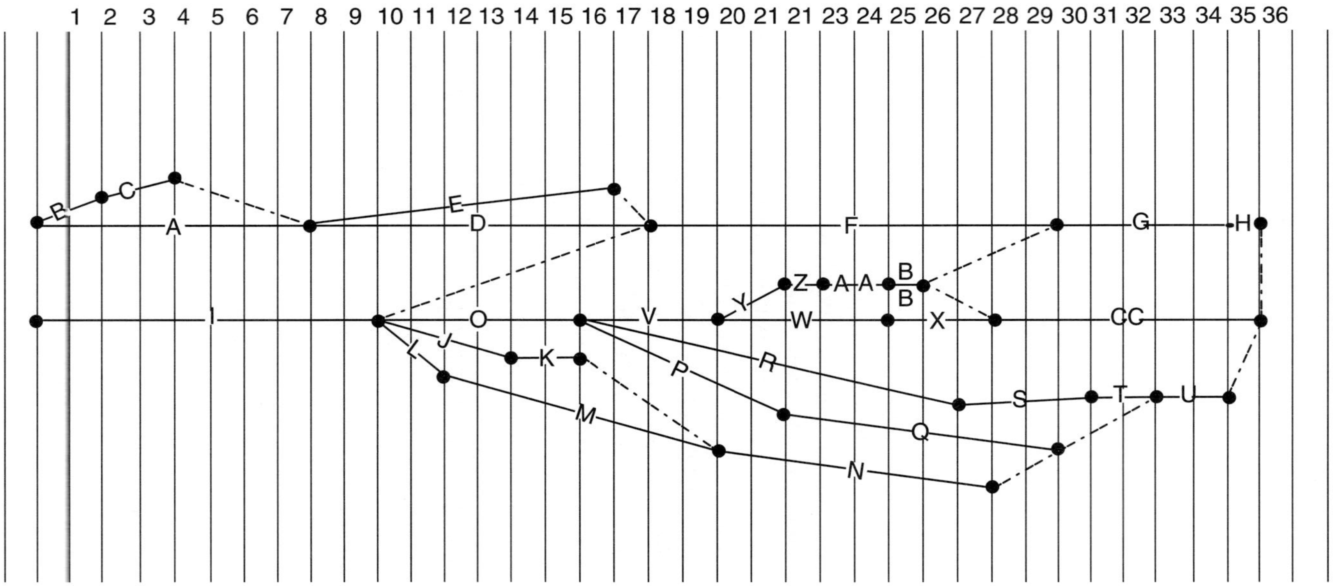

Figure 16-2

	Task Name	Duration
1	**DISK CLEANING MACHINE A**	**93 days**
2	Project Manager	93 days
3	**Prototype Design**	**19.5 days**
4	Component specs.	3 days
5	Component interface:	2 days
6	1st comp skchs	4 days
7	Select prfd skch	1 day
8	Mech dsn sketch	3 days
9	Fluid flow sktch	2 days
10	Elect dsn sktch	5 days
11	Software spec.	6 days
12	Revise comp skch	2 days
13	Design Audit	0.5 days
14	Finalize dsn sktch	1 day
15	Milestone	0 days
16	**Fluid Flow Dsn**	**55 days**
17	Fluid candidates	1 day
18	**Dsn Fld Test Fac**	**24 days**
19	Spec fld pref	2 days
20	Sketch test dsn	4 days
21	Pick test pts	1 day
22	Lay out dsns	5 days

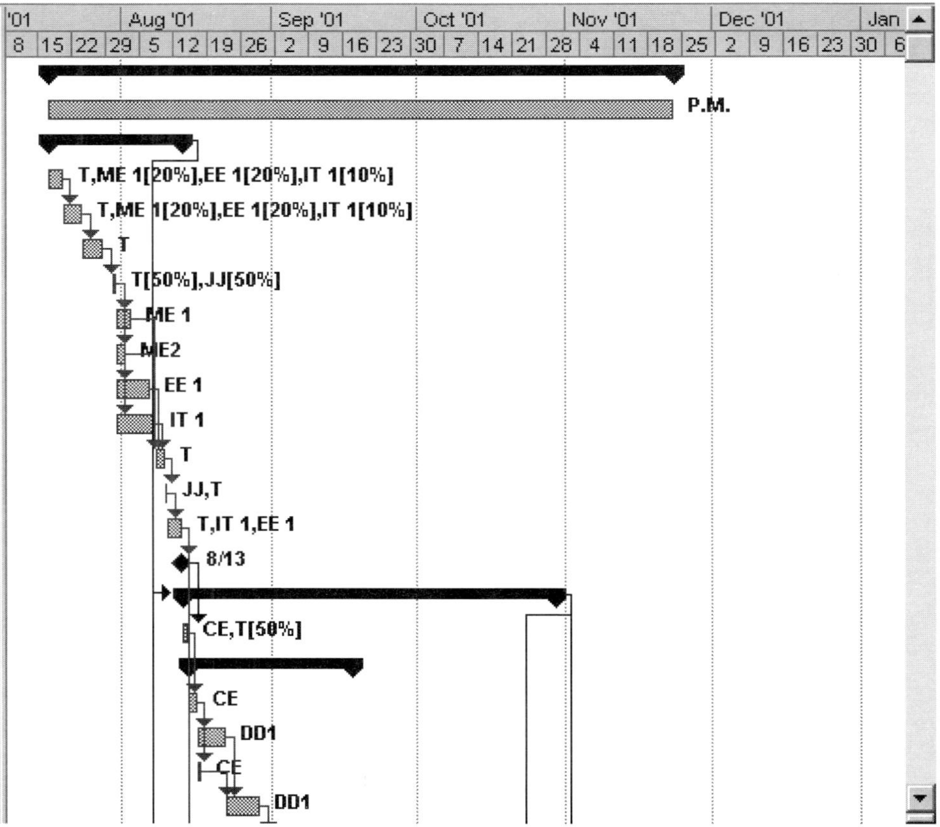

Figure 16-3A

		Task Name	Duration
23		Mfg test parts	10 days
24		Assemble	3 days
25		Perf test fluids	5 days
26		Select fluids	1 day
27		Lay out fl path	4 days
28		Pick components	1 day
29		Order std parts	10 days
30		Design special parts	11 days
31		Mfg spec parts	8 days
32		⊟ **Mechanical Design**	**36 days**
33		Composite lay out	6 days
34		Unit dsn frame	5 days
35		Unit dsn handling	7 days
36		Unit dsn housing	4 days
37		Parts design	10 days
38		⊟ **Work Order Make**	**13 days**
39		Parts1-7	13 days
40		Parts A, B, C	7 days
41		Part X	5 days
42		⊟ **Purchase Std Pts**	**5 days**
43		Group W	5 days
44		Group Z	3.9 days

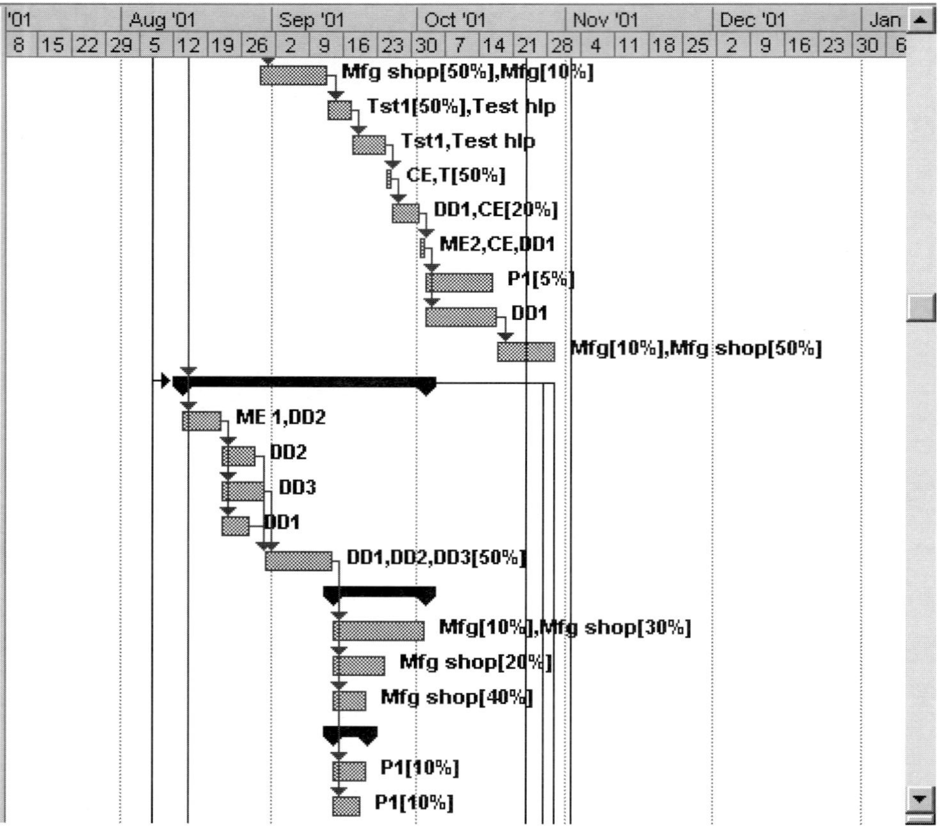

Figure 16-3B

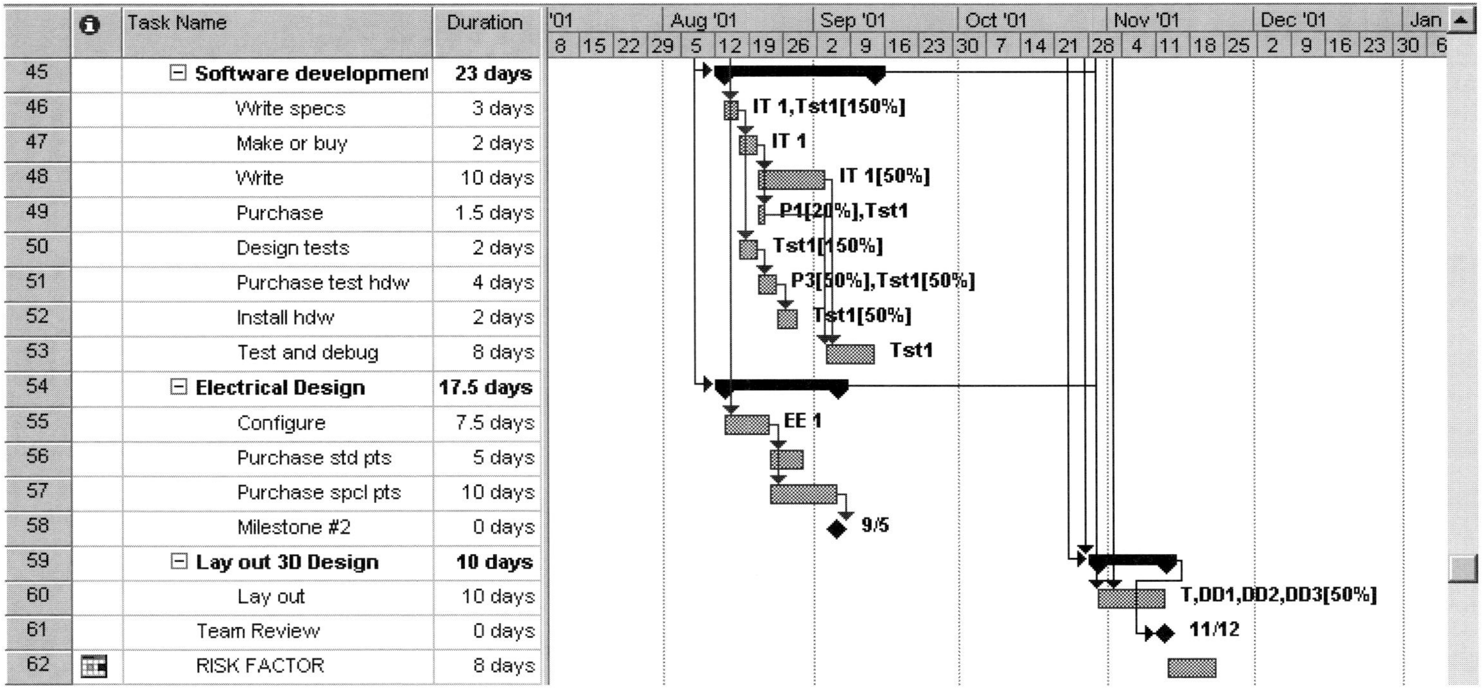
Task Name
Duration
'01
Aug '01
Sep '01
Oct '01
Nov '01
Dec '01
Jan
8 15 22 29 5 12 19 26 2 9 16 23 30 7 14 21 28 4 11 18 25 2 9 16 23 30 6
45 Software development 23 days
46 Write specs 3 days
47 Make or buy 2 days
48 Write 10 days
49 Purchase 1.5 days
50 Design tests 2 days
51 Purchase test hdw 4 days
52 Install hdw 2 days
53 Test and debug 8 days
54 Electrical Design 17.5 days
55 Configure 7.5 days
56 Purchase std pts 5 days
57 Purchase spcl pts 10 days
58 Milestone #2 0 days
59 Lay out 3D Design 10 days
60 Lay out 10 days
61 Team Review 0 days
62 RISK FACTOR 8 days
IT 1,Tst1[150%]
IT 1
IT 1[50%]
P1[20%],Tst1
Tst1[150%]
P3[50%],Tst1[50%]
Tst1[50%]
Tst1
EE 1
9/5
T,DD1,DD2,DD3[50%]
11/12

Figure 16-3C

Organization Chart
Major Project

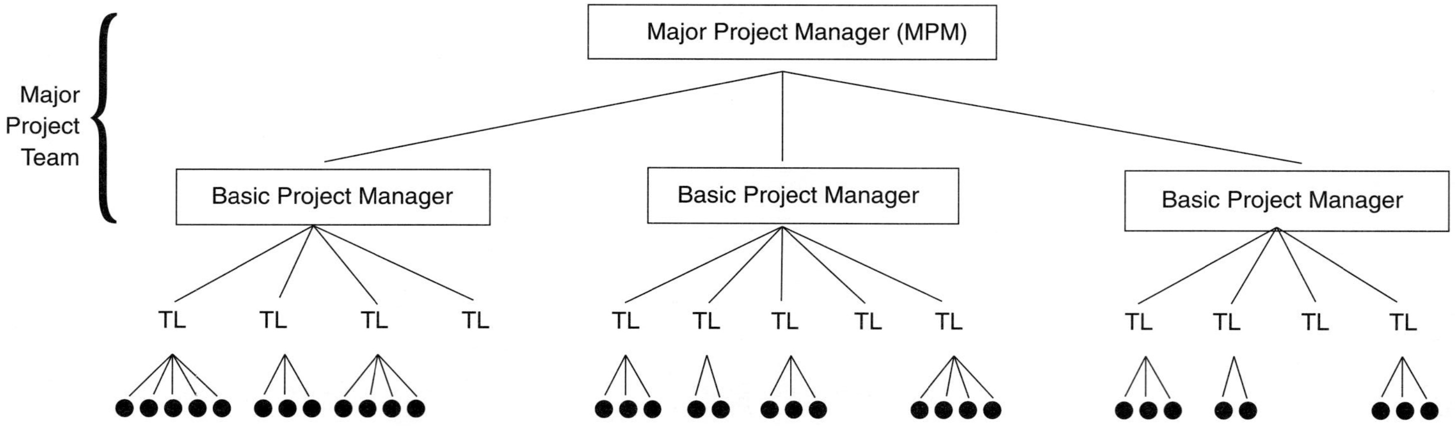

MPM = Major Project Manager
TL = Task Leader
• = Task Work Group Member

Figure 16-4

THE MACRO PROJECT

Generally, a macro project is easily recognized during the development of the scope statement; the key to its recognition lies in understanding the technologies involved in executing the project. If only one technology or methodology provides the foundation, it is generally a basic or a major project; the disk cleaning machine project was such a project. A framework of technology already existed to create this machine—the organization where it was executed had completed many similar projects.

When several different technologies or methodologies are involved in executing a project, it generally is a macro project. The multi-technology characteristic emerges at the beginning of the work breakdown structure effort. Due to the complexity of such projects, this characteristic is recognized at the scope level. In addition, an interdisciplinary team, which is led by a project manager who has a broad knowledge base of the technologies involved, is appointed to recruit a project management team and technically competent specialists to create a statement of work and develop the project's specification. At this point, many project histories will be reviewed and many different subject matter experts will be consulted over questions of feasibility, risk, and resource availability, as the macro project management team explores the project's costs. A specification then will be written that precisely defines the measurable output of the completed project. This specification may very well become an extensive document, but sometimes the desired output of a massive project can be defined quite simply. An example of such a simple definition is: "Design and build an atomic-powered power plant that will have a capacity to deliver 1 million kilowatts at 1,500 volts." A very sophisticated project management team, after much thought, research, and discussion, might have developed such a specification.

The work breakdown structure at the highest level would have been developed as the project's feasibility, risk, resource availability, and cost were considered. For an atomic power plant, the work begins with the technical design. This design defines the energy output of the reactor that is needed to feed the heat exchanger (boiler), which supplies steam to the turbine(s) to drive the generator(s) that will deliver the specified output. The tasks of reactor design and development, heat exchange design and development, turbine design and development, and generator design and development are decomposed as macro projects and major projects. Because many atomic power plant reactors have been built and much is known about this technology, the larger project might be manageable as a major project with many basic projects. However, if any advance design elements are to be incorporated into the new power plant—and it seems this always happens—it is itself a macro project.

At this level, a sophisticated project management team will begin to treat the submacro projects and major projects like tasks in a basic project. The team will lay out an estimate macro project Gantt chart, complete with preliminary risk factors, to get a rough idea about its feasibility, cost, and project duration. These estimates are very rough. They will not be finalized until this project has been broken down all the way to the basic project level and the basic project project managers have led their teams in planning the basic projects.

Most macro projects get into trouble with time and cost estimates and technical feasibility because they commit to the estimates derived at the upper level of the work breakdown. This is particularly true when some advances in technical applications are included in achieving project success. However, it seems so tedious to carry macro project planning down to the basic project "level" and is so time consuming that macro project managing teams do not do it. They explain away their project difficulties and overruns based on histories that always seem to include overruns. The Limerick Atomic Power Plant, near Philadelphia, is a wonderful exception.

The Limerick nuclear power plant was completed and went "on line" January 8, 1990. It is still regarded as perhaps the best designed and constructed nuclear power plant in the world. In the United States and around the world, nuclear power plant construction consistently overruns its budget and completion schedules. The Limerick plant construction was very carefully planned and managed. The project began in February 1986. It was completed under budget, precisely when the project management team intended it to be completed. This is a very rare accomplishment for a project of this size and complexity. It illustrates that with careful and detailed planning and management a very complicated project can be completed to specifications, on time, and within budget.[1]

The framework described here features several levels of projects and project management. At the lowest level is the basic project with its individual project manager. The specification that this project manager works with has moved down through several levels of work breakdown. At each level is a project manager or project management team that has received a specification from the previous level, and, working with the project managers who make up their project team, they have broken the specification down into lower level projects. Please note you can use the affinity diagram approach at all levels.

Intermediate projects within a macro project are managed by individuals or project management teams, depending on the number and complexity of the elements (projects) in the project that they manage. They have responsibility for helping subordinate project managers develop specifications (they act as project sponsors for these subordinates) and for coordinating the interactions and interdependencies among the subordinate projects. In addition, they attend the milestone meetings of these projects and hold milestone meetings with the project managers of their subordinate projects to ensure good communication and coordination.

[1]See *P. M. Network*, January 1991, Gotzis, T. P., "Limerick Generating Station No. 2".

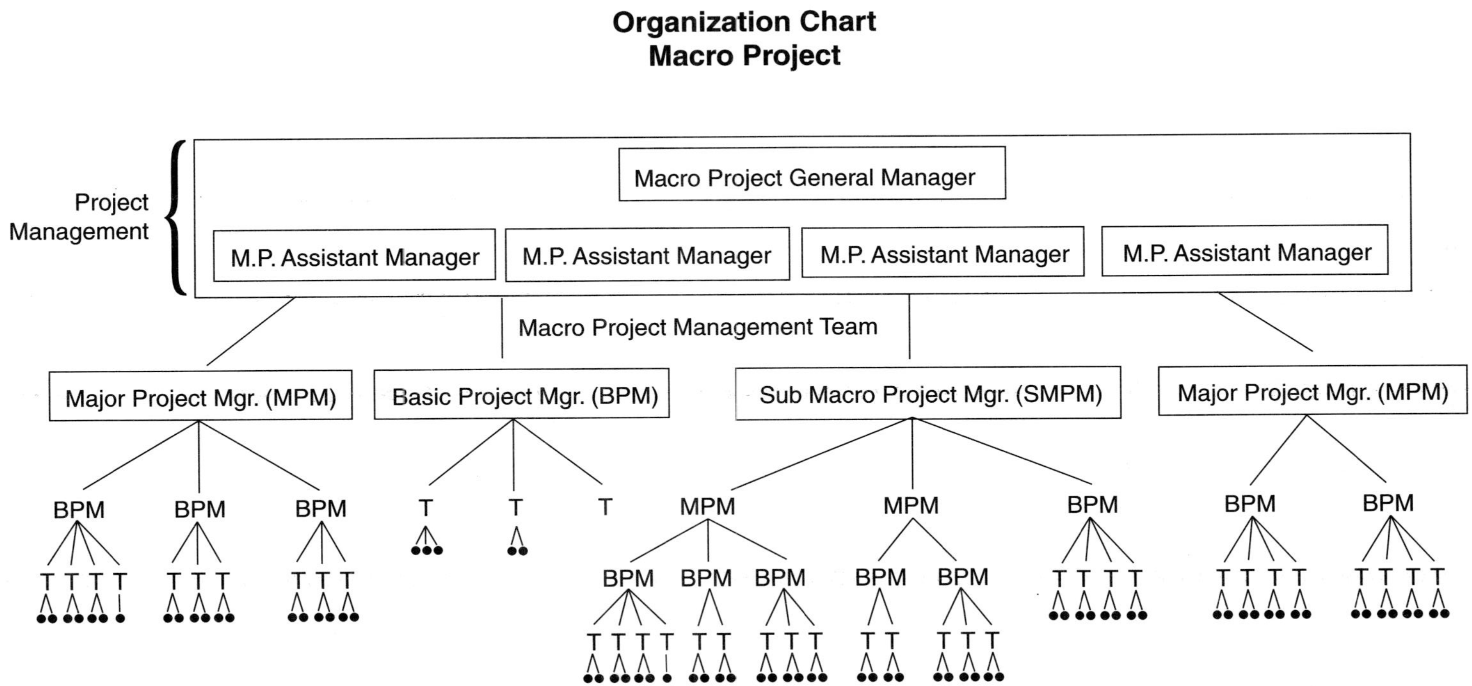

BPM = Basic Project Manager
TL = Task Leader
• = Task Work Group Member

Figure 16-5

Many project management organizations exist that contract to manage macro projects. These organizations also use a project manager team approach, leading or assisting the breaking down of the project into manageable levels. Each organization tends to define "manageable" differently; all create a plan and a Gantt chart covering the level to which they break down the project. Below that level, they depend upon the expertise of the project manager (often a contractor) to execute the project. A few of these organizations ask to see and be allowed to follow these subproject Gantt charts. Each project management organization coordinates the project through milestone meetings. The less breakdown used in the project, the more frequent and cumbersome the meetings, which often are scheduled weekly or even more often. These meetings substitute for the organization's lack of planning detail. Some project management firms use teams that are very good at coordination and communication (through frequent meetings), and at the "art" of expediting and adjusting plans. They do not generally get their projects finished on time, to specifications, and within budget, but they do generally get their projects finished.

Breaking macro projects down to the level of basic projects is sophisticated, but it is not fundamentally different from developing a basic project task list and Gantt chart. When this detailed level of planning is used, a structured project management hierarchy with good communication develops (see Figure 16-5). When this level of planning is done, projects can get finished to specifications, and be on time and within budget. The process is a simple, logical extension of IPM methodology.

SUMMARY

Projects can be categorized usefully as basic, major, or macro projects. The project type is determined by the number and variety of tasks required for the project's completion. A project that needs 30 or fewer task leaders and works within one technology or methodology fits the definition of a basic project. It has one project manager and one project management team that is made up of the project's task leaders.

A major project requires more than 30 tasks leaders and/or requires leaders who each have a different technical expertise as managers. A major project breaks down into several basic projects, each with their own basic project manager who leads the planning and execution of the basic project. Each basic project works to a specification that was developed by the basic project manager for the major project manager. The major project manager acts as the sponsor for each basic project and is the coordinator of the several basic projects within the major project.

The work breakdown structure for the macro project identifies several different effort areas, which are necessary for the project's execution and which must be coordinated to achieve the project's specified output. It differs from the work breakdown structure in a major project in that the areas of effort do not break down directly into basic projects but require several layers of breakdown before they are reducible to a family of basic projects.

To achieve success, macro projects require project management teams to define their specifications at each level and to coordinate the efforts of the leaders of subordinate projects.

Major and macro projects cannot reliably predict a project's feasibility, cost, and duration until the planning work on each of the component basic projects is completed.

DISCUSSION QUESTIONS

1. What are the major differences in project management roles for basic, major, and macro project managers?
2. What similarities exist in the way basic, major, and macro project managers manage projects?
3. When the project specification has been decided and agreed upon, what is the next biggest problem that the manager of a macro project faces?
4. Is it sometimes reasonable to treat a project either as a basic project or as a major project? How would you decide which managerial approach to use in this case?

GLOSSARY

Action item: An activity a team member performs following a team meeting to gather information for the next meeting.

Basic project: A project whose technological and process diversity is such that only one project manager and no more than 30 team members can handle it.

Beta (β) test: Second level testing of a newly developed product, process, or service, to demonstrate that the product meets the specified performance.

Collaborative decision-making: The process by which a group of workers shares their diverse knowledge and skills to solve a problem and arrive at a decision that all can accept.

Cost/benefit ratio: The ratio between the cost of producing a product, process design, or service procedure and its expected benefit (targeted to be less than one). A benefit is generally determined over a specified time period; it is represented in monetary terms.

Critical path chart: An arrow diagram chart displaying project tasks and task dependencies, plotted against a time scale. The time scale displays a task sequence that has no slack available to buffer the other tasks.

Direct cost: The cost of the labor, materials, and equipment required to execute a task.

Downstream task: A task that can be initiated only following the output of a prior task.

Facilitator: An individual who provides leadership to a workgroup, helping group members share their knowledge and experience to collaboratively arrive at decisions. The project manager plays this role at the team meetings.

Feasibility: The process of discovering if sufficient knowledge, skill, and resources exist within an organization to execute a specified project.

Flowchart: A diagram that displays a sequence of events that can lead to a specified outcome.

Function manager: The manager of a group of workers who perform a certain function, such as artwork and layout, engineering, programming, training, and so on, needed for a project task.

Gantt chart: A graphical representation of a project's schedule laid out on graph paper that lists project tasks in the left-hand column in descending order and displays task sequence and duration against a horizontal axis of days or weeks.

- **Working Gantt chart:** A Gantt chart used to describe a project that is in the process of being planned.
- **Basic Gantt chart:** A completed working Gantt chart that shows all of the planned tasks and risk factors.
- **Operations Gantt chart:** A chart that shows the actual flow of a project effort during the project's execution. It is based on the basic project Gantt chart.
- **Summary Gantt chart:** A project Gantt chart that only displays the major work packages as summaries of the basic Gantt chart task details.
- **Detailed Gantt chart:** Either a basic or operations Gantt chart that displays a project effort in terms of each individual task.

Internal customer philosophy: Task leaders communicating with one another to determine pertinent task information that will best help downstream task leaders work "smarter."

Kickoff meeting: The meeting where the project manager and the team members meet for the first time as a group so that the team can learn the steps involved in planning the project and can initiate the first step.

Leadership: The ability to organize and facilitate the efforts of a workgroup to identify and share an objective and to cooperatively and collaboratively work with diligence to achieve this objective.

Macro project: A project whose size and technologies dictate that a complex structure of major and basic projects are needed create the desired product. Its base is necessarily a complex of basic projects. Basic and major project managers, who are led and coordinated by a management team, run a mecro project.

Major project: A large project that is organized as a group of basic projects, which are executed in parallel or following one another sequentially. One person, a major project manager, coordinates the work of all the basic project managers.

Major work package: A term used to describe one large project area of effort of a certain work category that holds within itself several smaller areas of effort, each which further break down into tasks.

Milestone meeting: This meeting is held to review completed project tasks. It is scheduled at a natural break point along the task flow after a portion of the project has been completed, or when 20 to 40 project tasks have been completed. It is held to inform downstream task leaders of the finished work and to discuss their plans to begin work. All project stakeholders are invited to attend this meeting. It is an important communications activity.

PMBOK®: *A Guide to the Project Management Body of Knowledge* is a guide published by the Project Management Institute (PMI) as a resource to help project managers with their work.

Predecessor tasks: Tasks that must be completed before a successor task can begin.

Process improvement project: A project that is 1) designed to either reduce the cost of performing a process or the time taken to perform a process; 2) designed to improve the quality of the output of a process.

Product development or improvement project: A project for the design and development or redevelopment of a product that makes a significant, new contribution to fulfilling the customer's needs or solving a known problem.

Project closure: Those efforts undertaken to demonstrate that the project has met its objectives. Project closure includes holding the team review, delivering the project report, stopping charges billed against the project, and holding the team celebration.

Project execution: Doing the task work necessary to reach the project's objective(s).

Project launch: The efforts that constitute the first steps in executing the project plan, which are taken the day after the sponsor and customer have signed off on the plan.

Project Management Institute (PMI): An international organization of nearly 100,000 members with more than 200 local chapters. Membership is open to anyone having an interest in project management. PMI is the code name that the Project Management Institute uses to identify itself and its publications.

Project Management Professional (PMP®): The title, Project Management Professional, which is awarded by the Project Management Institute (PMI) to any member who has passed a series of tests based on PMBOK® and who has practiced project management for several years. (College training in project management can partially count for years of practice.)

Project product: A physical device, process, or service plan that meets the requirements of a project sponsor and customer.

Project progress documentation: A means of displaying a project's progress as measured by the completion of project tasks.

Project team member: A project team member is 1) a person responsible for performing one or several tasks on the project task list, or 2) a person leading a workgroup that is responsible for performing a task(s) on the project's task list.

Resource manager: The supervisor of a group of technical people from which project task leaders and workgroups members are recruited by the project manager.

Risk analysis: Procedures followed, task by task, to analyze a project's uncertainties. It is used to determine the amount of time to be allowed for these unforeseen problems in the form of a risk factor and to determine contengency plans.

Risk factor: A time duration bar shown along the critical path of the Gantt chart indicating a time buffer for the random task time overruns that can occur during execution of the preceding string of tasks.

Risk factor resources: The calculated probable costs associated with the task overruns that contribute to the risk factor.

Scope statement: A written statement describing a general problem area or an opportunity. It serves as a guide to initiate a project that will either reduce the problem or take advantage of the opportunity.

Slack: The time span between the end of a predecessor task and the start of a successor task when the start has been delayed because another predecessor takes longer than the task with slack.

Specification: A written statement that details the exact outcome of a project in measurable terms.

Sponsor: The person who first discovers the need for a project and initiates the project. A sponsor must be someone holding a position in the organization that enables him or her to tap into necessary project resources and to choose and direct a project manager. The sponsor acts as the project's customer (if the project is in-house) or as the representative for an outside customer.

Statement of work: A written description of the effort that has been agreed upon by the sponsor and project manager. It is used to migrate the project from a general scope statement to a precise project specification.

Successor task: A task that utilizes the output of a predecessor task and directly follows its predecessor(s).

Supportive work environment: It consists of sponsors, resource managers, and task leaders in the project workplace who accept the IPM method of executing projects and give it their full cooperation.

Task: A unit of effort to achieve a specific outcome that can be performed by one individual or workgroup without breaking it down into separable sections. Tasks are the building blocks of a project.

Task bar: The bar on a Gantt chart that represents the time duration of a task.

Task leader: A project team member-specialist who executes a task or leads a project's task workgroup.

Task stream: The successive flow of related tasks recorded between two Gantt chart date points.

Team norms: The rules of procedure that a team follows during team meetings to ensure orderly processes and effective communication and cooperation.

Technical skill: The ability to perform work requiring some special knowledge.

Time buffer: The sum total of all of a project's risk factors. A reliable project completion date can be forecast once the time buffer is known.

Upstream task: A task having a predecessor relationship—sometimes several tasks removed—to a reference task.

Walk-about management: The practice of the project manager making visits to workers who are actively involved in project efforts to offer encouragement and discuss their progress.

Work breakdown structure: A model that a project manager uses at the beginning of a project to capture each and every major effort to be performed for the project; the manager then decomposes the efforts into separate work packages.

Work package: Work that can be broken down into separable units, or tasks, that must be performed to execute a project.

Workgroup: Workers who are capable of working together to complete a task without the need of precise instructions.

INDEX